Portable Alpha Theory and Practice

*What Investors Really
Need to Know*

SABRINA CALLIN, CFA

WILEY

John Wiley & Sons, Inc.

Published by John Wiley & Sons, Inc., Hoboken, New Jersey.
Published simultaneously in Canada.

For general information on our other products and services or for technical support, please contact our Customer Care Department within the United States at (800) 762-2974, outside the United States at (317) 572-3993 or fax (317) 572-4002.

Wiley also publishes its books in a variety of electronic formats. Some content that appears in print may not be available in electronic formats. For more information about Wiley products, visit our web site at www.wiley.com.

This book contains the current opinions of the authors but not necessarily those of Pacific Investment Management Company LLC. Such opinions are subject to change without notice. This book has been distributed for educational purposes only and should not be considered as investment advice or a recommendation of any particular security, strategy or investment product. Information contained herein has been obtained from sources believed to be reliable, but not guaranteed. References to specific securities and their issuers are for illustrative purposes only and are not intended and should not be interpreted as recommendations to purchase or sell such securities. PIMCO may or may not own the securities referenced and, if such securities are owned, no representation is being made that such securities will continue to be held.

Past performance is not a guarantee or a reliable indicator of future results. Investing is subject to certain risks; investments may be worth more or less than the original cost when redeemed.

This book contains hypothetical examples which are for illustrative purposes only. No representation is being made that any account, product, or strategy will or is likely to achieve profits, losses, or results similar to those shown. Hypothetical or simulated performance results have several inherent limitations. Unlike an actual performance record, simulated results do not represent actual performance and are generally prepared with the benefit of hindsight. There are frequently sharp differences between simulated performance results and the actual results subsequently achieved by any particular account, product, or strategy. In addition, since trades have not actually been executed, simulated results cannot account for the impact of certain market risks such as lack of liquidity. There are numerous other factors related to the markets in general or the implementation of any specific investment strategy, which cannot be fully accounted for in the preparation of simulated results and all of which can adversely affect actual results.

Library of Congress Cataloging-in-Publication Data

Callin, Sabrina.
  Portable alpha theory and practice : what investors really need to know / Sabrina Callin.
    p. cm. – (Wiley finance series)
  Includes bibliographical references and index.
  ISBN 978-0-470-11808-5 (cloth)
  1. Portfolio management.   2. Investments.   I. Title.
  HG4529.5.C34   2008
  332.63′2042–dc22   2007045714

Printed in the United States of America.

10 9 8 7 6 5 4 3 2 1

Contents

Foreword

Sometimes you work for so long, or at the same company for so many years, that you lose perspective on what has been accomplished. I can remember the early years of financial innovation very well, but sometimes an outsider's comments are necessary to highlight what really has taken place. PIMCO's innovative and early move into portable alpha strategies was to me and my early associate Chris Dialynas a logical extension of an evolving active-management strategy that featured futures and the cash backing behind them. Not only were Treasury futures extremely cheap, but we felt that the cash backing our commitment could be invested at higher yields with little maturity extension or credit impairment. Soon thereafter the strategy was applied to pure stock index portfolios under the name of StocksPLUS. The fact that there was a portable alpha component to it never really occurred to us; or I should say the term *portable alpha* never really occurred to us. Nonetheless, the results were remarkable.

It was only later, when the academic literature began to recognize the ability of higher-return investments to enhance futures and index-related products, and the strategy of combining various asset classes into a higher-returning recipe, that the term *portable alpha* crossed our desks and became part of PIMCO's conventional wisdom. And it was only recently, when Peter Bernstein acknowledged in his latest book, *Capital Ideas Evolving,* that PIMCO had been the first to actively employ portable alpha strategies, that we looked back on what we had done from an outsider's perspective. Pretty cool, we all thought, to have been part of financial history without really knowing it!

I suppose it shouldn't have been such a surprise. PIMCO professionals have had a storied history of innovation for decades now. The following book—superbly orchestrated by Sabrina Callin and magnificently written by numerous PIMCO professionals—is a testament to that innovation and a further step down the road to bring an understanding of the concept to an investment public eager to learn how at least some of it is done. I congratulate this PIMCO team and urge you to absorb as much as you can, as well as to pursue follow-up inquiries with us personally. Our knowledge—in addition to our alpha—is portable. May it always be so.

WILLIAM GROSS

Preface

Portable alpha is one of the more talked-about topics in the asset management industry today. It is almost impossible to pick up a copy of an industry publication or a financial journal without finding some mention of the term *portable alpha* or related concepts. Many conferences have been dedicated to the topic, and some in the industry have even anointed portable alpha and alpha-beta separation as *the holy grail* of investing or a *new paradigm* in modern investment management. While portable alpha strategies have been around for over 20 years, the somewhat recent increase in investor risk appetites and comfort with the use of derivatives appears to have contributed to a proliferation of portable alpha strategies and related services. At the same time, significant growth in the derivatives markets has increased the number of potential applications for the portable alpha concept.

The idea that portable alpha strategies may provide a solution that enables investors to meet or exceed return targets is certainly appealing, as are the potentially powerful diversification benefits. In addition, for investors focused on liability-driven investing (LDI), portable alpha applications can offer compelling reductions in liability-relative risk. Of course, portable alpha strategies do not defy the basic laws of investment risk and return—there is still no such thing as a free lunch! In fact, when compared to traditional stock and bond investments, many portable alpha investment structures are much more complex, and the risks more challenging to measure and monitor over time. It is also true that portable alpha strategies necessarily involve the use of derivatives and at least one form of leverage. As such, investment- and operational-risk management is of critical importance. However, the end result can be very powerful and well worth the extra time and effort involved in understanding, evaluating, and investing in portable alpha strategies.

Why all the interest in portable alpha? Investors are more open than ever to new asset classes and new investment strategies, not only due to the fundamental merits of an expanded opportunity set and diversification but also due to an apparent concern about not meeting return targets. Adding fuel to the fire, there are a number of interested parties actively marketing the concept of portable alpha and alpha-beta separation as the solution to the challenges that many investors face.

When it comes to portable alpha investment applications, however, the real problem from the standpoint of investors is that all too many people in the industry seem to grossly oversimplify what is undeniably a complex concept from a number of different perspectives. The complexity and risks may be magnified when the alpha source and beta market exposure have a materially positive correlation, when the management of the two is separated between two or more different managers, or when the alpha source involves material risks that are neither familiar to most investors nor fully measured using traditional risk metrics. This is not to say that portable alpha strategies—including those that involve separate alpha strategy and beta derivatives management—are a bad idea or an unwise investment. Rather, a number of portable alpha strategies or approaches simply require more initial and ongoing due diligence on the part of investors and fiduciaries than might be the case with traditional and more familiar stock and bond investments.

PIMCO has been employing an expanding number of different portable alpha strategies for over two decades and is generally credited with being the first, or at least one of the first, to launch a portable alpha strategy with an alpha source that is entirely independent from the beta market exposure. PIMCO's StocksPLUS strategy (inception date 1986) is put forth by a number of practitioners and others in the industry as an example that the concept works over long periods of time and multiple market cycles— and clearly we agree.

In theory and in practice, the concepts behind portable alpha allow for improvements in investment efficiency as measured by return per unit of risk, reductions in downside risk, and other relevant real-world metrics that may not be realistically possible in a traditional investment management context. However, we also believe that it is critically important for investors to separate themselves from all of the hype that seems to be surrounding the concept and focus not only on the potential benefits but also on other relevant considerations that may be crucial to the long-term success of different portable alpha applications. The goal of this book is to do just that: explore the potential benefits, applications, costs, and risks, together with the practical aspects of implementing this important yet often complex investment application that has come to be known as portable alpha.

We recognize that the pace of market innovation seems to accelerate every day, not to mention the constantly changing market dynamics. Combine this with the fact that the portable alpha investment application in its broadest form can be extended to just about every aspect of investment management if not every investment strategy—and the topics that might be covered are almost endless. As a result, we are certain that there are (or will be) relevant considerations that we may have unintentionally omitted or not explored to the level of depth that may be required. To this end, we most certainly welcome constructive feedback for purposes of both future editions of this book and also our ongoing client-driven research and communication.

Sabrina Callin
Newport Beach, California
August 2007

WHAT'S IN THE BOOK

Content and associated objectives, by chapter

Chapter 1: Overview of Book and Key Concepts

Introduce the key concepts associated with portable alpha that are important for investors to grasp, and provide an overview of each of the chapters in the book.

Chapter 2—Portable Alpha Definitions and Trends

Review the details behind portable alpha investment applications, the evolution of portable alpha strategies over time, and the primary benefits of porting alpha.

Chapter 3:—Back to the Basics: Investments 101

Underscore the fundamentals of investing that are most relevant in a portable alpha context with a central focus on the related concepts of risk and return and the benefits of diversification.

Chapter 4—Asset Allocation and Portable Alpha

Explore the value that investors can derive by moving away from the classic approaches to asset management toward a framework that allows for improvements in diversification and risk budgeting through innovative approaches including portable alpha.

Chapter 5—Alpha, Beta, and Alpha-Beta Separation

Provide clarification with respect to the terms alpha and beta together with the key associated concepts for investors to consider in an alpha-beta separation and portable alpha context.

Chapter 6—Global Sources of Portable Alpha, Associated Risks, and Active Management

Highlight the different potential sources of incremental return that are available globally together with the associated investment risks, correlations and the potential value of skilled active management.

Chapter 7—Derivatives-Based Beta Management

Detail the investment and operational complexities together with the related costs and risks associated with the derivatives-based beta component of portable alpha strategies.

Chapter 8—Portable Alpha Implementation

Review integrated, semibundled, and segregated approaches to portable alpha implementation, including the structural elements and associated cost, investment risk, and operational risk considerations.

Chapter 9—The Real Holy Grail: Risk Measurement and Management

Focus on the real key to successful portable alpha strategy implementation—prudent ongoing risk measurement and management.

Chapter 10—Liability-Driven Investing

Explore liability-driven investing including approaches that incorporate the portable alpha and alpha-beta separation concepts.

Chapter 11—Portable Alpha Theory and Practice: Wrapping It Up

Summarize the key concepts put forth in the book with the goal of helping investors navigate portable alpha theory and practice.

Epilogue: Portable Alpha—The Final Chapter: Schemes, Dreams, and Financial Imbalances: "There Must Be More Money."

Acknowledgments

S pecific to the *Portable Alpha Theory and Practice: What Investors Really Need to Know* book project, we would like to acknowledge:

- Tammie Arnold at PIMCO and Laura Walsh at Wiley for believing in the project from the very beginning together with their unwavering and enthusiastic guidance and support every step of the way.
- Chris Dialynas at PIMCO for sponsoring and collaborating on the project and providing excellent direction and mentorship throughout the process.
- Emilie Herman at Wiley for superb editorial assistance and also her remarkable patience, perseverance, and understanding.

As is the case with most major endeavors, this book project was a team effort not only on the part of the authors and individuals noted above, but also with respect to other key professionals at PIMCO behind the scenes, each of whom invested a tremendous amount of time, energy, and effort, as follows:

- Christopher Abram
- Kevin Broadwater
- Emily Javens
- Michael Kiedel
- Wayne Lai
- Richard LeBrun
- Erika Hayflick Lowe
- Krista Maloney
- Suzanne Oden
- John Tran
- Peter Van De Zilver
- Steven Vames
- Masako Walsh

Of course, our knowledge on portable alpha and the related areas covered in this book certainly should be credited to many others, including but not limited to:

- Bill Gross and his team at PIMCO back in the early 1980s for creating the StocksPLUS portable alpha prototype.
- John Loftus for coining the term StocksPLUS and helping countless investors and other professionals grasp the key underlying concepts.

- Our colleagues in the industry and related academic fields for their substantial contributions to the theory behind and different applications and practical considerations for portable alpha.
- The team at the Chicago Mercantile Exchange for launching S&P 500 Index futures contracts over a quarter of a century ago.
- Last and most importantly, our clients for sharing with us their tremendous insight, trust, and guidance in the exciting and rapidly evolving world of investment management.

CHAPTER 1

Overview of Book and Key Concepts

Sabrina Callin

O ur goal in writing this book is to provide investors with a practical guide to portable alpha theory and practice, with a focus on the concepts that we believe are most important from the standpoint of investors. In effect, we are attempting to help investors avoid potential pitfalls by successfully navigating the benefits and complexities of portable alpha, available sources of return and their associated risks, related myths and realities, and also the key aspects of implementation. Portable alpha is a powerful investment application—but, just like investing in general, it is not nearly as simple in practice as it may sound in theory.

The asset management industry appears to be engaged in a paradigm shift, prompted by the 2000–2002 equity market sell-off and low bond yields, that is exemplified by but extends well beyond portable alpha and alpha-beta separation. Regardless of the cause, the marked increase in investor demand for and acceptance of new types of risks, tools, and strategies should lend itself to both greater alpha potential and improved diversification of risk. However, the same two rules that have always applied to investing apply in the new paradigm and specifically with portable alpha strategies:

1. It is almost always necessary to take some type of risk in order to generate return over the risk-free rate.
2. The identification, measurement, and diversification of risk is key to optimal investing.

According to Peter Bernstein in an interview about his new book, *Capital Ideas Evolving,* "The central role of risk, if anything, has grown rather than diminished. We really can't manage returns because we don't know what they're going to be. The only way we can play that game is to decide what kinds of risk we're going to take. Risk is the beginning."[1]

Most portable alpha investment strategies are designed to provide attractive returns in addition to the return of the underlying (beta) market exposure. The key question is whether the excess returns are coupled with an acceptable level of risk on a stand-alone basis and also within the context of the overall asset allocation or risk budget in both normal and atypical market environments.

As described in more detail in Chapter 2, portable alpha investment strategies generally obtain market exposure using derivatives contracts like futures or swaps (in some cases combinations of derivatives contracts or similar borrowing/financing arrangements), which do not require payment for the market exposure up front. An investor may be required to provide a relatively modest margin deposit, although rarely more than 5 to 10 percent of the total notional market exposure. This, in turn, leaves an investor's capital available to be invested in a separate, independent investment strategy that—in addition to the beta market return—is designed to generate attractive risk-adjusted excess return, or *alpha*.

Portable alpha applications may be particularly valuable in markets where traditional active management has not resulted in value-added for investors. The same is true in cases where the inherent diversification benefits between combinations of alpha strategies and beta market exposure(s) result in a substantial improvement in the risk/return profile for investors relative to traditional passive or active strategies. The portable alpha investment application can also be employed at the overall investment plan level, in which case there would not necessarily be a one-for-one replacement of traditional managers with portable alpha strategies. Rather, in these cases there might be a fundamental shift in the entire asset allocation, risk budgeting, and manager selection process.

In addition to the overriding themes regarding return, risk, and diversification presented here and throughout the book, some additional key concepts are worth addressing up front—concepts that are central to understanding portable alpha but may be easily overlooked or misunderstood amid all the excitement currently surrounding portable alpha and alpha-beta separation. These concepts include the practice of borrowing to achieve higher returns, leverage, and the confusion surrounding alpha and beta. Following the discussion of these key concepts, we have also included an overview of the specific topics covered in the book, by chapter, with the goal of providing not only the context (the key concepts) but also a road map as we embark on a journey toward our intended destination—a framework for investors to better understand and evaluate portable alpha strategies.

BORROWING TO ACHIEVE HIGHER RETURNS

It is interesting that, with all the focus on portable alpha and alpha-beta separation, it is sometimes assumed that the underlying concepts are entirely new. Certainly the significant development in the derivatives markets and in other financial market borrowing/lending arrangements has made it possible to employ a much greater variety of portable alpha strategies. However, ultimately portable alpha and related concepts like alpha-beta separation are all about borrowing in order to achieve a higher expected return. If you stop and think about it, there is not a single application that falls under this now very broad portable alpha umbrella that does not involve some form of borrowing as the primary means to increase expected returns. Sound familiar?

Modern portfolio theory, as introduced in the middle of the twentieth century, recognized two key factors that are fundamental to the benefits of and construct behind portable alpha:

1. Risk-free borrowing as a means to increase return for investors who have a greater risk tolerance.
2. Diversification as a means to increase return at the same level of risk (or to decrease risk at the same level of return).

The two are highly interrelated in the theoretical world in the following sense: Assuming that a portfolio exists that is identified as the optimal portfolio from an investment efficiency standpoint (that is, a portfolio that involves risk but benefits to the greatest possible degree from diversification and therefore is expected to deliver the maximum return per unit of risk), then every investor should hold that portfolio. However, every investor does not have an identical risk tolerance, for any number of obvious reasons. This is where risk-free lending and borrowing comes into play. If the risk of that *optimal portfolio* is too great, then an investor can mix the risk-free asset and the optimal portfolio in appropriate proportions such that the end result produces the desired level of risk. If the risk of the optimal portfolio is too low, then an investor can borrow (theoretically at the risk-free rate) and purchase more of the optimal portfolio, thereby increasing the return at the same level of return (over the risk-free rate) per unit of risk as that afforded by the optimal portfolio.

The potential benefits of the portable alpha investment application are very closely related to the concept of borrowing at the risk-free rate and also to the power of diversification, even though the application, in practice, is not identical to the underlying investment theory. On one hand, it is possible to gain access to an increasing number of market exposures by borrowing at a money market-based rate (typically LIBOR) as a proxy for the risk-free rate, simply by obtaining asset exposure via the derivatives markets (futures, swaps, option combinations, even repurchase transactions) or similar arrangements or, most recently, even via products that are structured by broker/dealers to facilitate borrowing on more lenient terms than those typically associated with the swap markets (at a cost, of course!). This means that investors with an appropriate level of risk tolerance can effectively borrow at close to the risk-free rate in order to obtain additional risky asset exposure (more than would be possible in the absence of the ability to borrow) and therefore a higher expected return that is directly related to the additional risk. On the other hand, it is not necessarily true that investors have identified the optimal portfolio to start with, and most certainly not true that it is possible to invest in the optimal portfolio via a simply executed borrowing arrangement.

In truth, the optimal portfolio that exists in theory is not easy to identify in practice. As a result, it actually is possible to increase the returns of an investment portfolio via a borrowing arrangement without a corresponding increase in risk and sometimes without an increase in risk at all—or even a reduction in risk. This is true due to the potential for improvements on two fronts: diversification and alpha—and therein lies the real power of portable alpha.

LEVERAGE—THE GOOD, THE BAD, AND THE UGLY

Portable alpha strategies typically employ the use of derivatives and at least one form (if not multiple forms) of leverage. Therefore it is not surprising that portable alpha strategies, in practice, share many characteristics in common with the use of derivatives and leverage. Both derivatives and leverage can produce powerful risk reduction, return, and other benefits for investors. However, as has been proven far too many times, if investors do not understand and/or do not carefully monitor and disclose the potential risks that may be associated with both leverage and derivatives, the results can be disastrous. The same is true of portable alpha strategies—including strategies that focus on the separation of alpha and beta based on the same underlying concepts.

This brings us to the important concept of leverage, which we focus on repeatedly throughout this book, as leverage is a central underpinning to the portable alpha investment application. Some investors hear the word *leverage,* (or things they associate with leverage, like *derivatives* or *overlays* or *portable alpha*) automatically stop listening and refuse to consider any associated investment strategies, under the assumption that leverage automatically involves substantial risk with the potential for an almost limitless (or least very significant) downside. By contrast, other investors appear to give very little consideration, if any at all, to the potential downside risk that may be associated with leverage, instead aggressively pursuing strategies and combinations of strategies that effectively stack leverage on top of leverage on top of leverage.

Investing in strategies that involve leverage and then (with the same underlying capital) also employing leverage/borrowing arrangements to obtain additional market exposure (leverage on top of leverage) may actually result in a marked improvement in the risk/return profile of a carefully constructed portfolio. The key is a portfolio that is carefully constructed such that investors and/or fiduciaries have a thorough understanding of all of the underlying risk factors and how those factors relate to one another. This generally necessitates the use of a variety of risk metrics (definitely *not* only volatility-related measures) to gain an understanding of the true downside risk. Unfortunately, this type of diligence is not always employed. In addition, the potential exists for investors without the appropriate tools for accurately assessing the risks to be lured by the high returns that leveraged strategies may provide during good times—only to be sorely disappointed by the associated losses when bad times inevitably come to pass.

The preceding examples of two very different views on leverage bring up a consideration related to governance. Some might argue that the conservative view is one that simply steers clear of investments involving any type of leverage. While this may be the easy way out (the least amount of work), if the goal of investing is to maximize return at a given level of risk or to minimize risk at a given level of return, this is not necessarily the most prudent investment decision, as leverage and derivatives can most assuredly be employed in such a way that these objectives are accomplished. Therefore, refusing to consider any type of leverage might, in a sense, be equated to refusing to either reduce risk or increase the expected return on assets at the same level of risk—hardly a good investment decision!

A relevant corollary may be the assumption that passive indexing is the most conservative approach to investing. This simply is not true if the passive choice actually has more risk and/or greater downside potential than an alternative strategy (such as a portable alpha strategy) that provides the desired market exposure with less downside risk and/or a lower overall risk profile.

For those who think that leverage is necessarily bad, it may be relevant to consider the fact that every individual who owns a home that they have not yet paid for in full (i.e., everyone who has a mortgage) is leveraged. Any corporation with outstanding debt also might be described as leveraged—which means that anyone who owns common stock owns a leveraged investment. Most institutional investors also invest in real estate, where the underlying investments are leveraged (borrowing is involved)—and so on and so forth. Leverage, in and of itself, is neither fundamentally good nor bad, neither risky nor risk-reducing. As is the case investmenting more broadly—indeed, many things in life—it all depends.

In reality, just as there is good cholesterol and bad cholesterol, there is good leverage (leverage that reduces risk and/or enhances return at an acceptable level of risk) and there is leverage that, while not necessarily bad, does result in magnified market risk or risk factor exposure that will result in magnified losses in the event of losses on the associated market exposure. To put it in simpler terms, leverage should probably be considered good if it allows an individual (or a unit of capital) to perform more efficiently and effectively than would have been the case without it. In the workplace, as an example, an employee who is able to effectively leverage himself is generally viewed as a highly productive asset to the organization.

However, the downside of leverage might be thought of as too much of one type of risk at the wrong time. Having leveraged exposure to a specific asset or market typically means you have more than 100 percent exposure to that risk factor or set of risk factors. This generally works out great in normal periods or in periods of low or declining risk/volatility. However, it does not work out very well in periods where the downside risk (which may also invoke liquidity risk and financing risk) rears its ugly head.

As with leverage in a broader sense, investors and investment management providers can use the portable alpha application to improve the risk/return profile at the investment strategy level and at the overall investment portfolio level. As such, we are strong advocates of not dismissing the portable alpha investment application simply because there is an element of borrowing that is often equated to leverage. To be very clear, though, many portable alpha investment strategies do involve an increase in risk (as is often the case with leverage) and sometimes a material increase in risk across a number of different dimensions, including but not limited to volatility, tail risk, downside risk, and operational risk.

Interestingly, it is sometimes said that portable alpha and alpha-beta separation enable investors to maintain exposure to the policy portfolio and at the same time increase the aggregate expected return on assets. The potential issue with this statement relates to the idea that policy portfolios are presumably constructed with the goal of achieving an optimal return at an acceptable level of risk. If a portable alpha strategy (or set of portable alpha strategies) is employed that materially increases not only the expected return but also the actual risk profile, does this really mean that the policy portfolio (as it was originally intended and approved) is maintained? It may be true that the market exposures specified by the policy portfolio are all still in place in one form or another (either through outright asset purchases or through leveraged market exposures), but the policy portfolio has certainly been altered if the aggregate risk is greater than the level of risk specified and acknowledged by those who approved the policy portfolio in the first place.

Portable alpha may provide investors with the opportunity to improve investment results either at the individual strategy level or at the portfolio level. However, investors should most definitely take care to make sure that the end result is not an unintended increase in risk.

THE CONFUSION SURROUNDING ALPHA AND BETA

Part of the confusion among investors when it comes to risk and return in a portable alpha context lies with the increasingly casual and often theoretically incorrect use of the alpha and beta terms in our industry. *Alpha* and *beta* are dependent terms derived from regression equations, as discussed in much more detail in Chapter 5. In an investments context, beta simply measures the sensitivity of a return series to a given factor—for example, the sensitivity of a stock or portfolio of stocks to the return of the stock market. Yet it is now common practice to refer to a given market index or risk factor as "beta," which makes it all very difficult to follow. Why? Because there are probably an almost endless number of market indexes and risk factors that can be used for purposes of measuring beta.

In addition, the actual beta (or betas, in the case of multifactor regression analysis) associated with a given investment or investment portfolio is wholly dependent on the factor or factors one uses for purposes of analyzing the returns. It is true that modern portfolio theory often references the stock market as a proxy for *the market portfolio* due to the practical reality that the market portfolio cannot readily be specified. However, it does not follow that there is one *beta* (sensitivity to the stock market) and that therefore the returns of all investments that are not explained by beta relative to the stock market are alpha.

To illustrate this point with a relatively simple example, let's say we measure the beta of a bond index, a commodity index, and a hedge fund composite index relative to a stock market index. What do we find? As shown in Figure 1.1, we find stock market beta in hedge funds, commodities, and even, at times, bonds! Is this surprising? Not necessarily.

What the chart essentially tells us is that during the period under review, hedge fund returns (on average) exhibited a relatively stable and materially positive correlation with equity returns; bond returns exhibited a relatively stable low to negative correlation; and commodity returns exhibited a relatively volatile, mostly positive, and sometimes negative correlation. All three investment categories clearly would have provided diversification

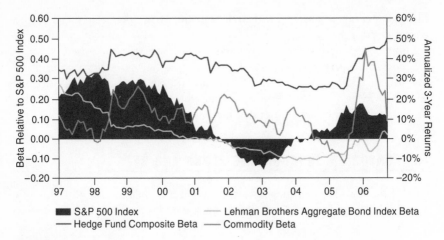

FIGURE 1.1   Rolling Three-Year Returns and Betas versus S&P 500 Index
Data source: PIMCO, Standard & Poor's, Hedge Fund Research Inc., Lehman
Brothers, Dow Jones.

benefits relative to equities in a portfolio context. Even though the hedge
fund index returns exhibited a materially positive correlation with equities,
the correlation was far from 1.0.

But what about the stock market beta? Should it be hedged? The answer:
It depends. Hedging the stock market beta (i.e., attempting to remove the
market sensitivity exhibited by an investment to a particular risk factor)
will most assuredly alter the return profile. The key point is that you can't
really describe an investment as a beta or an alpha because most investments
exhibit multiple betas (sensitivities) to multiple risk factors. What is most
relevant in a portable alpha context is not so much alpha and beta per se
but rather the benefits afforded by the diversification of risk factors and also
by an active manager's security selection and market timing skill.

Diversification allows an investor to improve his underlying return
profile, and portable alpha allows investors to increase the diversification
benefits at the investment strategy and portfolio level by seeking alpha from
sources and managers that are independent from the desired market exposure or market benchmark. We can (and in fact do in Chapter 5) look across
a wide variety of different combinations of market risk factors (inherent in
different market indexes and hedge fund styles) and measure the correlations among those risk factors. This type of historical insight, together with
a deep understanding of manager skill, the strategies employed, variation
in risk factor exposure, and maximum risk/risk factor exposure employed
in a particular investment strategy, can be very helpful in putting together

a portable alpha strategy that may be reasonably expected to result in an improved risk/return profile. However, it is very dangerous to assume that a strategy that has been designated as an alpha strategy will not result in a material increase in risk or even a fundamental alteration to the desired asset class exposure when coupled with a given beta market exposure.

All investment strategies that provide a material return over cash are also likely to involve material additional risk of some type, regardless of whether an investor or provider chooses to describe the risk or risk factors as betas. In some cases the primary risk factors are easier to identify than in others, but even so, as we show in the correlation charts toward the end of Chapter 5, most investments do exhibit measurable relationships with other investments (betas). Alpha is also only independent from the factor that is used to measure the associated beta. You cannot hedge the factor exposure and then expect the resulting return pattern to be uncorrelated with the remaining universe of other possible factor exposures, as is sometimes implied or even stated outright in presentations on portable alpha. Alpha and beta are, by definition, dependent terms. Nonetheless, the underlying concept still makes a great deal of sense due to the inherent potential diversification and associated risk/return improvements that can be achieved by combining an independent alpha source with a desired market exposure. At the end of the day, that is what it is all about!

PORTABLE ALPHA DEFINITIONS AND TRENDS

Portable alpha definitions and associated terminology can vary substantially depending on the person providing the explanation. This certainly keeps things interesting but, unfortunately, may also ultimately lead to confusion among investors. The goal of Chapter 2 is to provide an overview of the portable alpha investment application (as it is most broadly defined), including the derivatives-based beta market exposure and the investment strategy, or alpha engine, in which capital is invested. The primary benefits of *porting* alpha are highlighted, along with examples of portable alpha strategies and the original development of the concept. The chapter also addresses some of the common misperceptions surrounding portable alpha and the evolution of portable alpha strategies over time, including somewhat recent events that have spawned a flurry of interest in the concept and related applications.

A key overriding theme in the discussion of portable alpha definitions and trends—and in the entire book—is the importance that investors not lose sight of the potential for a material increase in risk in addition to the potential for attractive incremental return. After all, beyond all the excitement that currently surrounds portable alpha, investors are still held to the fundamental underpinnings of prudent investment management. The goal of maximizing return on capital invested can only be accomplished with very careful consideration of downside risks.

BACK TO THE BASICS: INVESTMENTS 101

Chapter 3 reviews the fundamentals of investing and modern portfolio theory that are particularly relevant as background for the portable alpha investment application. These basics include the construction of an optimal investment portfolio; utility functions and risk aversion; portfolio selection and the efficient frontier; the capital market line, including related risk-free borrowing and lending; the capital asset pricing model (CAPM) and factor models—all with a focus on the benefits of diversification.

The chapter also addresses the concept of risk premiums, and examines relevant differences between theory and reality, including the risk-free reference point, the market portfolio, market efficiency, the assumption of normally distributed returns, and the potential for a mismatch between the incentives of investors and investment managers. In addition, both option pricing and merger arbitrage strategies are reviewed in the appendixes to provide a basis for unstanding nonlinear return distributions. As innovative and new as many deem the portable alpha and alpha-beta separation concept, it is remarkable just how much of the underlying investment theory is best explained by some of the principles that were introduced almost half a century ago and are still as relevant today as ever.

ASSET ALLOCATION AND PORTABLE ALPHA

The fourth chapter switches to a focus on asset allocation and key related ideas, all of which are relevant as a basis to considering different portable alpha applications. An emphasis is placed on the lack of diversification in typical institutional investor asset allocations, and suggestions are put forth for improving portfolio level efficiency through diversification, a careful search for alpha, and a disciplined approach to managing asset allocations. Portable alpha implementation at the strategy and portfolio level is reviewed as a potential solution for improving investment returns and an important development in asset management. Challenges associated with volatility and correlation measures are addressed, as is the need for a much greater focus on sustainable spending as an investment objective. Equity risk premiums are specifically analyzed given the dominance of equity risk in most investment portfolios, and examples are put forth as to how investors can benefit from some of the preceding ideas and concepts.

Finally, investors and fiduciaries are encouraged to be open to new approaches to asset allocation, risk budgeting, portfolio benchmarking, and investing in general, including portable alpha approaches, that may involve a move away from the classic models. While such departures from the traditional may be met with hesitation, the benefits that are likely to accrue to long-term investors are compelling and should most certainly be considered.

ALPHA, BETA, AND ALPHA-BETA SEPARATION

Chapter 5 focuses on providing clarification with respect to the terms *alpha* and *beta,* which are often used in a context that may prove particularly problematic in a portable alpha and alpha-beta separation framework. Alpha and beta are defined as a basis for helping investors separate themselves from the marketing-oriented use of the terms today, especially as it relates to understanding the risk and return characteristics of portable alpha strategies. Example alpha and beta calculations are provided to illuminate the difference between alpha and excess return, and key potential issues with the separation of the alpha and beta are highlighted. The fundamental challenges to achieving a desirable level of alpha by independently selecting alpha and beta are addressed, including the interdependence of the two, difficulties in identifying alpha, and the complexities and associated costs and fees. Two different case studies are presented to help illustrate important points together with asset allocation and risk budgeting considerations. Benchmarking is also discussed, as is the existence of multiple betas in most types of investment strategies.

Alpha and beta are undeniably useful terms in the world of active investment management. However, they are rendered meaningless if a proper benchmark that reflects the primary risk factors of the associated investment strategy is not identified for purposes of calculating the alpha and beta (or betas). Even then, true alpha may still be elusive.

GLOBAL SOURCES OF PORTABLE ALPHA, ASSOCIATED RISKS, AND ACTIVE MANAGEMENT

One of the primary benefits of the portable alpha investment application is the almost limitless choice of risk factors and investment strategies that investors can access to outperform a money market (cash) rate and therefore to provide incremental return in a portable alpha context. However, as discussed in the sixth chapter, it is imperative that investors do not evaluate alpha strategies in a vacuum, as the capital invested in a portable alpha strategy is exposed to the risk factors that are inherent in both the alpha strategy and the derivatives-based beta exposure. Therefore, it is critical for investors to have a reasonably thorough understanding of the primary risk factors and risk factor ranges in each component, in addition to understanding the potential value-added that may accrue to investors as a result of tactical risk factor allocation and security selection. Fortunately, however, the expected returns from most strategies can be deconstructed in this way.

To this end, the primary strategies and associated risk factors that are currently employed as alpha sources are reviewed, including equity, fixed income, and different styles of hedge funds, together with the associated primary risk factors and the potential value of skilled active management. An entire section is also dedicated to exploring the additional value-added that may be associated with the global marketplace, using representative fixed-income and currency strategies for purposes of illustrating the key points. Common risk premiums across different strategies are highlighted, as is multifactor regression analysis as one means to help investors assess underlying risk factors when a representative investment benchmark is not readily identified.

Finally, a common base line is presented for purposes of evaluating potential alpha sources with a focus on (1) key characteristics and benefits, (2) sources of return associated risk factors, and (3) the relationship between the primary risk factors and the risk factors inherent in the derivatives-based beta market exposure.

DERIVATIVES-BASED BETA MANAGEMENT

Derivative instruments are the building blocks for portable alpha strategies and therefore a key ingredient to successful portable alpha implementation. In the seventh chapter our goal is to provide a good sense of the risks, costs and complexities associated with maintaining beta market exposure using derivatives. It is important to note that, in the most basic sense, derivatives represent a borrowing arrangement not entirely different from securities lending, as one example. As such, we explore this analogy as a means to better understanding the fundamentals behind derivatives-based beta management. The futures and swaps markets are reviewed before addressing the importance of skill when it comes to executing and maintaining derivatives positions, particularly during periods of market stress. Examples are given to illustrate the preceding points, and associated operational risks are also addressed.

The overriding message in this chapter is that derivatives management is not simple, andit should not be free, as has been suggested. Rather, there are any number of important considerations that are entirely relevant for investors to carefully evaluate in a portable alpha context. Derivatives are a very important tool—however, as is always the case with levered market exposure, not one that should be taken lightly.

PORTABLE ALPHA IMPLEMENTATION

The number of different implementation options for portable alpha strategies available to investors continues to grow, which is definitely a positive development, although it can be difficult to navigate the associated complexities, costs, and fees. In Chapter 8 we provide investors with a framework to help break down the various approaches into different components or elements including (1) the alpha strategy investment; (2) the beta derivatives exposure; (3) liquidity to meet margin or collateral calls associated with the derivatives-based beta exposure; and (4) consolidated risk management, risk monitoring, and reporting.

In addition, we describe the three basic approaches to portable alpha implementation: the fully integrated approach, the completely segregated approach, and something in between which we call *semibundled*. The advantages and potential disadvantages of each approach are addressed, together with an explanation of how each of the elements or components associated with portable alpha strategies may be implemented in practice. A case study is also presented to help illustrate some of the inherent complexities and downside risk that can be associated with portable alpha strategies. Portable alpha implementation is not simple. However, it is certainly possible for investors to deconstruct almost any approach into each of the key elements as a means to better understand the costs and risks, in addition to the benefits.

THE REAL HOLY GRAIL: RISK MEASUREMENT AND MANAGEMENT

Chapter 9 covers risk measurement and management, which may be critically important given the inherently levered nature of portable alpha strategies and other associated complexities. We emphasize the importance of understanding and controlling the risk factors that drive the performance and downside risk of both the alpha and the beta components. We also address the shortcomings of different statistical risk measurement tools that are based on the assumption of normally distributed returns and/or that ig-nore the risks that a portable alpha strategy or program may face in periods of crisis.

In addition, we explore recent work by Harry Markowitz on the use of CAPM in the real world, plus extensions of this analysis, looking at the dynamic impact of leveraging on the market portfolio, the pricing of risk, security prices, and including the potential for a destabilizing out-come. A detailed analysis of stress testing is put forth as a risk measurement tool that may be particularly relevant for portable alpha investment ap-plications, in addition to a thorough understanding of the tails of return distributions—and ultimately *just using good common sense.*

LIABILITY-DRIVEN INVESTING

While certainly not relevant for all investors, liability-driven investing (LDI) is right up there with portable alpha in terms of not only the number of conferences dedicated to the topic but also the number of investors who are focused on the potential benefits of such an approach. In many ways the two topics are actually interrelated, given the fact that many of the LDI approaches involve a component (duration *overlays*) that by most measures falls into the broad category of portable alpha. Of course, with LDI, the primary focus is specifically related to liability hedging and reducing balance sheet volatility as opposed to an improved return profile. That said, the ultimate goal is to reduce risk (relative to liabilities) at a given level of expected (asset) return and is therefore not entirely different from portable alpha strategies more broadly.

Chapter 10 provides an overview of LDI, including the landscape, objec-tives, and key examples, tying in the relevance of the portable alpha invest-ment application as appropriate. While both concepts may represent impor-tant shifts in focus by investors, the ultimate goal is apparent: better security for plan participants and a better ability to weather future market storms.

PORTABLE ALPHA THEORY AND PRACTICE: WRAPPING IT UP

Chapter 11 summarizes the central themes and concepts presented through-out the book, including the reasons why we feel that the time, energy, and effort required to truly understand and evaluate portable alpha investment applications, sources of return and risk, and different approaches to portable alpha implementation is likely to be a worthwhile endeavor.

CHAPTER 2

Portable Alpha Definitions and Trends

Sabrina Callin

The term *portable alpha* has been used to describe an increasing number of investment strategies in recent years. What exactly is portable alpha? More than anything, it is an investment application, one that can be employed in a variety of ways to generate potential value-added for investors. The rapidly increasing number of possible applications for the concept probably drives the variation in descriptions.

Nonetheless, to the best of our knowledge the vast majority of everything that is described today as portable alpha, alpha-beta separation, and alpha transport shares one common denominator: the use of derivatives (or similar borrowing arrangements) to gain market exposure, coupled with an investment in a separate and distinct strategy (or set of strategies) designed to generate excess returns, or *alpha*. The market exposure obtained using derivatives is typically described as the *beta*, while the underlying capital investment that effectively collateralizes the derivatives exposure is commonly referred to as the *alpha strategy* or *alpha engine*. The goal is for the combination of the parts—the alpha strategy and the derivative-based market exposure—to generate an attractive risk-adjusted excess return relative to a specified investment benchmark, generally the market index (beta) referenced by the derivatives contracts.

Derivatives allow investors to obtain market exposure at what is typically a money market interest rate-based borrowing cost (also referred to as a *cash* rate and generally proxied by the London Interbank Offered Rate, or LIBOR). As a result, the expected return from a portable alpha strategy is equal to the expected return of the beta market, less the borrowing cost associated with the derivatives, plus the expected return from the alpha strategy. It follows that any excess return generated over the return of the beta

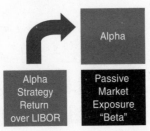

Alpha: Risk-adjusted excess return.

Desired **beta** market returns generally
obtained using futures or swaps at
LIBOR-based cost.*

NOTE: Resulting alpha may or may not be equal to alpha strategy returns over LIBOR.
       End result is dependent on correlation between alpha strategy and beta
       market exposure, realized financing cost, implementation considerations, and
       other factors.

*The cost of obtaining desired beta market returns via derivatives is generally tied to
 short-term LIBOR although the cost (+/–LIBOR) may vary to a material degree across
 different market exposures and market environments.

FIGURE 2.1   Simplified Portable Alpha Diagram
Source: PIMCO.

market will be roughly equal to the return of the alpha strategy over LIBOR,
before accounting for fees and other portable alpha implementation costs.
Figure 2.1 provides an admittedly simplified portable alpha illustration.

Of course, borrowing rates vary and some portable alpha programs
involve additional borrowing costs, liquidity facilities, lines of credit and the
like, in order to maintain the levered market exposure at times when the
alpha strategy cannot be tapped for required margin flows or collateral calls
associated with the derivatives. It is also true that any excess return over the
beta market return produced by a portable alpha approach may or may not
be equal to the alpha. Rather, the resulting alpha will depend on the risk
inherent in the alpha strategy in addition to the correlation between the beta
market and the alpha strategy, factors that should be carefully contemplated
by investors when estimating the possible distribution of returns on the
capital invested. More on this later.

THE VALUE OF AND COMPONENTS TO
PORTING ALPHA

The term *portable alpha* (or *transportable alpha* or *alpha transport*) references one of the key benefits of the portable alpha investment application—
the idea that alpha can be sourced from an entirely distinct investment and
then *ported* to the desired market exposure. This allows investors access to
a much broader opportunity set for alpha than is the case when an investor

is limited to selecting solely from managers with apparent skill in selecting securities and managing the risks in the desired market arena (for example, equity managers with demonstrated stock selection skill).

In addition to the broader investment opportunity set that portable alpha avails to investors, the diversification benefits from combining desired market exposure with an independent and unrelated alpha strategy can result in a compelling risk/return profile and the potential for a substantial reduction in downside risk. There are also unique benefits that the portable alpha investment application can provide to investors focused on liability-driven investing or other risk-neutral reference points that are different from the traditional absolute return framework where portfolio efficiency is measured relative to the risk-free rate. The result: an increasingly broad set of potentially powerful investment applications and, in many cases, a return profile that is more attractive or at least highly complementary to traditional investment strategies.

Although the term has only somewhat recently entered the common lexicon of the investment management industry—albeit with a vengeance!—a section discussing the topic in the *Investments* textbook authored by Bill Sharpe, Gordon Alexander, and Jeffery Baily, titled "Transportable Alpha," dates back to at least the early 1990s.[1] Despite the proliferation of different portable alpha strategies and applications in recent years, the two forms of portable alpha described in the *Investments* textbook still provide an excellent basis for understanding the key components of a portable alpha approach.

The first example involved a decision by a large pension plan to increase the aggregate expected alpha generated by plan assets by effectively adding active stock manager alpha to their fixed income allocation. In order to accomplish this goal without deviating from the desired asset allocation and associated risk profile, the pension plan increased exposure to a group of active stock managers who the trustees believed would continue to deliver high levels of alpha, decreased the exposure to the stock market by an equivalent amount using stock index futures, and also increased fixed-income exposure by an equivalent amount using Treasury futures contracts as follows:

- The capital allocated to the portable alpha approach was invested with the active equity managers expected to provide the equity market return plus additional risk-adjusted return (alpha).
- The extra stock market exposure was hedged by selling stock market index futures. (Short equity futures positions provide investors with the inverse of the stock market return plus a money market rate–based return.)

- The desired fixed-income exposure was obtained by purchasing Treasury futures. (Treasury futures provide the return of the underlying Treasury instruments less a money market rate–based borrowing rate.)

The end result, assuming the lending and borrowing rates are the same in the stock index and Treasury futures markets (and ignoring transaction, liquidity and other implementation costs), is simply the Treasury return plus the excess return generated by the active equity managers, as the short and long equity market exposures and the short and long financing rates cancel out as illustrated in Figure 2.2. Alluding back to the definition of the portable alpha investment application presented at the beginning of this chapter, the alpha strategy in this example is represented by the combination of the investment with the active equity managers and the short equity futures positions—similar conceptually to a market-neutral equity strategy whereby the expected alpha is generated from stock selection but there is no systematic exposure to the stock market itself.

The other transportable alpha example put forth in the *Investments* text was PIMCO's StocksPLUS approach, a strategy that collateralizes equity index derivatives with an actively managed short-term bond portfolio with the goal of providing clients with alpha in addition to the return of the stock

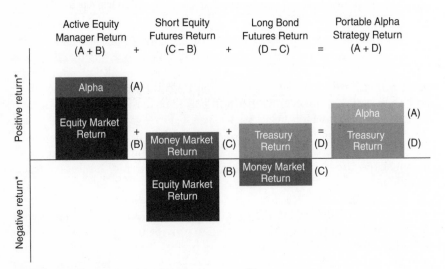

*Assumes equity market and treasury returns are positive.

FIGURE 2.2   Stock-Selection Based Portable Alpha Bond Strategy
Source: PIMCO; hypothetical example for illustrative purposes only.

market. In this case, as shown in Figure 2.3, the short-term bond strategy is designed to outperform a money market interest rate (with a materially similar risk profile to money market instruments), whereas the long equity index futures contracts provide the total return of the equity market less the money market–based borrowing rate. As a result, the combination of the two should produce the equity market return plus the alpha from the short-term bond strategy. In this case, the alpha strategy is simply the actively managed short-term bond portfolio.

The success of a particular portable alpha approach is generally defined by the end result. Is the result superior to a passive index investment and/or available actively managed traditional investment strategies from the standpoint of the associated return and risk? In the case of the pension plan example, success is largely dependent on the active stock managers' ability to outperform the equity market, even though the ultimate goal is bond market outperformance. In the case of the StocksPLUS strategy, success is dependent on PIMCO's ability to outperform the borrowing cost associated with the stock index futures. Importantly, however, even though the first application takes place at the investment portfolio or plan level and the second at the investment strategy level, both approaches can be broken

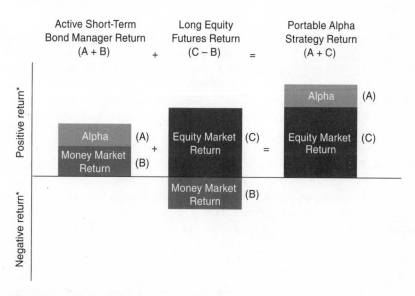

*Assumes equity market and treasury returns are positive.

FIGURE 2.3 Short-Term Bond–Based Portable Alpha Equity Strategy
Source: PIMCO; hypothetical example for illustrative purposes only.

down into the two components commonly referred to as beta and alpha in an alpha-beta separation context:

1. The derivatives-based market exposure, which provides the investor with the desired market or asset exposure.
2. The alpha strategy, which is designed to provide investors with additional incremental return. (It may or may not involve short futures positions or short sales of securities to achieve desired risk/return characteristics.)

As was the case with the transportable alpha examples originally put forth in the *Investments* text many years ago, everything that is described as portable alpha today includes those same two components.

THE DERIVATIVES-BASED MARKET EXPOSURE (BETA)

Derivatives have a negative connotation for some—generally in connection with capital losses experienced by people who invest in highly levered derivative positions in an attempt to magnify returns. Of course, placing blame on derivatives is hardly fair. Rather, the decision of whether to invest in a particular instrument, asset, or strategy ultimately lies with the investor and/or the manager, as do the results.[2] Certainly derivatives have inherent complexities that may not exist with outright purchases of physical securities like stocks or bonds. However, derivatives serve a very important function in the financial markets. Most important, for purposes of portable alpha investment applications, derivatives provide investors with the ability to efficiently finance or hedge market exposure. In this sense, derivatives can be likened to borrowing or lending activity that may be more readily familiar to most people.

Anyone who finances a car obtains the asset (the car) without paying for the asset up front. The financing cost is tied to a specified borrowing rate and paid over the life of the auto loan. There also may be a relatively small initial deposit required. Futures and swaps that are used by investors to gain market exposure work in much the same way as more familiar borrowing arrangements as explained in more detail in Chapter 7. The investor obtains the asset exposure without paying for it up front, and incurs a borrowing cost over the life of the derivatives contract. As previously noted, the borrowing cost is generally tied to a short-term money market rate, like LIBOR. There also may be an initial margin deposit required, which is typically held in high quality, liquid interest-bearing securities like U.S. Treasuries.

THE ALPHA STRATEGY

The use of derivatives to gain desired market exposure frees up investment capital that would have otherwise been required as payment for physical securities. As such, assuming the desired market exposure can be obtained at a reasonable cost on an ongoing basis via the derivatives market, an investor can invest the capital in a wide variety of different alpha strategies.

As a starting point to the decision process, it is important to identify an alpha strategy that is expected to outperform the borrowing cost associated with the derivatives-based market exposure (beta) and any other costs or fees associated with the execution of the portable alpha approach. In one sense, the alpha strategy decision is similar to traditional active investment management approaches—the investor is looking for a strategy that is expected to outperform an index (in this case, a money market borrowing rate). Also similar to investing more broadly, in order to outperform a money market rate, the investor is generally required to assume some type of risk.

Besides evaluating the return and risk profile of the alpha strategy on a stand-alone basis, there are other considerations that are highly germane to portable alpha investment applications. The primary additional considerations relate to liquidity requirements, capital preservation, and the relationship between the alpha strategy and the beta exposure that is obtained using derivatives. Specifically:

- Liquidity is very important given the unfunded nature of the beta component. In an up market, investors will receive cash inflows from the broker or counterparty that need be reinvested. Conversely, in a down market investors are required to provide cash or securities to the broker or counterparty. If the alpha strategy does not provide ready liquidity, it may be necessary for the investor to either carve out a portion of the capital allocated to the portable alpha program to meet potential liquidity needs or enter into some type of borrowing arrangement. *The liquidity element of portable alpha strategies is addressed in more detail in Chapter 8, together with other relevant implementation considerations.*
- The alpha strategy should be reasonably reliable for purposes of long-term capital preservation because the capital allocated to the alpha strategy also serves as collateral for the derivatives-based market exposure. Strategies that are untested across different market cycles and environments or involve less familiar risks may require careful analysis and stress testing to assess the true downside risk on an ongoing basis.
- The excess return that is generated from a portable alpha strategy is primarily a function of the return of the alpha strategy over the borrowing cost associated with the derivatives-based market exposure. However,

the capital that an investor allocates to a portable alpha strategy is exposed to the collective risk of both the alpha and the beta components. Therefore it is important to consider this when evaluating suitable alpha strategies and to select a strategy that, when combined with the derivatives-based (beta) market exposure(s), not only provides incremental excess return but does so at an acceptable level of risk from the perspective of the investor. In some cases—most likely when the alpha strategy is low-risk to start with and also exhibits little or no correlation with the beta market—the resulting risk profile may be virtually identical to the risk profile of the beta market. However, in other cases the risk profile can be very different indeed, as reviewed in more detail in Chapter 5.

COMMON MISPERCEPTIONS

The concept of portable alpha is often oversimplified, perhaps in an attempt to take something that is actually fairly complicated and make it digestible. Regardless of the reason, the end result is some number of misperceptions that may exist among investors.

One potential misperception is the idea that any investment strategy that is designed to outperform cash (in other words, to generate an *absolute return* relative to the risk-free rate as proxied by money market borrowing rates like LIBOR) and/or is categorized as *market-neutral* is a suitable candidate for use as collateral for any given derivatives market exposure in a portable alpha context. In reality, alpha strategy decisions and beta decisions are highly interrelated. This is true because the alpha strategy investment serves as collateral for the derivatives-based market exposure (beta), as previously described. It is also true because an investor relies on the combination of the two to produce the desired expected risk/return profile and results.

Almost every investment strategy is designed to produce an absolute return over cash—with the exception of very low-risk cash investments like Treasury bills, money market instruments, and funds—and every investment strategy that is designed to generate a return over cash presumably requires that the *investor* assume some type of risk. Just because an investment manager calls a strategy "absolute return" or decides to benchmark the strategy against the risk-free rate or a proxy does not mean that there are not risk factors inherent in the strategy that warrant careful consideration by potential investors. Even in a case where an attempt is made to isolate an active manager's true alpha (risk-adjusted excess return) by hedging out the associated benchmark or risk factor exposure, it is still important to consider the active management risk exposures that the manager is taking to generate the alpha in the first place, together with any residual market risk left over after the benchmark exposure is hedged.

This is especially relevant in a portable alpha context, where it is often the case that the capital allocated to the alpha strategy is combined with an equivalent amount of capital exposure to the beta. Putting the concept into a picture in Figure 2.4, for every $100 allocated to the portable alpha strategy, an investor obtains $200 worth of risk factor exposure—or potentially more if the alpha strategy also involves leverage.

If the combined set of risk factors result in undesirable leverage or downside risk, the result can be disastrous for the end investor. Of course, it does not automatically follow that $200-plus worth of risk factor exposure (as in the example in Figure 2.4) will result in an increase in risk, and it certainly does not follow that the risk is 100 percent additive. That is where the power of diversification comes in.

Importantly, though, investors should not assume that the risk of capital loss with a portable alpha strategy is the same as the risk of capital loss with a passive beta market investment, without carefully considering the likely distribution of returns from the combination of potential risk factor exposures in the alpha strategy and the derivatives-based beta market exposure. An increase in risk relative to a passive beta market investment may be perfectly acceptable and even desirable if there is a corresponding expected increase in return. However, ignorance of the risk assumed in an alpha strategy may not be well received as an explanation for the significant underperformance of a portable alpha strategy.

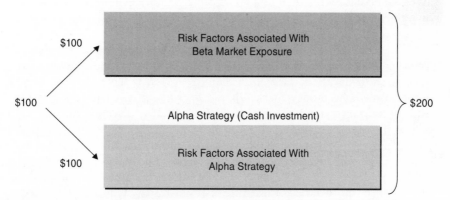

FIGURE 2.4   Portable Alpha Market Exposure Example
Source: PIMCO; hypothetical example for illustrative purposes only.

Another misperception is the idea that the portable alpha investment application allows an investor to transport alpha, once identified, to any desirable market exposure. The same is true when it comes to the idea that alpha can easily be separated by hedging out beta using derivatives. It is true that the derivatives markets have evolved to a substantial degree, such that it is now possible to replicate or hedge a much larger variety of market exposures using derivatives than was possible even at the beginning of the twenty-first century. That said, there still are a number of market exposures that are not readily available in the derivatives markets, at least not necessarily on an ongoing basis at a low cost, and the ability to employ a portable alpha approach is dependent first and foremost on the availability of a liquid, cost-efficient beta derivatives market. As such, while applications for the portable alpha concept are increasingly broad, investors will be well served by carefully considering the viability, on an ongoing basis, of obtaining (or, where applicable, hedging) market exposure via the derivatives market as a starting point to employing a portable alpha strategy.

THE EVOLUTION OF PORTABLE ALPHA

The first use of the investment application that has come to be called portable alpha dates back to at least the early 1980s, shortly after the introduction of U.S. Treasury futures. At that time the investment team at PIMCO was managing a number of investment portfolios benchmarked against broad U.S. bond market indexes that included U.S. Treasury securities. PIMCO recognized that Treasury futures provided an opportunity to generate attractive alpha for clients within their bond portfolios, as described by PIMCO's chief investment officer, William Gross, in the *Financial Analysts Journal* article "Consistent Alpha Generation through Structure."[3]

The idea was relatively straightforward: Opportunistically purchase Treasury note futures and collateralize the futures positions with high-quality, short-duration, *cash equivalent* securities. If the cash equivalents outperformed the money market–based borrowing cost embedded in the futures contract price (which tended to trade at a discount to Treasury bills at the time), then the total return from the Treasury futures plus cash equivalent strategy would exceed the return of the associated Treasury instrument, thereby generating attractive incremental returns for client portfolios. Importantly, because the Treasury futures collateral was limited to high-quality, short-duration instruments, the strategy was essentially risk-neutral relative to holding the associated Treasury instruments outright. Since that time, PIMCO has expanded this strategy, called "BondsPLUS," in an attempt to produce structurally based alpha for clients using a variety of different fixed-income derivative instruments.

Of course the portable alpha investment application is not limited to generating alpha within actively managed fixed-income portfolios. The application can be used within any type of investment portfolio to generate attractive incremental returns so long as there are liquid derivatives contracts available to provide the desired market exposure. Moreover, the application can be used as the basis for an entire investment strategy, as is the case with most of what people refer to as portable alpha today, where the desired market index exposure is obtained using derivatives, and the majority of the capital allocated to the portable alpha strategy is invested in one or more alpha strategies.

Equity portable alpha strategies that are designed to generate alpha relative to the large cap U.S. equity market by backing S&P 500 futures with a high-quality enhanced cash portfolio have been around since 1986, when PIMCO launched the StocksPLUS strategy cited in the *Investments* text as an example of the transportable alpha concept, as referenced earlier. According to Peter Bernstein on the topic of StocksPLUS and making alpha portable, in his 2007 book *Capital Ideas Evolving,* "So far as I know, this product was the first to seek alpha from a source outside the primary asset holding in a fund."[4]

What happened around this time that is relevant for the portable alpha investment application? The Chicago Mercantile Exchange introduced S&P 500 Index futures in 1982, over a quarter of a century ago, enabling the first stand-alone portable alpha equity strategies to emerge as an alternative to traditional equity management. The idea for StocksPLUS first came to light during a discussion at a PIMCO board meeting involving Bill Gross and also Myron Scholes, a PIMCO director at the time, about how PIMCO's core competencies as an active core bond manager might be expanded to other markets.

The introduction of S&P 500 futures provided a seemingly obvious answer, given the use by PIMCO of the BondsPLUS strategy as a source of alpha within fixed-income portfolios. Transfer PIMCO's active fixed-income management skills to the equity market by owning equity index futures backed by an actively managed, high-quality short-term bond portfolio. The idea seemingly had a great deal of merit for equity investors who were all too often (then and now) disappointed by the results of traditional stock selection strategies.[5] Instead of settling for the returns of the market (less fees) or risking a result of market underperformance (less higher fees) with a similar or even greater level of risk, StocksPLUS provided equity investors with a third choice that, by design, capitalized on equity investors' longer-term horizons to generate potential excess returns without a material increase in volatility or downside risk.

StocksPLUS and similar strategies, in effect, offer equity investors the ability to benefit from what one might describe as time horizon arbitrage. The borrowing cost embedded in the price of an S&P 500 futures contract is a short-term money market rate. However, equity investors generally have much longer time horizons than money market investors and do not require perfect safety and liquidity on a day-by-day basis. As a result, with the StocksPLUS approach there is no logical reason to invest all of the capital that collateralizes the equity futures in money market instruments. Rather, diversified, short-term bond portfolios are only slightly more risky than a money market portfolio when risk is measured by an increase in volatility or a possible loss of capital.

Yet diversified short-term bond portfolios have historically provided an attractive incremental return relative to the additional incremental risk over most periods of reasonable length. This occurs in part because there is a market segmentation effect that causes yields on money market instruments[6] to be lower than they might otherwise be, due to the strong demand from investors who need (or think they need) perfect safety of capital and same day liquidity. However, even though the higher return may be accompanied by slightly higher volatility, it is generally the case with high-quality fixed-income investments that there is a very low probability that investors will not receive a full return of capital plus interest—thus the time horizon arbitrage.

This is clearly evidenced in what is typically a steep slope in the short end of the U.S. Treasury yield curve and also the associated risk/return profile of six-month Treasuries measured relative to one-month Treasuries over the past 40 years, as shown in Figure 2.5.

In the case of U.S. Treasury bills, the risk or element of uncertainty that an investor bears in holding a six-month Treasury bill instead of a one-month Treasury bill is certainly very modest by most measures. In fact, if an investor plans to hold a Treasury bill to maturity, the return is known in advance and there is no incremental risk or uncertainty difference. However, in order to receive the certain result an investor must hold a six-month Treasury bill for six months, instead of one, and short-term interest rates may change over this period, thereby impacting the price of the six-month Treasury bill to a slightly greater degree than one-month Treasury bills during the first five months of the holding period. This moderately greater interest rate sensitivity is what causes the moderately higher volatility of returns with six-month Treasury bills relative to one-month Treasury bills over time.

The introduction and expansion of available derivative contracts that allow investors to efficiently gain market exposure at a money market–based

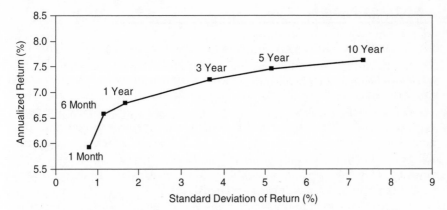

FIGURE 2.5 Annualized Return versus Risk for Various Maturities (Treasury Yield), One-Month Holding Periods, January 1968 through March 2007 *Data source*: Bloomberg Financial Markets, PIMCO.

cost opened the door to a number of related investment applications, and the acknowledgment of the associated benefits has certainly not been unique to PIMCO. There have been investors employing a variety of different portable alpha investment applications, either within investment portfolios as a source of alpha or as the basis for an investment strategy designed to generate alpha relative to a given market exposure, for a number of years. Some investors—generally institutional investors with significant staff, operational, and technological resources—have even used the concepts underlying portable alpha and alpha-beta separation as the basis for their asset and/or risk allocation at the aggregate investment portfolio or plan level.

Interestingly, even with a portable alpha approach that is as relatively straightforward as StocksPLUS, until somewhat recently there was often hesitation on the part of prospective investors largely due to an apparent lack of comfort with the use of derivatives. A different concern that some investors raised specific to StocksPLUS related to the idea that an investment in a short-term bond portfolio (one step away from a money market fund on the risk/return spectrum) for purposes of generating equity market alpha somehow seemed incongruent or even risky. Perhaps the answer really was that, prior to 2000, even relatively simple, portable alpha equity strategies with very little incremental risk just did not seem worth the hassle to some investors. The equity market was delivering 15, 20, even 30 percent per year; pension plans were overfunded; return targets were easily met; and in this environment, additional return from equity market investments may have seemed less critical.

A NEW PARADIGM?

There has undoubtedly been an increase in the use of portable alpha applications by investors over the years. This is evidenced in the growth of strategies like StocksPLUS whereby one investment provider manages both the derivative-based beta market exposure and the alpha strategy. It is also evidenced by an increasing number of investors who have applied the concept of portable alpha to part or all of their investment portfolios with the goal of improving the efficiency or risk-adjusted return, as was the case with the pension plan highlighted in the *Investments* text, and also the case with British Petroleum's pension plan led by Marvin Damsma, as described by Peter Bernstein in *Capital Ideas Evolving.*[7]

However, it was not until shortly after the advent of the twenty-first century that there appeared to be a dramatic increase in interest in the portable alpha concept among both investors and providers. The primary event that preceded the intense focus on portable alpha, alpha-beta separation, and the like appears to have been the equity market downturn that started in 2000 and wreaked havoc on investment portfolios in the ensuing two years. That upheaval was particularly intense for pension plan asset portfolios on a liability-relative basis, as illustrated in Figure 2.6, where pension liabilities are proxied by the Ryan Labs liability index and pension asset portfolios are proxied by a 60 percent allocation to the S&P 500 and a 40 percent allocation to the Lehman Brothers Aggregate Bond Index (LBAG).

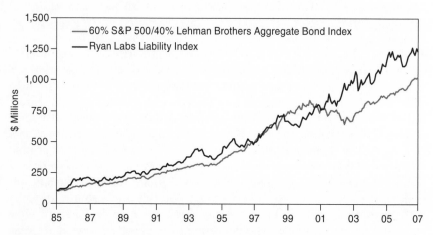

Hypothetical example for illustrative purposes only.
Assumes monthly rebalance to 60% S&P 500/40% Lehman Brothers Aggregate Bond Index.

FIGURE 2.6   Growth of $100 Million as of March 31, 2007
Data source: Ryan Labs, Standard & Poor's, Lehman Brothers.

The value of the average investment portfolio declined to a material degree during this period, erasing much of the gains realized during the dramatic equity bull market of the mid- to late 1990s. At the same time, as is typically the case during periods of equity market stress, interest rates fell, causing pension plan liabilities to rise and moving many pension plans from a position of surplus, with more than enough assets to meet estimated future liabilities, to a deficit with a material percentage of unfunded liabilities, as described in detail in Chapter 10.

Investors not only experienced what for many was a substantial decline in the value of their asset portfolios, but also faced a lower prospective return environment given the decline in interest rates from levels that were already relatively low by historical standards. The low interest rate environment was also coupled with low levels of equity dividends and, for many, lower expectations regarding future stock market price appreciation. Necessity breeds invention, and investors as a group began actively and even aggressively pursuing investments in alternative asset classes and investment strategies with the goal of meeting or exceeding asset return targets and, in many cases, increasing portfolio diversification. As discussed in Chapter 10, many pension plans also started focusing on liability-driven investing in an effort to improve the match between their asset portfolios and the long-term liabilities that the assets were intended to cover, and also in the interest of reducing actual and perceived plan sponsor risk associated with pension plan liabilities.

The substantial decline in the equity market that occurred between 2000 and 2002 was certainly not a positive event from the perspective of most investors. However, the challenges that were largely caused or at least brought to light by the unusually prolonged and severe equity market downturn seemingly spurred a relatively broad-based paradigm shift in investment management, whereby investors as a group focused like never before on the potential benefits of new asset classes, innovative investment strategies—often involving derivatives and leverage—and the benefits of diversification. This is not to say that an entirely new technology was created. Rather, asset classes and investment applications—most of which had been around for some time—that had the potential to help investors achieve their return targets and other objectives were suddenly on everybody's radar, despite the fact that most were more complicated than traditional investments, or at least less familiar to most investors. Investing has always been about taking risk, but now investors are seemingly more open than ever to different types of risks and strategies, including portable alpha.

From our perspective, the pace of the shift was really quite remarkable. Investors, on average, moved very quickly from the stance that the StocksPLUS approach was somewhat complicated to actively considering strategies that collateralize equity or other index derivatives with a wide variety of riskier, less liquid alpha strategies.

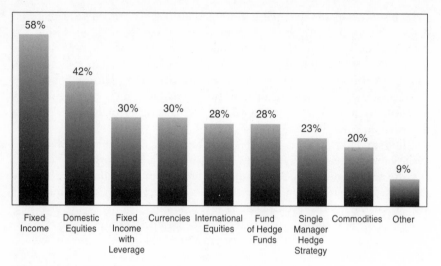

Note: Based on 112 funds that currently use portable alpha strategies.

FIGURE 2.7   Portable Alpha Strategies—Sources of Alpha in 2006 Greenwich Survey
Data source: Greenwich Associates.

The combinations of derivative-based market exposures and investment strategies that providers are offering and investors are employing within a portable alpha context has expanded dramatically in recent years and shows no signs of slowing down. Figures 2.7 and 2.8 summarize the results of a late 2006 Greenwich Associates survey of institutional investors that were invested in portable alpha strategies. Equity derivatives backed by some type of fixed-income alpha engine was the most common form of portable alpha application by a wide margin. However, both sides of the portable alpha equation are rapidly evolving.

THE IMPORTANCE OF RETURN—AND RISK

Perhaps the greatest appeal to investors of the portable alpha investment application following the equity market sell-off at the beginning of the twenty-first century relates to the much-touted marketing line that investors need not settle for equity and bond market returns plus the excess returns of 0.5 percent to 1 percent (after fees) that traditional active stock and bond managers purportedly deliver, on average. Rather, investors—as the marketing message goes—will be much better served by capturing the so-called

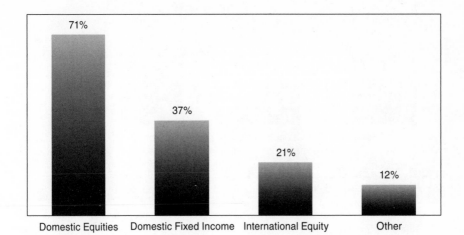

Domestic Equities   Domestic Fixed Income   International Equity   Other

Note: Based on 112 funds that currently use portable alpha strategies.

FIGURE 2.8   Portable Alpha Strategies—Sources of Beta in 2006 Greenwich Survey
Data source: Greenwich Associates.

alpha of 4 percent-plus from a hedge fund or fund-of-funds strategy and transporting that alpha to the equity and bond markets. The end result: equity market return plus 4 percent and bond market return plus 4 percent, and all problems solved for investors, just like the fairy godmother did for Cinderella with the wave of her magic wand after her evil stepmother and stepsisters tore Cinderella's gown to shreds and then left her behind with no hope of attending the Prince's ball.

In the institutional investment management arena, where fiduciaries are particularly concerned about meeting asset return targets, and where the combination of forecasted asset class returns, traditional active manager alphas, and predefined policy portfolios fall short, the idea that portable alpha investment applications may provide a solution is undoubtedly very appealing. Specifically, assuming an 8 percent annual return for equities plus 1 percent alpha after fees and a 5 percent return for bonds plus 0.5 percent alpha after fees, an investor with a traditional 60/40 equity and bond allocation falls short of an 8 percent return target on an expected basis by 0.4 percent, as demonstrated in Figure 2.9. Add a 4 percent excess return to both the expected passive stock and bond market returns and the investor moves from a modest expected shortfall to a reasonably healthy expected surplus relative to the prespecified asset return target, as shown in Figure 2.10. And they lived happily ever after . . .

Equity Index + 1%
Excess Return

Bond Index + 0.5%
Excess Return

Return Target = 8%

8%   +   5%   =   7.6%

60/40 U.S. equity/bond hypothetical asset allocation falls short
of return targets using traditional active managers.

FIGURE 2.9   The Challenge: Return Targets May Be Difficult to Meet
Source: PIMCO; hypothetical example for illustrative purposes only.

The crucial element that is missing from this example, which is also
the key defining factor of modern portfolio theory and a central theme
throughout this book is *risk*.

Is it reasonable to expect that a hedge fund will outperform the money
market–based financing rate associated with obtaining stock and bond exposure through the derivatives markets? Most investors are likely to answer
with a resounding yes. In fact, according to a Greenwich Associates survey of U.S. public and corporate pension plans in late 2006, respondents
on average expected hedge funds to deliver a return over the ensuing five
years (2007–2012) that is roughly in line with the returns expected from
U.S. equities and moderately below the returns expected from international
equities. So the math that results in a 4 percent return over cash as put forth
in the aforementioned marketing-oriented presentations on portable alpha
do not seem that far out of line with investor expectations. Do most people

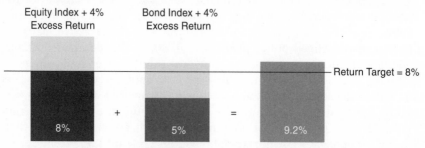

Equity Index + 4%
Excess Return

Bond Index + 4%
Excess Return

Return Target = 8%

8%   +   5%   =   9.2%

60/40 U.S. equity/bond hypothetical asset allocation, using hedge
funds plus equity and bond overlays, exceeds return targets.

FIGURE 2.10   The Potential Solution: Portable Alpha
Source: PIMCO; hypothetical example for illustrative purposes only.

expect hedge funds to deliver equitylike returns with cashlike risk? Probably not, and that is where the evaluation process gets more complicated.

To illustrate this point, it may be helpful to start with a simpler example. If investors expect hedge funds to deliver a return that is roughly equal to the return of U.S. equities, then the same expected return result highlighted in Figure 2.10 could be achieved by investing in U.S. equities as the alpha strategy for both bonds and stocks. In order to achieve this result using U.S. equities as the alpha strategy, the allocation would be 160 percent equities and 40 percent bonds. Interestingly, this type of portable alpha strategy would be most efficiently executed by keeping the capital invested as is—60 percent in equities and 40 percent in bonds—and then purchasing an additional 100 percent of equity market exposure using equity index futures. There are two reasons that this is true:

1. It is much cheaper currently to finance equity market exposure through the derivatives market than bond market exposure.
2. It is generally less expensive to liquidate bonds than stocks as needed to meet margin calls associated with the derivatives exposure.

The other alternative would be to finance the original 60/40 stock and bond exposure through the derivatives markets and then invest the capital in the alpha strategy—in this case equities—which is the more typical way that portable alpha programs are executed (capital invested in alpha strategy, desired beta exposure obtained via the derivatives markets). The key from an investor's standpoint is the probability that the actual result—the expected bond return and equity return plus the 4 percent expected excess return—will deviate substantially from the expected result on the downside. In this case, while we cannot know what the future holds (thus the uncertainty and risk), we do have a long enough period of historical returns for both stocks and bonds to derive probabilities based on historical actual results.

The probability of a loss over a one-year period is 24 percent, and the probability of a loss over a three-year period is 14 percent, based on the historical distribution of returns over the 29-year period ending December 31, 2006[8] from a strategy that was 160 percent exposed to the equity market and 40 percent exposed to the bond market, where the additional 100 percent equity exposure was financed at a U.S. three-month LIBOR financing rate. Using the histogram in Figure 2.11 to illustrate the results over one-year historical time periods, we find that there was a 22 percent incidence of negative returns, an average negative return of –18 percent, and a worst-ever loss of –40 percent, with a mean return of 19.5 percent and a volatility around the mean of 27.5 percent.

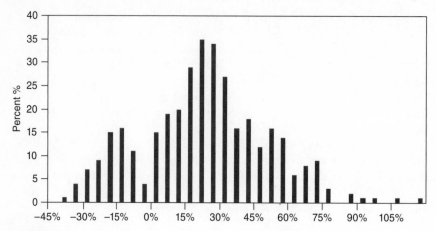

FIGURE 2.11 Twelve-Month Returns of 160/40 Portfolio
Source: PIMCO.

Over three-year time periods—again referencing a histogram, this time in Figure 2.12—we find that there was a 13 percent incidence of negative returns, an average negative return of −11 percent, and a worst-ever loss of 26 percent, with a mean return of 18 percent, annualized, and a volatility around the mean of 16 percent.

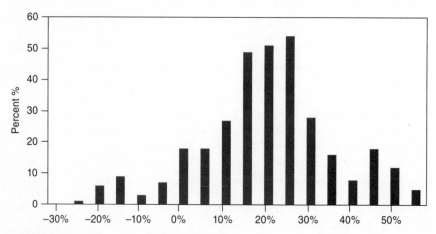

FIGURE 2.12 Thirty-Six-Month Total Returns of 160/40 Portfolio
Source: PIMCO.

Is this an acceptable level of risk for the very attractive expected incremental return? The answer presumably varies from investor to investor, as it should. One commonly used reference point for evaluating the efficiency of an investment strategy or portfolio as it relates to risk and return is the Sharpe ratio, which measures the ratio of incremental return for the incremental risk relative to the risk-free rate. The higher the ratio, the more return per unit of risk. The Sharpe ratio for this 160/40 equity and bond strategy over the past 29 years was 0.40, compared to a Sharpe ratio of 0.55 for a portfolio that had 60/40 exposure over the same time period. As such, the levered equity portfolio (the portable alpha portfolio in our example) produced a lower Sharpe ratio than the unlevered portfolio. This should not be that surprising, because there is a borrowing cost (LIBOR) associated with the leveraged exposure and there is not much of a risk-reducing diversification benefit in adding 100 percent equity market exposure to a portfolio that is 60 percent equities to start with.

Of course, as is always the case, investment results are highly dependent on the time period in question. What if we backed up exactly five years from the year-end that immediately followed the Greenwich survey referenced earlier (the five-year period that ended December 31, 2006), and compared an investment portfolio that was invested 160 percent in equities and 40 percent in bonds to the 60/40 portfolio over this time period? The results are shown in Figure 2.13.

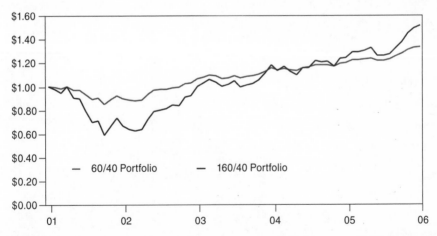

FIGURE 2.13 Growth of One Dollar Investment in 60/40 versus 160/40 S&P 500/LBAG, 2001–2006
Data source: PIMCO, Lehman Brothers, Standard & Poor's.

While this is an admittedly unusual period, the point about returns being time period dependent is strikingly obvious. At the end of the first year of the analysis (December 31, 2002), an investor with a 60/40 allocation would have lost 10 percent while the 160/40 portable alpha investor would have lost 33 percent. Yet, given the period of extraordinary positive equity market returns that followed the period of extraordinary negative returns, the investor in the leveraged portable alpha strategy would still have been better off from a return-on-capital standpoint at the end of the five-year period, with a total return of 8.6 percent annualized versus only 6 percent from the 60/40 strategy. Of course, equity market declines are not always followed by equity market rallies, as shown in the Japanese equity market total return data in Figure 2.14. As of December 31, 2006, the Japanese equity market as defined by the TOPIX index was worth only 67 percent of its value on December 31, 1989.

Moving back to the portable alpha example involving 100 percent exposure to hedge funds, 60 percent exposure to equities, and 40 percent exposure to bonds, the hedge fund alpha strategy is almost certainly going to provide more diversification than would be the case in our example involving 160 percent equity market exposure and 40 percent bond market exposure, and diversification is key to reducing risk. Are the diversification benefits great enough to eliminate the additional risk relative to a portfolio that simply holds 60 percent in equities and 40 percent in bonds all together? It depends—and most specifically depends on the inherent risk in the hedge fund strategy and the correlation between the hedge fund strategy (or

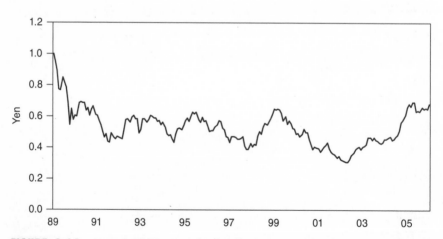

FIGURE 2.14   Growth of One Yen Investment in the TOPIX Total Return Index
Data source: Bloomberg Financial Markets.

strategies) and equities, given the fact that a 60 percent/40 percent portfolio is dominated from a risk standpoint (over 90 percent) by equity market risk, as illustrated in Figure 3.7 in the next chapter.

How correlated with the equity market are hedge funds? Clearly the answer varies not only by type of hedge fund strategy but also from hedge fund to hedge fund. However, as many researchers have shown, there are a number of hedge fund categories that have demonstrated a materially positive correlation with equities, at least in recent years as illustrated in Figure 2.15.

This does not mean that the end result of any given strategy that combines hedge funds with bond and/or equity derivatives exposure will not be a good one, or that the resulting risk/return profile will not be attractive. It is true that the ill-fated Amaranth[9] was used by investors as an alpha strategy within a portable alpha context. However, there are also undoubtedly numerous examples of very successful—in terms of the end result and the risk/return profile—portable alpha programs that employ hedge funds as alpha strategies. The key, as is always the case with investing, is for investors

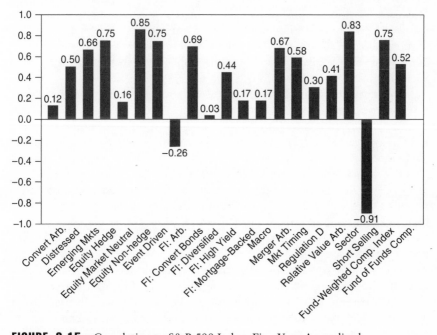

FIGURE 2.15 Correlation to S&P 500 Index, Five-Year Annualized (2002–2006)
Source: HFRI.

and fiduciaries to vigilantly evaluate not only the expected return profile but also the expected risk profile and, most importantly, the downside risk potential, before investing and on an ongoing basis.

CONCLUSION

We applaud the paradigm shift that has resulted in increased investor willingness to consider innovative investment strategies. The result may be an improvement in risk/return profiles—a shift outward in the efficient frontier (as described in Chapter 3), so to speak—for investors as a group. Indeed, one of the key benefits is the much broader opportunity set for value-added and diversification relative to traditional investment strategies. However, we have also watched the paradigm shift with a degree of trepidation because of the potential stumbling blocks for investors associated with newer and more complex investments and investment strategies.

Not surprisingly, we feel that the concept behind portable alpha makes a great deal of sense, whether it is implemented within an investment portfolio, as the basis for an investment strategy, or at the overall asset allocation level. However, portable alpha implementation is not simple—not even in its simplest form, and certainly not in more complex applications as discussed in more detail in Chapter 8. The degree of complexity associated with each component and a given portable alpha application in the aggregate also varies substantially, as do the costs and fees.

This does not mean that portable alpha strategies are riskier than other investment strategies that seek to outperform broader markets. Some strategies are riskier and some are not, and even those strategies that are more risky may present a very attractive risk/reward trade-off for investors. It simply means that investors must explicitly acknowledge the intricacies of portable alpha strategies and adjust the evaluation process and even the investment process accordingly. For example, strong investment and operational risk controls are crucial to maintaining appropriate market and risk factor exposures, particularly during periods of market stress, and many of the more complex portable alpha strategies have only been tested in periods of low and declining market volatility.

The portable alpha investment application may offer investors the ability to capitalize on longer-term horizons and diversification to a better degree than most traditional investment strategies. However, portable alpha is not a magic bullet that somehow eludes the basic laws of investment risk and return.

CHAPTER 3

Back to the Basics: Investments 101

Alfred Murata and Sabrina Callin

Investment: Sacrifice of certain present value for (possibly uncertain) an expected greater future value.
        —Sharpe, Alexander, and Bailey, *Investments*

Most individuals and entities have future explicit or implicit liabilities that they are attempting to satisfy—retirement spending goals, college educations, pension obligations, and so on—and investing for the future is not so much an option as a necessity. But understanding the *need* to invest and deciding *how* to invest are two very different things. Not surprisingly, the details behind any given investment decision-making process vary substantially in practice. In theory, however, the optimal portfolio for a given investor is dominantly a function of the investor's return objectives, time horizon, liquidity requirements, and risk tolerance. While the true risk-free investment may vary from investor to investor, investing fundamentally relates to the trade-off between expected risk and return, and the benefits of diversification.

Risk and uncertainty can be substantially reduced by investing in instruments such as U.S. Treasury bills that bear a low risk of a capital loss, are highly liquid, and provide a predetermined return on capital (based on the coupon and prevailing rates at the time of purchase) when held until maturity. In fact, U.S. Treasury bills are generally the de facto designated "risk-free" asset in investment textbooks. However, there is a trade-off associated with highly liquid investments that substantially eliminate the risk of incurring capital losses: a lower expected return. It is generally necessary to take some type of *risk* in order to generate incremental return over the risk-free rate. This does not come as a surprise, of course. Risk tolerance is the guiding factor behind any well-designed investment decision-making process and the identification, measurement, and diversification of risk is critical to optimal investing.

In practice, the task of defining and quantifying risk (of capital losses, of not meeting future obligations, etc.) may be much more complex than it is in theory. It is also true that return profiles and correlations among investment risks, asset classes, and strategies are far from stable in many cases, making the ex-ante construction of a portfolio that will produce the optimal ex-post result an acutely challenging task. Furthermore, textbook applications of investment theory typically imbed any number of assumptions that are necessary to illustrate an important concept, yet do not hold true for most investors in the real world.

Nonetheless, the central underpinnings of investment theory that we explore in more detail in this chapter—with a central focus on the related concepts of risk and return and also the benefit of diversification—are as relevant today as ever, and particularly so for understanding both the potential benefits and complexities of portable alpha strategies. Risk typically goes hand in hand with an expected return premium over the risk-free rate—and, generally speaking, the higher the expected return, the greater the underlying risk. Thanks to financial innovation, however, the universe of available risk factors continues to expand along with the array of different instruments, vehicles, and associated investment strategies, increasing the potential value that can be derived from intelligent investing and diversification.

THE OPTIMAL INVESTMENT PORTFOLIO

The investment process generally starts with a careful assessment of return objectives, time horizon, liquidity requirements, and risk tolerance. The investor's level of sophistication is also relevant, as are related preferences and restrictions specific to different types of securities and investment strategies. These considerations, and any other pertinent information, help establish the initial parameters for the construction of a tailored investment policy and portfolio. An investor who has a very short time horizon, requires absolute safety of principal, and also needs perfect liquidity will be limited to investment choices that are effectively risk-free, even on a day-over-day basis. An investment portfolio that consists entirely of money market securities or similar cashlike investments may be optimal for this type of investor. However, for most investors with longer time horizons, the optimal portfolio will include a diversified set of investmentss that collectively result in a higher risk of a capital loss, greater volatility, and lower liquidity than a portfolio consisting entirely of cashlike investments.

Harry Markowitz published his groundbreaking paper in 1952 in the *Journal of Finance* titled "Portfolio Selection" and is generally credited with setting the basis for modern portfolio theory as we know it today. According to fellow Nobel laureate Bill Sharpe, "Markowitz came along, and there was light. Markowitz said a portfolio has expected return and risk. Expected return is related to the expected return of the securities, but risk is more complicated. Risk is related to the individual components as well as the correlations."[1]

One of the most analyzed problems in finance theory is optimal portfolio construction, where the goal is to maximize return at a given level of risk tolerance. In a world in which an investor is certain of the future, the optimal portfolio construction problem is trivially reduced to that of structuring a portfolio that will maximize the investor's return. Unfortunately, the future is not certain and consequently, in addition to the considerations specific to the investor, the solution to the optimal portfolio construction problem will depend upon (1) a set of possible future scenarios for the world; (2) a correspondence or mapping function, linking possible future scenarios to the returns of individual securities; (3) a probability function of the likelihood of each of the possible future scenarios of the world; and (4) considering 1, 2, and 3, a way to determine whether one portfolio is preferable to another portfolio. Reduced even to this level of abstractness, the optimal portfolio construction problem is difficult to solve, and consequently, finance theory uses assumptions in each of the four elements.

UTILITY FUNCTIONS AND RISK AVERSION

Even if an investor has a view on items 1, 2, and 3 in the preceding paragraph, it may still be unclear how to construct an optimal portfolio due to difficulty in comparing individual portfolios. The least controversial and most basic assumption is to assume that an investor prefers more wealth to less wealth. Consequently, an investor would prefer portfolio A to portfolio B if portfolio A resulted in more wealth regardless of which future scenario of the world was realized. However, the assumption that an investor prefers more wealth to less wealth will not provide much assistance in determining whether portfolio A is preferable to portfolio C if certain future scenarios favor portfolio A while other scenarios favor portfolio C. A commonly used methodology is to assume that investors attempt to maximize their expected utility, which is a function of the investor's utility in each possible scenario, where the utility in each scenario is an increasing function of the investor's wealth.

Finance research generally assumes that investors are risk-averse, meaning the additional utility gained from an additional dollar of wealth is less than the reduction of utility caused by a loss of a dollar of wealth. An implication of risk aversion is that investors would generally prefer to have consistent levels of wealth regardless of what future scenario is realized, rather than having higher levels of wealth in some scenarios and lower levels of wealth in other scenarios.

One commonly studied utility function is the quadratic utility function, where expected utility is an increasing function of expected future wealth, and a decreasing function of the variance of future wealth. The degree of risk aversion in the quadratic utility function example relates to the trade-off between expected return and variance, where investors with higher risk aversion would need a greater increase in expected return to be indifferent to an increase in variance of future wealth. While the mean-variance model implied by the quadratic utility function is not perfect, it is generally thought of as at least having some applicability for most investors.

PORTFOLIO SELECTION AND THE EFFICIENT FRONTIER

Optimal portfolio selection is predicated on the ability to measure both the expected return and expected risk of individual assets or investment strategies and also the covariance or correlation among assets and investment strategies. Standard deviation is the statistical measure most commonly used to quantify risk as reflected by the historical or expected return dispersion. In absolute risk terms, standard deviation helps investors measure the variability of returns and therefore, assuming a normal return distribution, the potential upside as well as downside (negative return or capital loss) deviation. The key concepts behind portfolio selection and the efficient frontier may be best illustrated by walking through a hypothetical example where the goal is to construct an optimal portfolio, minimizing risk at a given level of expected return or, alternatively, maximizing expected return at a given level of risk.

Figure 3.1 displays the expected return and standard deviation of returns for a collection of assets. As a starting point, let's assume that the investor is limited to allocating a nonnegative amount of the portfolio to two securities, A and B, as illustrated in Figure 3.2.

A 100 percent allocation to security A will result in a portfolio with an expected return of 6.0 percent and a standard deviation of 8.0 percent,

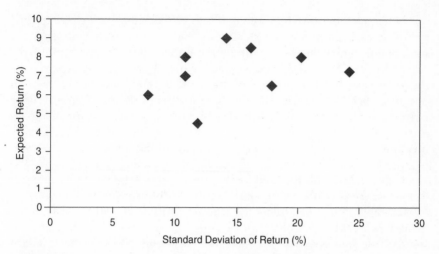

FIGURE 3.1 Expected Return versus Standard Deviation for the Investment Universe
Source: PIMCO; hypothetical example for illustrative purposes only.

while a 100 percent allocation to security B will result in a portfolio with an expected return of 8.0 percent and a standard deviation of 11.0 percent. The curved line joining securities A and B denotes the expected return and standard deviation of a portfolio with a nonnegative portion of the portfolio invested in security A, and the remaining portion invested in security B.

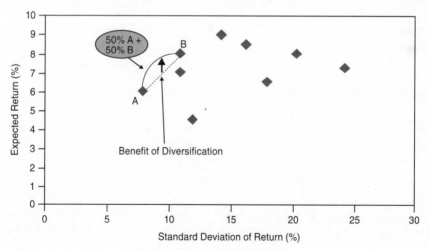

FIGURE 3.2 Allocation of Portfolio to Two Securities
Source: PIMCO; hypothetical example for illustrative purposes only.

Note that the curved line joining securities A and B has a higher expected return at each given level of standard deviation of return than does the straight line joining the two securities. The amount of separation between the curved line and the straight line joining security A and security B represents the benefit associated with diversification and depends upon the correlation of returns between securities A and B. If returns of security A and security B are perfectly correlated (which means that a strong return for A implies a strong return for B), then there would be no diversification benefits by investing in both of the securities, and the curved line joining security A and security B would be identical to the straight line joining them.

Figure 3.3 extends the results of Figure 3.2 to the case where the investor can invest the portfolio in any of the securities in the investment universe.

The curved line represents the *efficient frontier,* the portfolio with the highest expected return that can be constructed given a specified level of standard deviation. Note that there is a lower boundary in the standard deviation of returns that can be obtained due to correlation in security returns, whereas there is no upper boundary on the expected return that can be obtained, since the expected return of the portfolio can be increased by shorting a security with a lower expected return and investing the proceeds in a security with a higher expected return.

Figure 3.4 builds on this concept of the efficient frontier and applies the concept of the utility indifference curve to find the efficient portfolio.

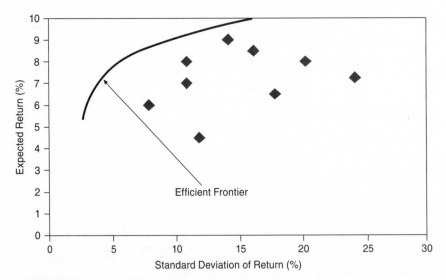

FIGURE 3.3   Efficient Frontier
Source: PIMCO; hypothetical example for illustrative purposes only.

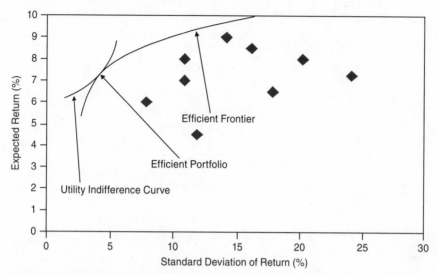

FIGURE 3.4 Efficient Portfolio
Source: PIMCO; hypothetical example for illustrative purposes only.

The shape of the investor's utility indifference curve depends upon the investor's degree of risk aversion. Nonetheless, the indifference curve is upward-sloping, as the investor is only willing to accept greater risk if the expected return is increased. The efficient portfolio can be found where the investor's utility indifference curve is tangent to the efficient frontier. Consequently, by investing in the efficient portfolio, the investor's utility will be maximized.

THE CAPITAL MARKET LINE

Harry Markowitz's efficient frontier was further extended by James Tobin to allow for risk-free lending and borrowing. Figure 3.5 displays the *capital market line,* which is the efficient frontier when investors have the opportunity to borrow or lend at the risk-free rate.

Under the assumption that investors can borrow or lend at the risk-free rate, all investors allocate their portfolios into only two assets: a portion to the market portfolio, the optimally diversified portfolio of risky assets for reasons noted subsequently; and the remainder to the risk-free asset. Investors who are willing to take more risk will increase their allocation to the market portfolio, while investors who are willing to take less risk will increase their allocation to the risk-free asset. The most risk adverse

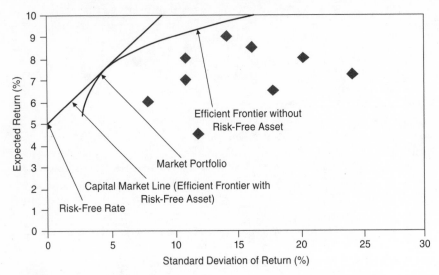

FIGURE 3.5 Capital Market Line
Source: PIMCO; hypothetical example for illustrative purposes only.

investors will invest wholly in the risk free asset and investors with even a greater risk tolerance than that represented by the market portfolio will theoretically borrow at the risk-free rate in order to obtain more than 100 percent exposure to the market portfolio. By structuring their portfolios in this manner, investors will maximize their expected return at a given level of risk.

Various metrics can be used to evaluate investment performance. Nevertheless, it is well understood that investing the entire portfolio in the risk-free asset is always a potential investment strategy. Consequently, a reasonable metric for analyzing investment performance should observe the portfolio return in excess of the risk-free rate, or *excess return,* rather than solely focusing on the *absolute* performance or return of the portfolio. A commonly used risk metric is the Sharpe ratio, which is equal to the excess return of the portfolio relative to the risk-free rate divided by the standard deviation of the portfolio—effectively a measure of excess return per unit of risk. Given that investors are assumed to be risk-averse, the higher the Sharpe ratio, the better. Note that under the assumptions previously discussed, on an ex-ante basis, any portfolio on the capital market line would have the maximum Sharpe ratio possible, by definition. But a portfolio that lies off the capital market line may have a higher realized ex-post Sharpe ratio than that of a portfolio on the capital market line.

Many financial models are one-period models, where the underlying thesis is that one can apply insights from a single period to the real world. Under these models, it is assumed that there is a security that provides a risk-free rate of return which will be identical regardless of what future scenario is realized. Consider a world where there are only two securities: a risk-free security that provides an identical rate of return in all scenarios, and a risky security that provides high rates of return in certain scenarios and lower rates of return in other scenarios. Depending upon the investor's risk preferences, the expected return, and the standard deviation of the securities, the investor can determine the optimal allocation between the risk-free and risky securities. The investor will increase the allocation to the risky asset as its expected return increases relative to that of the risk-free asset, and will decrease the allocation to the risky asset as the standard deviation of the risky asset increases.

CAPM AND FACTOR MODELS

As we observed, regardless of an investor's level of risk aversion, the optimal portfolio should, according to the underlying investment theory, lie somewhere on the capital market line. Thus, each investor's optimal portfolio would be wholly invested in the risk-free asset, wholly invested in the market portfolio, or partially invested in the market portfolio and partially invested in the risk-free asset. Given that it is theoretically suboptimal for any investor to invest in any risky asset outside of the market portfolio—since such investments would lie below the Capital Market Line—the market portfolio must be comprised of all risky assets. In addition, the proportion of each risky asset in the market portfolio must be proportional to each asset's market capitalization.

The capital asset pricing model (Sharpe 1964), or CAPM, references the market portfolio for purposes of pricing securities in a state of market equilibrium based on the idea that, at equilibrium, each security will be equally desirable. (If this was not the case, investors would purchase a more desirable security and sell a less desirable security, thereby bringing the price of the security back into equilibrium). Furthermore, each security's risk can be decomposed into idiosyncratic risk and systematic risk factors. An example of a systematic risk factor is stock market risk. A recession may negatively impact the stock market as a whole, whereas the possibility that a particular biotechnology company's drug trial will not be successful is a risk factor that is idiosyncratic to (uniquely associated with) that particular company.

Under the assumptions of CAPM, investors can diversify away the idiosyncratic risks of each security by investing in the market portfolio. Thus investors will not be compensated for taking on greater idiosyncratic risk. Consequently, the expected excess return of each security will be proportional to the amount of the security's market risk relative to that of the market portfolio, which is defined by the security's beta, as described in more detail in Chapter 5. Note that the market risk of the market portfolio relative to itself is equal to 1, so the beta of the market portfolio is equal to 1, while the expected excess return of the market portfolio is equal to the expected return of the market portfolio less the risk-free rate.

Capital asset pricing model analysis can be extended in various dimensions, including the addition of supplementary risk factors. For example, Fama and French extended the underlying concept to a three-factor model, where the equity market risk factor is supplemented by a large/small cap risk factor and a high/low book value risk factor. Regardless of the number of additional factors used to explain security or portfolio valuations, the central idea of these models is that investors should receive excess return over the risk-free rate as compensation for assuming market risk.

THE BENEFITS OF DIVERSIFICATION

As previously illustrated in the examples involving the efficient frontier, investors should take advantage of opportunities that will reduce a portfolio's risk level while retaining the same expected return threshold, in the same way that investors should take advantage of opportunities to increase a portfolio's expected return without increasing risk. The principal way to reduce portfolio risk without increasing an allocation to the risk-free asset is through diversification, which can also result in an increase in return without a corresponding increase in risk.

The benefits of diversification can be illustrated using a two-security example. If security X and security Y have a perfect negative correlation, that means that security X's returns are always weak when security Y's returns are strong, and vice versa. However, if knowledge of security X's return does not provide any information regarding security Y's return, then security X and security Y exhibit zero correlation. And if security X's returns are always strong when security Y's returns are strong, that means that the two securities are perfectly correlated. Given the fact that underlying economic factors affect the valuation of many securities, returns of many securities and corresponding investment strategies are positively correlated with one another.

The addition of securities that are expected to provide identical returns should reduce risk in the absence of the use of leverage and assuming the securities are not perfectly correlated. Nevertheless, the diversification benefit of adding more securities to the portfolio tends to decrease as the number of securities in the portfolio increases. At some point, the diversification benefits of adding securities to the portfolio will tend to be overwhelmed by the drawbacks of transaction costs and complexity.

Two approaches are generally used to determine which securities will add the greatest benefit of diversification to the portfolio. One approach is to use historical data to find out what security correlations were in the past, and to use this data when constructing the diversified portfolio. An alternative or supplement to the historical approach is to devise several risk factors that should affect security valuations, estimate each security's sensitivity to each of the risk factors, and then use these estimates to derive portfolio correlations.

RISK PREMIUMS

A *risk premium* is the rate of return in excess of the risk-free rate that an investor can expect to earn by investing in a security other than the risk-free security. Theoretically, many securities should provide an expected return in excess of the risk-free rate in order to induce investors to choose such securities over risk-free assets, since investors are assumed to be risk-averse. It is important to recognize that while these securities may provide an *expected* return in excess of the risk-free rate, they do not produce a *certain* return in excess of the risk-free rate. Consequently, an investor will not always end up realizing higher returns than the risk-free rate by investing in securities with positive risk premiums, since there is always a possibility that the downside of risk will emerge. In addition, it not possible to determine what the risk premium embedded in a security actually is, since the risk premium is not directly observable.

Many market participants attempt to use historical returns as a proxy for future returns to estimate risk premiums. This approach is not perfect, since historical returns only provide information on what returns happened to be in one possible scenario, as highlighted in Chapter 4 specific to the expected risk premium associated with the stock market. Nevertheless, it is reasonable to assume that many securities and portfolios of securities have positive risk premiums. By way of example, available risk premiums include but are not limited to liquidity risk, currency risk, commodity risk, equity risk, credit risk, interest rate risk, vega (volatility) risk, financing risk, and even accounting, regulatory, and tax treatment risk, as described in more detail in Chapter 6.

Looking back at the investment definition, it follows that anything that introduces uncertainty into the investment equation can be thought of as a risk to the investor. Clearly an investment in stocks, even highly diversified portfolios of stocks that eliminate idiosyncratic risk, involves an uncertain outcome regarding the return on an investor's capital. It might be true that stocks have outperformed bonds, inflation, and cash, on average, over time. However, the actual result is highly dependent on the time period. Invest just before a market decline, say August 31, 2000, and it is going to take a very, very long time to achieve a positive return on capital, let alone to actually outperform the risk-free rate. How long exactly? As illustrated in Figure 3.6, it would have taken over six years for an investment in the S&P 500 on August 31, 2000, to regain its original value, and well over six years to reach a point where that particular equity market investment actually exceeded the return of a risk-free investment.

In today's increasingly innovative investment arena, it is possible to assume risk premiums in a wide variety of ways, often through the use of derivative instruments or structured products that seek to provide investors with exposure to specific risk premiums currently deemed valuable or, alternatively, to hedge investors against an explicit risk that they may want to remove or reduce. Thus investors no longer must hold a security or portfolio of securities to receive exposure to one or more risk factors. In addition, an investor who chooses to hold a security or portfolio with exposure to a given set of risk factors often has the ability to remove one or more

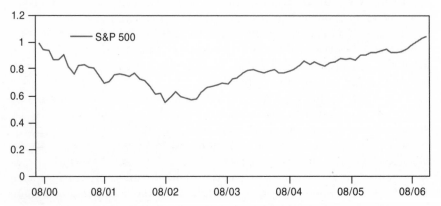

FIGURE 3.6 S&P 500 Growth of a $1 Investment in S&P 500, August 2000 to November 2006
Data source: Standard & Poor's.

of the risk factors inherent in the underlying investments through hedging transactions.

THEORY VERSUS REALITY

Investment theory, by definition, has to be simpler than reality (thus the simplifying assumptions!) in order to illustrate the key points without losing the audience altogether in the complexity of it all. This was true in a less complicated world, and it is most certainly true today as investment decisions have become much more complex with the broadening array of investments, vehicles, structures, and security types available to investors.

This does not mean that the theories are of no use—rather, the opposite is true. The underlying theory provides a very important starting point to what is ultimately an impossible task: constructing the optimal investment portfolio when the outcomes from investing in any given risky portfolio are not only unknown, but are generally subject to a very large list of uncontrollable variables. The point of this chapter is to review key aspects of the underlying theory that are relevant for purposes of understanding and implementing various forms of the portable alpha investment application. It is not to prove or disprove any particular theory or even to work through the associated statistics or proofs as might be necessary in an academic forum. That said, there are a few points where theory departs from reality which are important to illuminate for our purposes, including the risk-free reference point, the market portfolio and efficiency, the distribution of security returns, and the potential for a mismatch between the investor's incentives and the investment manager's incentives.

The Risk-Free Reference Point

One of the key assumptions underlying most investment theory is that the rate of return generated by the risk-free security is a nominal return that does not depend upon which state of the world is realized. The representative asset that provides the risk-free rate is often thought to be something similar to a short-term Treasury bill, as previously described. While investing in short-term Treasury bills may not present a risk of capital loss or an uncertain nominal return assuming the Treasury bill is held until maturity, this approach—buying and holding Treasury bills until maturity—may not be the least risky strategy from the standpoint of all investors.

Consider the example of a pension plan that is obligated to make a series of payments extending out well into the future. By investing a pre-determined amount in a longer-duration portfolio of high-quality fixed-income securities that pay a fixed interest rate and bear a minimal risk of capital loss, together with other characteristics that may be beneficial in terms of matching the return on the asset portfolio to the estimated future value of the liabilities, the pension plan may substantially reduce the probability that it will not have enough money to make its required distributions in the future. In contrast, if the pension plan adopts a strategy of investing a similar amount in Treasury bills, the mismatch between the duration of the Treasury bills and the duration of plan liabilities will be much greater and therefore more risky to the pension plan. In this case risk is not defined by volatility of the return on assets but rather by the potential dispersion between the value of assets *relative* to liabilities as discussed in more detail in Chapter 10.

Nonetheless, a Treasury bill or money market rate like LIBOR is generally a good proxy for the return on capital from an investment that effectively bears no risk of capital loss over even very short time horizons, and thus limits uncertainty in this regard. LIBOR is also generally the basis for the interest rate at which investors borrow and lend via the securities and derivatives markets. As an example, in practice the fair value or no-arbitrage pricing of equity index futures contracts (both long and short positions) references LIBOR as the embedded interest rate.

The Market Portfolio and Efficiency

In the relatively simple state of the theoretical world, it is often assumed that there is an optimal portfolio of risky assets, the previously referenced market portfolio, and the proxy most commonly used for this portfolio is the stock market. While this may seem to be a gross oversimplification looking out at the vast universe of risky assets and investment strategies that provide an expected return over the risk-free rate, this has not always been the case. Rather, at the time that modern portfolio theory was conceived stocks really were *the* risky liquid asset available to investors, as opposed to relatively illiquid investments like real estate holdings or commodities that were not readily assessable to most.

Even today, stock market risk dominates most investment portfolios when portfolio risk is decomposed into the various components. To this point, it may be surprising to some that equity market risk accounted for more than 90 percent of the risk of an investment portfolio with a constant capital allocation of 60 percent to U.S. stocks and 40 percent to U.S. bonds over the 20-year period ended December 31, 2006, while bond market risk only accounted for around 3 percent of the aggregate risk profile. This is illustrated in Figure 3.7 and described in much more quantitative and qualitative detail in the September 2005 paper "Risk Parity Portfolios: Efficient

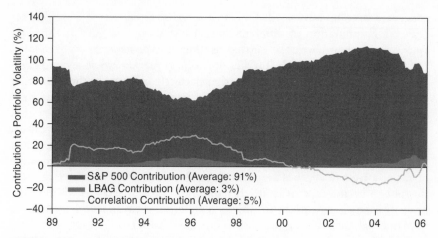

FIGURE 3.7 Contribution to Portfolio Volatility, 60 percent S&P 500 / 40 percent Lehman Aggregate, Three-Year Period Ended December 31, 2006 *Data source:* PIMCO, Standard & Poor's, Lehman Brothers.

Portfolios Through True Diversification," by Edward Qian at PanAgora Asset Management.[2]

So is the use of the stock market as the proxy for "the market" so far off? Yes and no. Yes, in the sense that stock market risk is the dominant risk by far in most investment portfolios. No, as a matter of technical accuracy and also because investors are increasingly looking for ways to better diversify the risk in their portfolios. In fact, better diversification is one of the objectives that is driving the interest in portable alpha. Regardless, it is not realistically possible to come up with a good estimate for the market portfolio. Stock market capitalization is relatively straightforward. But move beyond the stock market to include private equity, all of the various fixed-income instruments that are traded over the counter in markets all over the world, real estate holdings (private homes, apartment buildings, office space, shopping malls, etc.), different types of commodities, art, even fine wine—and it gets complicated very quickly!

Fortunately there is an entire industry devoted to providing market indices comprised of the investable securities in a particular asset class, sector, style, etc. which can, in turn, be used as the basis for passive investment strategies and as a benchmark for investment managers for whom a particular market portfolio is representative of their investment universe, neutral investment point and investment risk. As such, while a proxy for the market portfolio is needed for purposes of illustrating important theoretical concepts, most investors will be better served by the use of a market index or a combination of different market indices or risk factors that best approximate their particular desired risk factor exposures.

A related concept to the market portfolio is market efficiency and equilibrium securities pricing. Is the market perfectly efficient in the sense that the price of every security at any point in time most accurately reflects the ex-post future value to investors from holding it? Of course not—that is where the risk or uncertainty comes into play and why we, as investors, demand risk premiums. Do stock prices at a point in time reflect the collective wisdom (or lack thereof) of market participants as to the future value of the security? Well, it is certainly difficult to come up with a reason for this not to be the case. It is another question altogether as to whether the price of a stock at a point in time is a function of available information, fundamental factors, technical factors, behavioral factors, or other factors. Indeed, it has been proven that investors can consistently outperform market indexes, although the success rate varies substantially from index to index as do the reasons for the success. In some cases, outperformance may be due to security selection and market timing skill while in others it may largely be related to the assumption of additional risk. Luck is also a component that cannot be ruled out. Regardless, the fact that market participants are a diverse group with varying time horizons, levels of skills, and objectives, combined with the ever-expanding universe of (often complex) investment opportunities, certainly lends itself to the idea that active management can result in risk-adjusted excess returns.

Security Return Distributions

Generally, individual security returns can be specified by an expectation and some kind of probability distribution around this expectation. Therefore, it is often assumed that investment returns are normally distributed and risk is best quantified by standard deviation. While many securities may be reasonably assumed to have returns that are approximately normally distributed, there are many securities, portfolios of securities, and investment strategies in which the assumption of normally distributed returns is grossly inaccurate.

One may claim that many economic variables that influence security returns, such as GDP growth and inflation, are approximately normally distributed. Consequently, securities whose returns may be linearly related to such economic variables (for example, the enterprise value of a firm) may have return distributions that are normally distributed as well. Nevertheless, many securities have optionlike characteristics and consequently have returns that are not best approximated by a normal distribution.

In fact, even the most common types of securities can be described as having optionlike characteristics resulting from the division of a firm into two components, debt and equity. Equity can be viewed as a call option on the enterprise value of the firm (with the strike price being equal to the amount of debt outstanding), while debt can be viewed as being worth the nominal amount of debt outstanding less the value of the put option on the enterprise value of the firm (again, with the strike price being equal to the amount of debt outstanding). Even if the returns of the enterprise value of the firm are normally distributed, the returns of each of the components—debt and equity—will not be perfectly normally distributed. Deviations from the assumption of normally distributed returns become more pronounced as the degree of optionality in the security increases.

In the case of this equity and debt example, the risk of a substantial loss associated with the unlikely but possible tail event of the bankruptcy of one firm can be substantially reduced by limiting the exposure in a portfolio to individual issuers (to limit idiosyncratic risk) and also by diligent credit/company analysis to avoid investments altogether in companies that may be prone to financial distress.

While diversification, where possible, is an obvious solution to limiting downside risk, some strategies explicitly expose investors to concentrated (often levered) risk by design. For example, it is certainly possible to construct a portfolio that has a high likelihood of outperforming a given benchmark index by a small amount and a small likelihood of dramatically underperforming the index, by design. While such a skewed payoff profile may or may not be particularly compelling for an investor, interestingly it may be very compelling for an investment manager who is managing portfolios on behalf of outside clients. From the standpoint of the investment manager, this strategy would allow outperformance of competitors who are not using such strategies, with a high likelihood over a short to intermediate time horizon, even though such a strategy also results in the investor bearing the risk of a substantial loss at some point over a longer time horizon.

Many strategies that are employed as part of hedge fund portfolios also may exhibit these types of characteristics. In this case, investors may be willing to assume this type of risk profile where, based on the underlying probabilities, the returns should be positive under normal market circumstances. However, investors must recognize that the outside chance exists for meaningful negative returns during unusual market environments. To further illustrate this point by way of example, Appendix 3.2 highlights the mechanics of a merger arbitrage strategy.

In addition, there are many investment strategies that, as a whole, have a high degree of associated optionality that is not captured in traditional risk metrics like standard deviation or volatility. In effect, options provide a form of insurance that the holder is willing to pay for and the seller is willing to provide, not unlike other forms of insurance. As an example, a stock market investor may purchase a put option that allows him to sell his equity market exposure after a specified decline in the stock market. The stock market investor does not necessarily want the stock market to decline, but he values the insurance that his losses will be limited to a prespecified capital loss in the event that the market does fall. The challenge from a statistical perspective is that the premium collected from selling options may have a smoothing effect on returns, thereby actually reducing volatility, all else being equal. This is true even though—on a stand-alone basis—selling options, just like selling insurance, very specifically represents a transfer of risk from the buyer to the seller. It is just a risk that may not be evidenced from a statistical perspective for some period of time. In order to fully appreciate this concept, it may be necessary to explore the concept of option pricing in more detail, as we do in Appendix 3.1.

It is also true that the actual underlying risk of securities that are illiquid by nature may not be reflected in traditional metrics, like standard deviation, which rely on the idea that the potential future dispersion in returns can be estimated by measuring the historical dispersion of monthly returns. If there is no market for a security, the metrics that are used to assess the value of the security on a month-over-month basis are unlikely to fully reflect or incorporate the wide variety of factors that can lead to return volatility in liquid securities markets.

Consequently, because the most common risk and diversification measurement statistics—like standard deviation or volatility, variance, covariance, and correlation—are all based on the assumption of normally distributed returns, it is imperative that investors understand the strategies and associated risks investment managers are employing and adjust the risk measurement process accordingly for purposes of optimal portfolio construction and risk measurement.

Potential for a Mismatch of Incentives

A final point specific to the departure of theory from reality that may be relevant in a portable alpha context and more broadly relates to the potential for a mismatch between the incentives of the investor and the incentives of the investment manager. As noted earlier, finance research generally assumes that investors are risk-averse, meaning the additional utility gained from an additional dollar of wealth is less than the reduction of utility caused by a loss of a dollar of wealth. By contrast, investment managers or other agents who manage funds on behalf of outside clients may *not* be risk averse, especially when their compensation is a function of the returns they produce.

For example, many hedge funds are paid an incentive fee, which is often a percentage of the profits generated for client portfolios, with no incentive fee collected if performance falls below a certain threshold, which is often a zero percent return. This type of fee arrangement is intended to align the incentives of the manager with those of the investor by the sheer fact that the manager is only paid when positive incremental returns are generated. However, given that a hedge fund will not earn an incentive fee if performance falls below the threshold, if the fund is already performing poorly, the fund manager may have an incentive to increase the level of risk in the portfolio in hopes of increasing the likelihood of earning an incentive fee. Consequently, when structuring investment management contracts, investors should be careful to ensure that their agents' risk preferences are aligned with their own.

CONCLUSION

Peter Bernstein said it best in an interview about his recently published book, *Capital Ideas Evolving* (John Wiley & Sons, 2007), on the topic of the relevance of financial theory for the current practice of investment management:

> *There are two things that make financial markets function. Financial markets are a bet on the future, so in their gut they're risk taking. The other is that financial markets can't function without information. When you put these two together, you're making a bet on an unknown future but you're basing that bet on information. The theories follow from these two important features. Markowitz said you have to think about risk as well as return, because you don't know what the outcome is going to be. You do that by diversification, trying to maximize the trade-off between risk and return.*[3]

The optimal portfolio varies from investor to investor dominantly as a function of an investor's return objectives, time horizon, liquidity requirements, and risk tolerance, together with his expectations about the unknown future. Of course, the optimal portfolio construction problem is difficult to solve when investors are not certain of the future.

Two main impediments to solving the optimal portfolio construction problem are the uncertainty in the distribution of security returns and the difficulty of comparing portfolios that leave the investor better off in different states of the world. Ex-post does not necessarily follow the mean risk/return profile that is expected ex-ante. Nonetheless, modern portfolio theory helped pave the way for investors to establish a framework for optimal investing and to carefully evaluate the trade-off between risk and return as well as the benefits of diversification.

The same basic concepts that are relevant in the construction of the theoretically optimal investment portfolio are relevant for the portable alpha investment application. Portable alpha is a potentially powerful investment application that may result in an increase in return at a similar level of risk or an increase in risk but at an improved Sharpe ratio or risk/reward trade-off. Alternatively, portable alpha investment applications can also result in increased risk without a corresponding increase in return, which is not likely to be a desirable result. The key from an investor's perspective is to optimize the increased diversification benefits and alpha opportunities made possible by the concept behind portable alpha and also to never lose sight of the fundamental relationship between risk and return.

APPENDIX 3.1 OPTION PRICING

There are two types of options: call options and put options. A holder of a call option has the right, but not the obligation, to purchase an asset at a specified price (which is called the *strike price*) at or before a specified expiration time, while a holder of a put option has the right but not the obligation to sell an asset at a specified price at or before a specified expiration time. Note that the value of an option is always nonnegative, since the holder of a call option can ensure that he will not lose money by deciding never to purchase the asset at the specified price, while the holder of a put option can ensure that he will not lose money by deciding never to sell the asset at the specified price.

A common technique to value options is to use dynamic or stochastic programming, which essentially means that one uses the current price of the asset, works forward in time to come up with some sort of probability distribution of the asset price in the future, then determines the value of the option in the future (as a function of the value of the underlying asset), and then works back in time to determine the value of the option today.

The one point in time when one can be certain of the value of a call option is the last instant in time (which is called the *expiration date*) at which the holder of the option has the right to purchase the asset at the specified price. Thus, at the expiration date, if the investor decides to take advantage of the opportunity to purchase the asset at the specified price (this process is called *exercising the option*), the investor will receive a payoff equal to the current price of the asset, less the strike price. However, if the investor decides not to take advantage of the opportunity to purchase the asset at the strike price, the investor will receive a payoff of zero. Given that the investor is assumed to be profit maximizing, the payoff has a floor of zero, meaning no money will be owed by the buyer/owner of the option at the expiration date.

Figure 3.8 shows the payoff of the call option as a function of the asset price and the strike price on the expiration date, where the payoff of the call option will be equal to zero if the asset price is not above the strike price, and will equal the asset price less the strike price if the asset price is at least equal to the strike price on the expiration date.

While market participants will have little disagreement regarding the value of the call option at expiry, given that the asset price is known at that time, market participants may have dramatically divergent opinions regarding the probability distribution of the future underlying asset price. For example, market participants who view the underlying asset as currently undervalued should expect the asset to have a higher price in the future, relative to those market participants who view the underlying asset as currently overvalued. To overcome this seemingly intractable problem, Black and Scholes introduced an option-pricing model that used the concept of a *risk-neutral* portfolio to eliminate the impact of market participants' subjective views of the value of the underlying asset and consequently allowing a solution to the option-pricing problem.

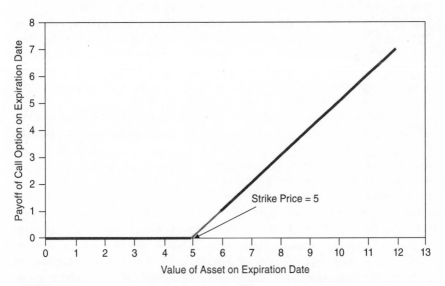

FIGURE 3.8 Payoff of Call Option versus Value of Asset on Expiration Date
Source: PIMCO; hypothetical example for illustrative purposes only.

A central idea of the Black-Scholes model is the formulation of a *risk-free* portfolio, such that the exposure of the value of the option to fluctuations of the underlying asset price can be hedged. For example, the value of a call option increases as the value of the underlying asset increases, and decreases as the value of the underlying asset decreases. Thus, to hedge the call option's exposure to the value of the underlying asset, the holder of the option would sell short a quantity of the underlying asset, so that the value of the portfolio consisting of long the call option and short the underlying asset would not fluctuate as the price of the underlying asset changes.

The second fundamental idea of the Black-Scholes option pricing model is the concept that since the value of the hedged portfolio does not depend upon the value of the underlying asset, the expected return of the hedged portfolio should equal the expected return of the risk-free asset. Consequently, the assumptions of the Black-Scholes option-pricing model imply that the option can be priced using stochastic programming techniques under which the expected return of the underlying asset is equal to that of the risk-free rate.

Note that the quantity of the underlying asset to short, or the hedge ratio, constantly fluctuates as a function of various parameters. If the asset price is very high compared to the strike price, then it is likely that the option will be exercised on the expiry date (since it will be optimal to exercise the call option on the expiration date if the asset price exceeds the strike price), leading to a hedge ratio close to 1 (as a $1 increase in the underlying asset price will increase the value of the option by close to $1). Conversely, if the asset price is very low compared to the strike price, then it is likely that the option will expire worthless on the expiry date (since it will not be optimal to exercise the call option on the expiry date if the asset price is below the strike price), leading to a hedge ratio close to 0 (as a $1 increase in the underlying asset price will barely increase the value of the option).

Consequently, under the Black-Scholes option valuation framework, the value of the option can be decomposed into two components, the *intrinsic value* of the option and the *time value* of the option. The intrinsic value is the value of the option assuming that the option is to expire immediately, whereas the time value of the option is equal to the additional value that is embedded in the option resulting from the opportunity to wait until the future to determine whether to exercise the option. Figure 3.9 displays a graph of the value of a call option as a function of the underlying asset price prior to expiration.

Conceptually, the time value of the option comes from maintaining the appropriate hedge ratio over time—selling the underlying asset as the value of the underlying asset increases, and buying the underlying asset as its value decreases. The more the underlying asset fluctuates, the more opportunities

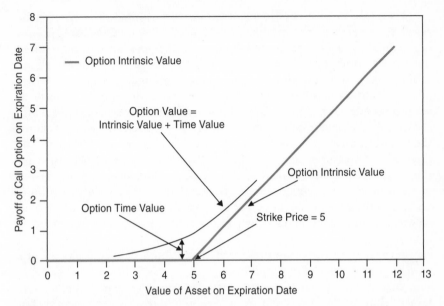

FIGURE 3.9   Payoff of Call Option versus Value of Asset Prior to Expiration Date
Source: PIMCO; hypothetical example for illustrative purposes only.

there are to buy low and sell high. Consequently, the value of an option increases as volatility increases.

APPENDIX 3.2 MERGER ARBITRAGE EXAMPLE

Merger arbitrage is a trading strategy that seeks to profit from security mispricings relating to potential merger transactions. Typically, merger arbitrageurs wait until a merger transaction is announced and initiate trades to take advantage of mispricings relating to previously announced but unconsummated merger transactions.

The simplest merger arbitrage transaction relates to merger transactions where the potential acquirer seeks to acquire the potential target for a specified amount of cash. In order to induce shareholders of the target company to tender their shares and consent to the takeover, the proposed takeover price generally embeds a significant premium over the target's share price prior to the announcement of the takeover bid. After the takeover bid is announced, the target's stock price generally increases toward the proposed takeover price, but often remains below the proposed takeover price.

There are three general considerations that explain the deviation between the target's market trading levels and the proposed takeover price in cash tender offers: the time value of money, the possibility that the target will not be acquired, and the possibility that the target will be acquired at a different price from the previously announced takeover price.

The time value of money affects the present or current value of all securities, and the proposed target stocks are no exception. Consequently, the greater the time until the deal closes (when stockholders can exchange their shares for cash), or the higher market interest rates are, the greater the discount between the current trading levels of the target's stock price and the tender offer bid level, solely due to the discounting of cash flows relating to the time value of money. In the extreme case where investors attributed no risk to the deal closing at tender offer level, the target's stock should be viewed as a zero-coupon bond, where the maturity date is the date that the deal closes.

Regardless of the purported merits (from both the acquirer's and the target's perspective) of a proposed merger transaction, one can never be sure that the proposed transaction will be consummated. Generally, the target's shareholders must approve the proposed merger agreement by tendering their shares, and often the acquirer's shareholders must approve the agreement as well, either explicitly by voting in favor of the merger agreement, or implicitly by supporting the acquirer's management. In addition, it is significantly more difficult to consummate a merger if the target's management does not consent to the merger, since the target's management can implement legal hurdles to make consummation of the merger more difficult. Besides the parties that are directly involved in the discussion—the target, the acquirer, and their respective shareholders—other entities may either increase or decrease the likelihood that the merger will be successful. Such entities include the Federal Trade Commission, environmental groups, state regulatory commissions, and labor unions.

Even if the target's management and third parties consent to the acquisition, market events or competing bids may interfere in the merger. For example, most merger agreements are subject to further due diligence on the part of the acquirer, which may allow the acquirer to adjust the previously announced takeover price or even rescind the offer as a result of additional information acquired during the due diligence. Other potential acquirers may also present more attractive bids for the target company.

Figure 3.10 displays the reward breakdown of a particular merger arbitrage opportunity.

In this example, prior to the announcement of the takeover bid, the target's stock was trading at $20/share. The acquirer proposes to acquire the target for $30/share, a 50 percent premium over the target's share price

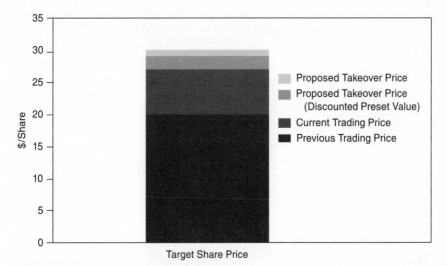

FIGURE 3.10 Merger Arbitrage Analysis
Source: PIMCO; hypothetical example for illustrative purposes only.

prior to announcement of the takeover bid. Note that due to the time value of money, the $30/share takeover price only amounts to $29/share today, since it will take time for the takeover to close. Nevertheless, in this example, the target's share price has only increased from $20/share to the current $27/share, leading to a potential $2/share ($29 minus $27), or 7.41 percent, excess profit for shareholders in the event that the merger is consummated.

However, if the takeover bid is withdrawn, the target's stock may fall to the prebid level of $20/share, leading to a potential loss of $7/share ($20 minus $27) or 25.94 percent for current shareholders. Merger arbitrageurs attempt to take advantage of opportunities similar to the one presented in this example in order to earn excess returns. Of course, risk arbitrage strategies by their very definition seek to capitalize on perceived mispricings that—while not 100 percent risk-free as is the case with true arbitrage—have a high probability of a moderately positive return (that can be magnified with leverage) and a low probability of a potentially material negative return (that can also be magnified with leverage).

CHAPTER 4

Asset Allocation and Portable Alpha*

Rob Arnott and Brent Harris

> [I]t is the long term investor . . . who will in practice come in for
> the most criticism, wherever investment funds are managed by
> committees or boards or banks. For it is the essence of his
> behavior that he should be eccentric, unconventional and rash in
> the eyes of average opinion. If he is successful, that will only
> confirm the general belief in his rashness; and if in the short run he
> is unsuccessful, which is very likely, he will not receive much
> mercy. Worldly wisdom teaches that it is better for reputation to
> fail conventionally than to succeed unconventionally.
> —John Maynard Keynes, Chapter 12, *The General Theory of
> Employment, Interest and Money*, 1936

Many of us serve as agents, shepherding others' resources. The agent's
time line—measured in quarters or years—and the fiduciary time line,
measured in decades, differ starkly because of the time horizon over which
an agent is judged and the peer groups against which we are compared.
What client would agree to grant an investment manager a 20-year free run,
after which her success will be judged?

This chasm between the relevant fiduciary time line and the agent's time
line and optimal asset allocation link is exacerbated by the fact that we all
have clients. The portfolio manager reports to the chief investment officer,

---

*Portions of this chapter are adapted from a 2002 *Journal of Investing* article by
Mr. Arnott.

who reports to the CEO of the asset management firm, who reports to the client's investment officer, who reports to the treasurer or chief financial officer, who report to the CEO of the client organization, who reports to the investment committee of the board of directors. Each step in the reporting process increases the pressure to focus on short-term results, both in absolute returns and relative to our respective peers.

For the agent who wishes to add value over the long fiduciary time horizon, the challenge is clear. Firstly, no agent should exceed the client's risk tolerance. The role of the agent is to move clients in directions that are likely to be profitable, to grow the assets to serve the clients' obligations. But if the clients do not stay the course, during the inevitable bad years which even the best strategies will experience from time to time, then their risk tolerance has been exceeded. All too often, we can recognize this only in retrospect, after the damage has been done.

Meanwhile, risk itself is ill-defined. It has many dimensions, notably the risk of losing money, the risk of underperforming our peers, and the risk of lagging the net present value of the liabilities that the assets are intended to serve. The challenge is to gauge how far on the continuum from conventionality to independence that clients can be taken without exceeding their risk tolerance. If an agent goes down this path, then it is important to be right, always and every time, in order to keep the client's trust and confidence.

The efforts of the agent to serve the needs of the end client while managing risk in a more disciplined way has stimulated two of the most important developments in institutional investing in the past decade: an increasing focus on strategic and tactical asset allocation, and an increasing pursuit of what may be broadly defined as portable alpha strategies. The two are tied together by the simple fact that asset allocation decisions and the quest for alpha are *separable*. We can source return from any market or strategy and then combine it with another market exposure using futures or swaps with the end goal of achieving an attractive risk/return profile—and perhaps one that is not readily available through traditional indexing and active management strategies.

A WORLD OF LOWER RETURNS

We are currently in a world of lower prospective returns compared to recent decades. This reality goes hand-in-glove with a world of lower yields. Stocks yield less than 2 percent, against a historical range since World War II from 1 to 8 percent, with an average of 4 percent. Bond and cash yields are below their historical norms, as are yields on Treasury inflation-protected securities (TIPS), high-yield and emerging markets debt, real estate investment trusts (REITs), and the list goes on. Lower current yields mean higher *past* returns (falling yields will have delivered capital gains, in addition to those previously higher yields) and lower *future* returns (lower yields, exacerbated by the risk of capital losses from rising yields). Hope is not a strategy and past is not prologue; expecting more return does not make it happen. Extrapolating the past, in which much of the reward was a consequence of capital gains from falling yields, is a terrible way to forecast the future.

Consider Table 4.1. Two of the three best-performing markets from 1995 to 2000 performed poorly from 2001 to 2006, while two of the three worst markets from 1995 to 2000 performed well in the past five years. It is noteworthy and important that the S&P 500 is close to the bottom of the range for the 2001–2006 period and even now is priced at low yields, by historical standards. As a result, most investors struggled during this six-year period, a time when the unconventional investor had a wide array of excellent investment opportunities.

Note also that the correlation between the S&P 500 and the classic 60/40 stock/bond U.S. balanced portfolio is 99 percent (not entirely surprising,

TABLE 4.1 Return, Risk, and Correlations with 60/40 Portfolio (1995–2006)

	6-Year Returns (Cumulative)		12-Year Characteristics	
Asset Class	2001-2006	1995-2000	Standard Deviation	Correlation with 60/40
Emerging Market Stocks	222%	–23%	23%	68%
REITs	218%	82%	14%	32%
Emerging Market Bonds	100%	121%	13%	59%
Commodities + TIPS	85%	46%	16%	7%
High-Yield Bonds	71%	47%	7%	52%
S&P 500 Equal Weighted	68%	179%	16%	90%
TIPS	52%	45%	6%	2%
Unhedged Foreign Bonds	52%	49%	5%	–6%
Convertible Bonds	46%	82%	12%	75%
Long-Term Gov't Bonds	45%	86%	8%	2%
Lehman Aggregate	38%	62%	4%	10%
GNMA Bonds	36%	64%	3%	15%
S&P 500	19%	219%	15%	99%
Money Markets	18%	38%	1%	8%
Hedged EAFE	13%	61%	15%	70%

It was only a bear market for those who were wedded to an equity-centric "normal portfolio."

███████ = Worst three (excluding S&P Equal Weight Index)
███████ = Best three (excluding S&P Equal Weight Index)
Source: Bloomberg, Global Financial Data.

given the dominance of equity risk in a 60/40 portfolio, as illustrated in Figure 3.7) and even international stocks—Europe, Australasia, and Far East (EAFE), removing the foreign exchange (FX) impact—exhibited a 70 percent correlation, which has been rising fast in our increasingly interconnected global markets. As such, a move from 60/40 to 60/30/10, where the 10 percent is reallocated from bonds to international stocks, increases our level of risk and expected return but does not truly diversify our holdings. Nor do investments into emerging markets stocks or convertibles—at least not during recent periods.

Those who say that we must be willing to take risks to earn lofty returns are clearly correct. The highest-return markets do have higher volatility than most. But those who say that a willingness to take risk will deliver high returns are just as clearly wrong. The high-risk markets are mostly clustered toward the top and bottom of the distribution in Table 4.1, with low risks predominating in the mid range. Five of the six best-performing markets of the past five years were all high-risk (with volatility in double digits), as were two of the three worst markets (offering the same as money market investments, more or less). By the same token, five of the six best-performing markets from 1995 to 2000 were high-risk, as was the worst-performing market in that span.

So how does an agent fulfill his fiduciary obligations? It's actually surprisingly easy: Manage return expectations, and then manage client assets seeking to meet *reasonable* objectives. In a world of lower yields, hence lower future returns, it is important to ratchet down return expectations. If this is not accomplished, clients are set up for disappointment and *agents are set up to be judged against an unrealistic self-imposed target*. As for managing the assets, conventional investment choices lead inevitably to conventional results. When yields are high and markets are low, this is just fine: Conventional returns are excellent in such a world. In today's world, this sets the stage for disappointing results. There are four paths to improved returns:

1. *Willingness to stray from conventional investments and investment strategies.* If we do so, selectively and opportunistically, with disciplined risk management, and on a scale large enough to matter, we can often find investments that can actually serve to reduce our portfolio risk due primarily to their low correlations with equities. Commodities, for instance, are a high-risk asset class when viewed in isolation, but, as we can see in Table 4.1, a commodity index futures collateralized by TIPS exhibited negligible correlation with a 60/40 investment portfolio, and as such may represent a powerful opportunity for diversification and portfolio risk reduction without a reduction in expected return.

2. *A careful and prudent quest for alpha.* This can be done aggressively, if we have a record of successfully identifying and employing profitable managers and strategies in advance of their future successes. Or it can be done conservatively, by seeking out and eliminating sources of negative alpha. The stark gap between the S&P 500 and the equal-weighted roster of the very same 500 companies, as shown in Table 4.1, suggests that some of the trendy stocks that dominate in our indexes—like the tail that wags the dog—do not match the performance of the average stock. Similarly, the equally stark gap between money market returns and the returns of almost all other fixed-income categories suggests that there may be considerable benefit in seeking other ways to assure a reasonable degree of capital preservation, rather than turning to money market instruments as our defensive reserve.

3. *Disciplined management of our asset mix.* This can be as simple as rebalancing or as aggressive as tactical asset allocation (TAA). We can choose to move money out of the expensive—and comfortable—markets, and redeploy that money into markets that are more attractively priced, frequently because they are out of favor. Whether we find tactical decisions to be attractive or not, it is clearly costly to allow the asset mix to drift with the whims of the capital markets. This all-too-common delegating of the asset mix decision to the capital markets might be termed *inadvertent* tactical asset allocation, because the shifts in mix are as wide as with TAA, but we reach peak exposures at market tops, just ahead of market drops, and minimum exposure at a market low.

4. *Leverage.* If the cost of borrowing is less than the rewards for our investment strategies, our returns should improve. But leverage may increase risk far faster than it increases returns. Success is leveraged upwards, but unfortunately, disappointment is leveraged downwards.

THE CLASSIC MODEL FOR PORTFOLIO CONSTRUCTION

The classic approach to fund management places the asset allocation decision first and foremost, then secondarily deals with the quest for alpha. This involves deciding how much to allocate to domestic stocks; how much to bonds; how much to international; to emerging markets; to alternative strategies, such as real estate, venture capital, hedge funds, and commodities; and to whatever else may be deemed worthy of a role in the portfolio. Goals are vague and mimicry of peers is paramount as performance relative to peers often matters far more than performance relative to the liabilities that portfolios are intended to serve.

Once the macro asset allocation decision is made, the next decision is the *active* asset allocation decision. Do we want to allow the mix to differ from our intended policy mix? If so, how much drift is tolerable? How (and how often) do we rebalance back to the policy mix? Do we permit deliberate tactical departures from our policy mix? If so, by how much, and based on what disciplines or strategies? Do we apply defensive option or option replication strategies (e.g., collar strategies or portfolio insurance) that directly or indirectly alter our asset allocation?

Once the various nuances of asset allocation have been dealt with, the next question is typically the split between active and passive: how much should be allocated to the quest for alpha? For instance, if 60 percent is allocated to domestic stocks, then do we want 20 or 40 percent invested with active managers, correspondingly leaving the remaining 40, or 20 percent in passive index replication? This decision often reflects the tolerance the investment committee of the board might have for alpha shortfalls, when and if they occur.

Once we decide how much to commit to active management, we need to decide which managers to employ in each asset category. We want the best domestic stock and bond managers, the best international managers, the best managers for the cash reserves in the portfolio, and so forth. This should be based on the expected alphas and correlations of the managers, but the easy path to judging the expected alphas and correlations is to look at the past. What managers have a sensible, well-reasoned investment process, backed up by strong past results?

CHALLENGES WITH THE CLASSIC MODEL

One of the first things we notice in this process is that there's too much room for slippage. Cash reserves build up in the equity and bond portfolios and sit idle, waiting for allocation to a manager or distribution to meet the obligations of the fund.

The drain on performance is startlingly large. Suppose (1) a fund has 5 percent average cash reserves, (2) the fund's managers have an additional 5 percent average cash reserves, and (3) cash lags a fully invested balanced portfolio by 3 percent per year. The cost would be 30 basis points per annum at the fund level.

Apart from the problem of uninvested cash reserves, the allocations to the various asset classes will drift with the movements of the capital markets, unless a conscious, disciplined rebalancing program is put in place. If an investor has $50 each in stocks and bonds, and stocks rise by 20 percent with bonds unchanged, the mix has shifted to nearly 55 percent in stocks. The allocations to the managers change with (1) the relative performance of their asset class, (2) the relative performance of their style, and (3) the relative alpha of the managers, so that the managers with the strongest past performance dominate our holdings. To this array of challenges, we add the cost of manager terminations and hirings, which is considerable (that cost has variously been put at 1 percent *or more* of the assets moved from one manager to another, depending on asset class and manager style).

We find it peculiar that funds will choose not to consider deliberate departures from the policy mix, but will cheerfully countenance *accidental* departures from the policy mix through asset mix drift. Both contribute the same tracking error relative to the policy mix, yet one seems to offer some possibility of adding to returns, while the other seems closer to sheer folly—in the extreme, a conscious shirking of fiduciary responsibility. The two intellectually honest choices would seem to be (1) to engage in a disciplined framework for active tactical asset allocation, based on a well-reasoned process, or (2) to engage in a systematic process of rebalancing, if not through active trading in futures, then at least through careful management of the cash flows into or out of the fund. Unfortunately, most funds do neither.

The second thing that we notice in this process is that the quest for alpha is held hostage to our asset allocation. We cannot freely capture alpha from the best and most reliable sources, unless those sources are found in precisely the asset mix that we choose to hold.

PORTABLE ALPHA, LEVEL ONE

Suppose we find:

- A hedge fund manager who we think can reliably deliver returns roughly equivalent to LIBOR plus 600 basis points with an interesting leveraged-arbitrage strategy, uncorrelated with the major risk factors in our existing portfolio.
- A junk bond manager who we think can add about 400 basis points to the high-yield bond indexes, albeit with a 0.20 beta to the stock market.
- Domestic stock and bond managers who we think can add 150 basis points and 100 basis points to their respective index results.
- International managers who are expected to do as well as domestic managers, but their alpha is offset by the withholding taxes, which takes the net alpha to about zero.

For purposes of an example, let's assume that the policy asset mix is comprised of 50 percent in domestic stocks, 20 percent in international stocks, and 30 percent in domestic bonds. We can get the alphas from the domestic stock and bond managers just described. But we have zero allocated to alternatives, where the arbitrage-based hedge fund manager might be viewed as an interesting manager. We also have difficulty dealing with the junk bond manager because of her exposure to both stock and bond market behavior (which pool of assets do we invest with her, anyway?).

We are left with 150 basis points from our domestic stock managers, 100 basis points from our bond manager (if our selections pan out as expected), less various bits of slippage in the portfolio. If we wind up 100 basis points (1 percent) ahead of passive results, it's a success. Table 4.2 shows how this works at the portfolio level. We cannot invest anything with the other two managers we identified, who have some reasonable possibility of adding materially to our returns, without violating our asset mix policy. Or can we?

Suppose we invest with the hedge fund manager, and buy stock index futures with notional value matching that of the hedge fund allocation. Because stock index futures produce returns that closely match the difference between the stock index total return and LIBOR now we have an expected return of S&P 500 plus 600 basis points.[1] We can fund this manager out of our equity allocation.

Suppose we take the high-yield bond manager, and short stock and bond futures in an amount that reflects the average stock beta and bond duration of that manager (for purposes of this example we assume that short positions equal to 20 percent and 60 percent of the high-yield exposure are required, respectively). Now we have effectively converted the manager to a cash-plus-400-basis-points manager. Suppose we now buy MSCI EAFE

TABLE 4.2 Alpha Management, the Classic Model

	Market Exposure				
	S&P 500 Exposure	Bond Exposure	Hedge EAFE Exposure	F/X Exposure	Expected Excess Return
Hedge fund manager	No fit in fund; policy allocation to alternatives is zero.				
Junk bond manager	No fit in fund; policy allocation to hybrid assets is zero.				
50% domestic stock managers	100%				1.5%
30% domestic bond managers		100%			1.0%
20% International stock managers			100%	100%	0%
Combined Fund Result	**50%**	**30%**	**20%**	**20%**	**1.05%**

Data source: Research Affiliates LLC, PIMCO; hypothetical example for illustrative purposes only.

TABLE 4.3   Portable Alpha, Level One: Strategy-Level Porting

| | Market Exposure | | | | |
	S&P 500 Exposure	Bond Exposure	Hedge EAFE Exposure	F/X Exposure	Expected Excess Return
20% hedge fund manager					
Plus S&P futures	100%				
Net result	100%				6.0%
20% junk bond manager	20%	60%			
Minus stock futures	(20%)				
Minus T-bond futures		(60%)			
Plus EAFE-tracking Futures/forwards			100%	100%	
Net result	0%	0%	100%	100%	
30% domestic stock managers	100%				1.5%
30% domestic bond managers		100%			1.0%
20% international stock managers	Not required. Covered by ported junk bond manager.				
Combined Fund Result	**50%**	**30%**	**20%**	**20%**	**2.75%**

Data source: Research Affiliates LLC, PIMCO, hypothetical example for illustrative purposes only.

index futures. Now we have converted the manager yet another step to an international-stocks-plus-alpha manager. We can fund this manager out of the international stocks portion of our fund, *even though the manager has neither international holdings nor equity holdings!*

The end result? As illustrated in Table 4.3, we have more than doubled the incremental expected return on our portfolio in addition to the expected return from a passive allocation from just over 1 percent to 2.75 percent. It's a simple, yet powerful, concept.

PORTABLE ALPHA, LEVEL TWO

What about a more ambitious decoupling of asset allocation and alpha? Let's find the managers and strategies that offer the most reliable prospective risk-adjusted returns (as best we can gauge the future!). We pay absolutely no attention to which asset class category we want to use to fund the manager. If we have a manager who has an interesting strategy, which we expect will deliver a reliable alpha, then let's hire him! How much should we invest with him? As much as we think is appropriate and prudent. If we have another investor with a complementary strategy, using totally different instruments, let's hire her, too. How much to invest? Again, as much as we think is appropriate and prudent.

Now we have a basket of managers and strategies, all of which are interesting, all of which we hope can add good value for us, and none of which was selected based on the asset class within which they work. What do we do about this tangled mess of risks and asset classes? Assuming we have perfect transparency with respect to the associated risk factors for each of the strategies, we can use futures and swaps to remove the market exposures that we don't want, and introduce exposure to the markets that we do want. If we take the simple difference between the exposures we've *got* and the exposures we *want*, we have a simple recipe for the futures we *need*. Putting these futures in place gives us exactly the asset allocation that we want, plus the roster of alpha sources (managers and strategies) that we think offer us the best prospects for the future.

In Table 4.4, we illustrate this approach. The allocations to the individual managers are made *without any reference to the policy asset allocation!* We then simply sum the anticipated structural risk factors of these managers,

TABLE 4.4   Portable Alpha, Level Two: Fund-Level Alpha Porting

	Market Exposure				
	S&P 500 Exposure	Bond Exposure	Hedge EAFE Exposure	F/X Exposure	Expected Excess Return
20% hedge fund manager					6.0%
20% junk bond manager	20%	60%			4.0%
30% domestic stock managers	100%				1.5%
30% domestic bond managers		100%			1.0%
Combined Result Preporting	**34%**	**42%**	**0%**	**0%**	**2.75%**
Plus S&P futures	16%				
Minus T-bonds futures		(12%)			
Plus EAFE-tracking Futures/forwards			20%	20%	
Combined Fund Result	**50%**	**30%**	**20%**	**20%**	**2.75%**

Data source: Research Affiliates LLC, PIMCO; hypothetical example for illustrative purposes only.

and put in place whatever futures are needed to bring the effective asset mix back in line with the policy targets.

(*Note:* For purposes of these simple examples, we are assuming that the leveraged arbitrage strategy pursued by the hedge fund manager does not include any systematic market exposures or risk factors. More realistically, any strategy that is designed to deliver returns of LIBOR plus 600 basis points is likely to involve risk factors that should be carefully contemplated at the policy portfolio level for reasons discussed throughout this book. Likewise, the junk bond strategy may incorporate different types of beta other than stock market and interest rate exposure/sensitivity. As a result, solely for purposes of keeping the illustration of the concept relatively straightforward, the examples used here only calculate expected returns and not the more complicated expected risk profile of the portfolio.)

PITFALLS OF PORTING

In at least one sense, portable alpha may be simpler to manage at the portfolio level (portable alpha, level two), once it's in place, than the classic structure. This is due to the fact that the classic structure requires constant tweaking of asset mix for rebalancing and tactical purposes; of the manager mix, to prevent unintended style bets from creeping into the fund; and of the placement of cash flows, both into and out of the fund. Management of a portable alpha structure has the following features:

- Allocations to managers are based on perceived likely risk-adjusted performance.
- Cash flows into the fund are placed with the manager or strategy that is deemed most likely to boost the risk-adjusted performance of the fund (more on this later).
- Cash flows out of the fund are taken from the manager or strategy in which confidence is waning, the strategy deemed least likely to help the risk-adjusted performance of the fund.
- Estimated risk exposures of the fund, assuming transparency of the risk exposures of the managers, are updated relatively easily.
- Futures positions for porting can be recalculated and readjusted as often as we update the risk exposures of the fund.
- Rebalancing to the intended policy mix becomes almost automatic. No committee approvals process is necessary, no need to debate the relative merits of the rebalancing trades, and no weighing how best to lighten one asset class in favor of another (e.g., which manager, among those we really like and want to retain, do we cut because we need to rebalance?).

All of this makes sense and has an elegance which cannot be achieved in the more conventional structure. That said, portable alpha at the fund sponsor level certainly has its costs and complications. The most obvious problem is the requirement to fundamentally rethink and restructure the way that fund management is carried out. Classes of managers and sources of alpha that would have been considered out of bounds are now very easily considered as candidates for the portable alpha–based portfolio.

This fundamental difference from the classic structure carries with it the mirror-image problem: If a move to a portable alpha framework is relatively easy but requires a fundamentally different mind-set and structure for asset management, then a move *back* to the classic structure requires an equally fundamental change in the mind-set and structure for asset management. In other words, as sensible and powerful as the portable alpha paradigm for institutional asset management may be, all levels of management must buy into the concept before it is pursued, since a flip-flop on something as fundamental as the basic paradigm for asset management will be very disruptive.

There is also a need to manage and roll the futures positions relating to the porting process. Because the underlying portfolio is wildly different from the target policy mix, 40 percent is the *gross* amount of futures exposure required to shift the effective mix of the fund to match the policy targets, in our example in Table 4.4. If futures rolling costs are 5 to 20 basis points per year; this means that we forfeit up to 8 basis points per year of our incremental return in the preceding example in order to port the potential alpha sources into the target asset mix. Of course the actual cost associated with obtaining or hedging market exposure via futures and swaps can vary to a material degree around LIBOR over time and by market index exposure.

There are both direct and hidden costs associated with shifting exposure from one market to another. If a portable alpha structure costs us, let's say, 5 to 20 basis points in derivatives rolling costs, this may not be considered a burdensome cost against an incremental extra return over a passive allocation of 275 basis points, as it is in Table 4.4. That lofty excess return may have been impossible, indeed unimaginable, in a context without portable alpha. But it is a cost that begins to matter if the *actual* result is closer to neutral, if our expected alphas fail to materialize. And it is a cost that matters a great deal if our pre-porting alpha is negative!

There are other nuances. Most investors do not manage portable alpha programs centralized at the portfolio level. So there is an element of maverick risk associated with doing something new and different: Top management may react badly if it does not work according to expectations. Collateral must also be posted, and if losses are incurred, funds must be recalled from the externally managed portfolios instantly, to meet 24-hour margin calls. This is the main reason that most sponsors who embrace portable alpha strategies prefer to let their managers take care of shifting their alpha from an unwanted market into the intended market.

Managers who are familiar with the process are unlikely to make awkward mistakes along the way. In other words, manager selection matters a great deal in a portable alpha framework, just as it does in the classic framework. Indeed, it matters *more* than in the classic framework, by an amount that reflects these rolling costs plus other potential implementation, borrowing, risk management, and reporting costs, as described in detail in future chapters. That said, the opportunity for meaningful alpha is likely to be much greater with a portable alpha framework than it is with the classic structure, because of the panoply of potential alpha sources that are newly at our disposal.

RISK BUDGETING: AN IMPRECISE SCIENCE

One of the inelegant elements of the classic model is the active/passive allocation decision. Whether we place 10 percent of our fund with a manager who adds incremental return and an additional 2 percent to the risk of a passive investment, or place 20 percent of our fund with a manager who increases our risk by 1 percent, the contribution to overall portfolio risk is the same. But the active/passive decision is typically made in a fashion that suggests that both managers are equally risky. That is patently false.

Regardless of whether we choose to move to a portable alpha structure, risk budgeting is part of the fund management process. If we don't manage the risk-budgeting decision consciously, our allocations among managers and strategies will do it for us. It makes sense to take this decision in hand and to use whatever tools we have at our disposal to make sensible decisions based on our best estimates of future returns and portfolio risks.

One of the pitfalls in managing a risk-budgeting process is that risk itself is an imprecise science. This holds true on both the tracking error side and on the correlations side. Long Term Capital Management (LTCM) collapsed in 1998, despite a targeted 15 to 20 percent risk budget for the overall portfolio. This happened for three simple reasons.

1. Strategies that were assumed to be uncorrelated because they had been uncorrelated in the past, turned out to be positively correlated in a turbulent liquidity crisis. This meant that their normal risk was not 15 to 20 percent; rather, it was 20 to 25 percent.
2. They overlooked the simple fact that the capital markets have volatility that is not static. With volatility within the markets doubling and tripling, now they were at 40 to 75 percent volatility.

3. Lethally, they overlooked the fact that multisigma events happen in the capital markets, when indeed they are commonplace. A 60 percent annual volatility means monthly volatility of nearly 20 percent. Wow! Against a flawed *expectation* of 20 percent annual risk, that's already huge. But what if we have a 5-sigma event? With 20 percent monthly risk, a 5-sigma event is a deadly 100 percent loss. This was the LTCM experience, and their fatal flaw.

In statistics, in normally distributed data, this never happens. Volatility doesn't change. Correlations might be misestimated, but they don't change. And 5-sigma events don't happen in our statistical models. In the real world of the capital markets, however, all three happen from time to time. The growth/value divergence in small cap stocks from December 1999 to February 2000 was over 5,000 basis points. That's a 6-sigma event. The large cap/small cap divergence in 1998 was 4,000 basis points. That's a 4-sigma event, lasting an entire year. The market crash in 1987 and the mini crash in 1989 (21 percent and 8 percent, respectively, in a single day) were 20-sigma and 7-sigma shocks, when measured against daily market volatility of the prior year.

Daily shocks of 5 to 10 sigma are rare in any single investment, but they happen somewhere in the world reasonably often. Monthly shocks of 4 to 6 sigma are rare, and annual shocks of 3 to 5 sigma are rare. But, again, they happen somewhere in the financial world with some regularity. So there are several problems with risk estimation, hence with risk budgeting, which should lead us to budget risk more conservatively than we might in a normal (i.e., statistically, a normally distributed) world.

- Estimated correlations are imprecise. If we have 60 months of data, the standard error in our estimate of correlations between strategies, alphas or markets is roughly 0.13. This means that if we think two strategies are uncorrelated, they may have a true correlation of –0.2 or +0.2, with about a 5 percent chance of either. And correlations change over time. All of which means that we should probably assume that the true correlation, looking to the future, is higher than the correlation that we observe in the historical data.
- Correlations in up and down markets are often different (as LTCM discovered to their chagrin, and that of their clients). It is imperative to look at both.
- Volatility estimates are less imprecise. If we have 60 months of data, volatility has a standard error of less than 10 percent. That's pretty good. Indeed, to the surprise of many nonstatisticians, it's a good deal better than the uncertainty on the correlation side. But it does mean that

if we are targeting a 2 percent incremental risk level, no one should ever be surprised if the actual outcome is 1.8 percent or 2.2 percent, *even if market volatility is steady.*
- Volatility changes over time. If volatility falls in half and then doubles, we may see our targeted incremental risk level plunge to 1 percent or soar to 4 percent. The measured risk over time, in this illustrative case, is not 2 percent, but actually leaps to 2.9 percent.* This is one reason that incremental risk is rarely as low as we intend it to be.
- Market shocks can create multisigma events. The overall fund should be managed to a level of risk where the investment committee overseeing the fund will not overreact to even a 3-sigma shock, because a 3-sigma shock will happen from time to time, with far more regularity than we would find in any normal distribution.

The imprecise science of managing risks is a far-reaching subject that is important in a portable alpha context—whether applied at the strategy level or at the portfolio level—particularly given the inherent importance of the risk and correlation estimates to the selection of combinations of alpha strategies and derivatives-based market exposures. This whole topic is explored in further detail in subsequent chapters.

SUSTAINABLE SPENDING IN A LOWER-RETURN WORLD

One of the key problems with the *classic model*, finding alphas in the same markets that we seek risk exposure, is that the conventional asset mix is not likely to deliver the returns that we need. Many of the recent problems in the newly underfunded pension, endowment, foundation world stem from (1) return expectations that are unrealistic and (2) a desire to spend more than market returns can support. Whether we *need* a particular rate of return, or hope for performance that can sustain outsized spending, we should not necessarily *expect* that return.

Our industry pays scant attention to the concept of *sustainable spending,* which is key to effective strategic planning for corporate pensions, public pensions, foundations, endowments—and even for individuals. Sustainable

---

*If we have 1% volatility in one year and 4% volatility the next, we would measure the volatility as the square root of the average of the two variances: average (0.01%,0.16%) is 0.085%. That variance is equivalent to 2.9% standard deviation, not 2%!

spending typically starts with sustaining the real value of the assets. This requires realistic return assumptions. *Hope is not a strategy.*[2] We need to know how much we can spend on a near-risk-free basis, in order to know how much of our intended spending comes from wishful thinking, from hope. This exercise sets the stage for a reasoned, risk-controlled quest for the incremental returns that we hope to achieve.

Sustainable spending is not a fixed rate of return on assets. It changes as real yields change. While most universities have used a 5 or 6 percent spending rule for many years, the investment markets have sometimes been priced to make this an easy goal, and sometimes (e.g., now) a very difficult goal. For the same reasons, pensions cannot hope to duplicate the 1990s experience of replacing pension contributions with pension fund returns.

THE CONSTITUENT PARTS OF A SPENDING POLICY

In recent years, many otherwise-sophisticated institutional investors have taken the view that they need a higher rate of return than the return that is assuredly available in the lowest-risk strategies (long Treasury bonds can match the cash flow needs for most pension funds, or long TIPS portfolios for most endowments and foundations), and therefore need more in risky assets in order to earn their risk premium, based on a dangerous assumption that higher risk will lead to higher returns. Do the riskier assets assuredly offer higher long-term returns? While theory suggests that there *should* be a risk premium, there is nothing in securities law that *assures* a risk premium. Indeed, relative to current yields on TIPS, the risk premium on stocks appears dismally small.

If we cannot be assured of a substantial risk premium, isn't it better to commit to a spending stream that we can *assuredly* earn, boosting that spending only when future happy surprises increase our sustainable spending? As a fallback, should we at least acknowledge that we're spending future investment returns that we may or may not earn? For example, if we can assuredly earn a real return of 2 percent and want to spend 5 percent, then we need to find an incremental 3 percent. This must come from (1) a risk premium earned on our selected departures from our risk-minimizing portfolio, (2) an alpha from our superior choice of investment managers and strategies, or (3) additional contributions to our asset base.

Today, the average corporate pension fund is using a *pension return assumption* averaging just over 8 percent in its earnings statement. What if the assets earn 5 percent, not 8 percent, in the years ahead? Then earnings are overstated by 3 percent of fund assets *per year*. The average public fund is using a discount rate of just under 8 percent, which tacitly means that it's expecting its nonbond assets to deliver around a 10 percent return. On this basis the average public fund is about 80 percent funded. With the bond markets yielding about 5 percent, this means that most sponsors are expecting to earn an additional 3 percent—at the overall fund level—either from the equity risk premium, from assuming other risks, or from alpha. But what if the assets earn only 5 percent? Then funding ratios are closer to 55 percent, and the public funds must make up the difference from tax revenues.

THE RISK PREMIUM AND THE BUILDING BLOCKS OF RETURN

The conventional view is that there is a large risk premium for equities and other risky assets and strategies. Therefore, many sponsors expect to make up some of the difference with riskier assets. The current risk premium *cannot* be assessed by looking at past excess returns. This would lead us to boost our expectations at market tops and lower them at market bottoms. But we can look at the building blocks of return.

For most assets, return has just three components: income, growth, and revaluation. The first two are straightforward: What is the current yield? What is the normal long-term rate of growth in income that we might expect in the future? Here it is crucial to rely on objective facts, not wishful thinking, in setting our growth expectations.

The third piece is more speculative: Should we expect the market to pay more or less for each dollar of income in the future than it does today? Can we trust the future risk premium to resemble past excess returns? Do junk bonds or emerging markets debt offer more yield than conventional bonds? Of course. Do they deliver a higher return? While default losses have been smaller than the yield premium in the past, current quality spreads are unusually narrow. Do stocks offer more return than conventional bonds? Only if the growth in earnings and dividends makes up for the lower yield of stocks. While this has generally been true over time, from current levels this may be a less reliable risk premium than in the past. The bottom line is that, from current market levels, we do not find a large risk premium in most of the markets that we typically rely upon for this extra return.

THE ROLE OF ALPHA IN SETTING EXPECTATIONS

Alpha is the incremental risk-adjusted return earned as a consequence of manager skill (as opposed to any incremental return being a consequence of assuming additional risk). Since institutional investment managers essentially *are* the market, the average alpha earned by the managers must be reasonably close to zero. If almost all corporate and public funds assume alpha as part of their return stream, then they must, like the citizens of Lake Wobegon, all be above average. The sensible view on alpha is to *seek* it, to be grateful when it is earned reliably over time, but not to *assume* it as part of the normal course of investing.

CONTRIBUTIONS

If we spend above a sustainable level, we must make up the difference in contributions, unless we can earn enough to cover the additional spending, either from a sensible risk premium or from alpha. Unfortunately, many sponsors are now being led to increase the aggressiveness of their investments, by dint of their assumptions. A low-return environment encourages many to make up the difference with increased allocations to risky assets, which are assumed to be likely to provide the higher returns. But higher-risk investments sometimes result in *lower* returns. *That's what risk means!*

- For corporations, this means they must contribute to help fund each new year's growth in future pension obligations. By fiddling with liability discount rates, the government may help companies push these contributions out a few years more. But that only increases the burden on future generations of management or compromises the security of the future generations of pensioners. The corporate pensions community regrettably got accustomed to long contribution holidays in the 1990s, which created the illusion that pension plans require no contributions to meet their obligations.
- For endowments, this means that capital campaigns may be needed to top up the assets, to cover any spending that exceeds the risk-minimizing real yield offered by the markets. The bull market of the 1980s and 1990s allowed the acceptance of a 5 percent spending stream as a "conservative" choice, even though much of the lofty real returns during these decades were from revaluation, not from the more sustainable income or growth components of return. If spending is 5 percent and real returns fall to 2 or 3 percent, then the endowments simply cannot operate in perpetuity, as many expect. Fortunately, as long as the shortfall is not too large, many endowments can turn to their alumni to rescue the endowments and their intended spending plans.
- For foundations, which typically have no source of supplementary contributions, this means that most foundations may ultimately not earn the 5 percent real return required to maintain the real value of the corpus

of the foundation portfolio. This means that most foundations, while enjoying a very long life span, may not fulfill their intended role in perpetuity, forever serving the needs of the projects selected by the trustees.

For the long-term investor, return expectations of 8 and 9 percent may not be achieved in a world of stock yields below 2 percent and bond yields of 5 percent. If the intended spending rises with inflation, as it often does, then sustainable spending falls well short of 5 percent, absent contributions. None of this can be comforting to those who would like to rely on lofty return assumptions, to justify chunky spending or skinny contributions. But it is far better to plan for the future on assumptions that are sound, rather than relying on hope as our strategy for the future.

THE IMPLICATIONS OF A SLENDER RISK PREMIUM

For investors, a slender return or a slender risk premium is not attractive at all. For those of us seeking investments that are priced to offer material benefits to compensate for risk (we prefer a solid risk premium), bigger is better.

It is a fact that even the equity risk premium is unknown—we all too often estimate it (badly) merely by extrapolating the past. *Should* there be a risk premium? Of course. Is it written into contract law for any assets we buy? Of course not. A 5 percent risk premium is often taken as fact, but it's only a hypothesis. If we take a 5 percent risk premium as a fact rather than a hypothesis, this wrongly seems to free us to focus on asset selection, since we've now dispensed with the risk premium and, by extension, the resulting asset mix decision. Few serious observers of the capital markets would argue that the future risk premium for stocks relative to bonds can rival the lofty excess return that stocks have delivered in the past.

The 81 years covered by the Ibbotson data has seen stocks deliver a real return of 7.1 percent, against 2 percent for bonds. That's terrific! But a big part of this return is attributable to the tripling of price-earnings (P/E) ratios in the past 81 years. Most observers would, at a minimum, subtract that from future return expectations. The constituent parts for return paint a different picture for the future. Dividend income provided 4.2 percent of the 7.1 percent real return for stocks, real dividend growth provided 1.3 percent, and rising valuation levels provided another 1.5 percent. If we set aside the 1.5 percent that stemmed from rising P/E ratios and falling dividend yields, we're down to 5.5 percent. If we recognize that the current dividend yield is 1.8 percent, not 4.2 percent, we're down to 3 percent, barely 1 percent better than we can get with inflation-indexed government-guaranteed bonds.

If the future real return on government bonds is 2 percent, then we need pretty heroic growth assumptions to get a risk premium of over 2 percent. Accordingly, let's assume that the risk premium is somewhere pretty far south of 5 percent. It may be 2 percent; it may be zero. But, it's not 5 percent.

STOCKS FOR THE LONG RUN?

If stocks offer a 5 percent risk premium relative to bonds, then it makes no sense for any long-term investor to invest in less risky assets. The long-term investor, if prepared to wait 20 years, has almost a 95 percent chance of winning with stocks, if they offer a 5 percent risk premium. But this notion of stocks for the long run is predicated on that lofty risk premium. If stocks normally deliver better returns than bonds by 4 or 5 percent per year, compounded over time, the arithmetic is compelling. If the margin is smaller, then the arithmetic quickly becomes less interesting. Consider Figure 4.1, drawn from a 2005 *Financial Analysts Journal* "Editor's Corner."

These graphs examine worst-reasonable outcomes. We define "worst-reasonable outcome" as the fifth-percentile outcome, which we have a 95 percent chance of beating. If stocks have 15 percent volatility relative to

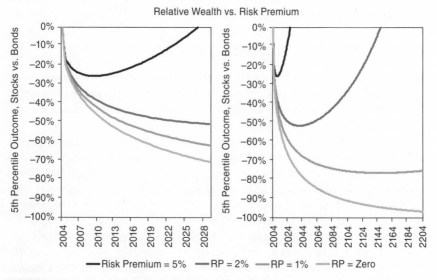

FIGURE 4.1   The Arithmetic of Long-Term Returns
Source: Research Affiliates LLC; hypothetical example for illustrative purposes only.

bonds, and a normal excess return of 5 percent, then the fifth-percentile outcome is a 19 percent shortfall.[3] That is, we'd have a 5 percent chance of stocks underperforming bonds by 19 percent or more in a year. In the second year, our fifth-percentile outcome is *not* another loss of 19 percent. Because risk expands with the square root of time, our fifth-percentile outcome is 34 percent below the mean, which has now grown another 5 percent, to a 10 percent gain. So our fifth-percentile outcome is a loss of only 24 percent, barely 5 percent worse than the one-year case. In fact, with a 5 percent risk premium, our worst reasonable outcome bottoms out at a 26 percent shortfall after five years. In other words, if stocks can reasonably be expected to deliver 5 percent more than bonds, our worst-reasonable outcome is that we're underwater relative to the bonds by 26 percent after five years. After five years, the picture quickly becomes brighter. And after 25 years, we have better than a 95 percent chance of winning with stocks, relative to bonds. In a nutshell, that's the basis for the *stocks for the long run* thesis.

But how realistic is this 5 percent risk premium? If bonds yield 5 percent, we need to get a long-term return of 10 percent from stocks to get a 5 percent risk premium. If stocks yield 2 percent, then stocks have to deliver long-term earnings and dividend growth of 8 percent. That's a lot to ask: Per-share earnings growth in the twentieth century (no slacker for growth, as centuries go) averaged just over 4 percent, of which fully 3 percent was inflation. Suppose earnings growth is only 5, 4, or 3 percent. Those figures will correspond to a 2 percent 1 percent, and 0 percent risk premium. After 25 years, we're 50 percent, 60 percent, and 70 percent behind the bonds, respectively, and still headed south. While this is the bad-news fifth-percentile outcome, it is well within the realm of possibility.

With a 2 percent risk premium, this worst-reasonable outcome never gets much worse than that 50 percent shortfall, and finally surpasses bonds in a bit under 150 years, as the second graph shows. This is also about the time that the worst-reasonable outcome with a 1 percent risk premium hits its low point, at 77 percent less wealth than the bond investors, and begins to slowly creep upwards. After 200 years, we're still way behind bonds. Notably, both of these scenarios require earnings growth that is faster than we've seen over a century of steadily rising prosperity. With earnings growth of 3 percent, we'd have no risk premium, for which the worst-reasonable outcome can never hit bottom.

In short, *stocks for the long run* works if the risk premium is large, *which it has been at times in the past and is not today.* The 2002 *Financial Analysts Journal* article "What Risk Premium is 'Normal'?"[4] showed that the normal risk premium over the past two centuries has probably been about 2.4 percent. If that is right, then 100-year investors can expect their stocks to beat their bonds, with 95 percent confidence. If the current risk premium is lower than 2.4 percent, we'd need a longer horizon to have this much confidence in the superiority of our stock holdings. Naturally, if we're willing to settle for a 60 percent likelihood of success, the span we'd need to wait is considerably shorter. But what we're being asked to believe is that the wait for stocks to assuredly outpace bonds is a reasonable span for patient investors. Not true, unless stocks are priced to deliver a large risk premium relative to bonds.[5]

DIVIDENDS AND A SLENDER RISK PREMIUM

Many investors think that dividends don't matter if the growth is sound. After all, dividends grow over time; bond coupon payments do not. Eventually, the former surpasses the latter, forming the basis for the superiority of stocks—for the long-term investor. How long must we wait before our income on stocks matches our income on bonds? Consider Figure 4.2. Investing $100 in bonds delivers $5 of income; in stocks, it delivers $2 in dividend income (or less). If dividend growth merely matches the 4 percent rate of the twentieth century, then our dividend income catches up with the income we're earning on bonds in *just under a quarter of a century*. If growth is more robust, at 5 or 6 percent, the wait is shorter but still requires

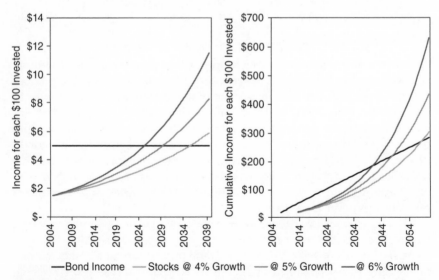

FIGURE 4.2   The Arithmetic of Compounding Growth of Income
Source: Bureau of Labor Statistics, Research Affiliates LLC.

nearly two decades of patience. It's a long wait, but the patient investor wins with stocks.

How long do we wait for the *cumulative income* to catch up? If dividend growth matches the 4 percent growth of the twentieth century, we need over 40 years for our cumulative income to have kept pace. In those 40 years, our $100 bond investment will have paid us $200 (assuming we could reinvest at the same 5 percent when today's bonds mature), and our stocks will have finally paid us $199. Even at higher growth rates—with little historical support for such optimism—we have to wait roughly 30 years. While the long-term investor eventually wins, it's a daunting wait. These exhibits vividly show us what a skinny risk premium looks like! The risk premium rules of thumb that we've been taught to rely on are a shaky foundation for shaping our future expectations.

BENCHMARKING AT THE PORTFOLIO LEVEL

In 2004, Peter Bernstein laid down a gauntlet for our industry to stop misusing "normal policy benchmarks." Many observers have misconstrued his remarks as suggesting that we *stop* using benchmarks altogether. Yet the past misuse of benchmarks does not mean that they should be abandoned. Rather, they should be used correctly. This is easier said than done!

Performance benchmarking is one of the most influential developments in institutional investing in the past quarter-century. But it has been used to suppress risk against a benchmark, rather than to select and manage acceptable risks that are likely to deliver profits. If the benchmark is a poor fit with the obligations that are served by a portfolio, then *an irrelevant risk is reduced or eliminated,* at the likely cost of lowered absolute returns.

Benchmarking is not without merit. What can be measured *will* be measured, and indeed *should* be measured. Benchmarking allows us to measure the value that a manager adds and the risk he is taking to produce additional return. Sophisticated investors use benchmarks to control their exposure to various markets, and to select managers based on their abilities to reliably add alpha. However, a benchmark should bear some resemblance to the obligations that a portfolio is intended to serve and should be used to *gauge* risk, not to *suppress* it.

Let's look at pension plans as an example. strategic advisor Keith Ambachtsheer is a co-founder of CEM Benchmarking Inc., which has been tracking the cost-effectiveness of pension funds around the world since 1991. He notes that in a sample of 76 large U.S. defined-benefit plans in the CEM database to the end of 2006, the average five-year tracking error of a fund relative to its policy benchmark was 1.4 percent. Over the same period, the tracking error of a fund's policy benchmark relative to its plan liabilities was 17.1 percent. This astounding gap led directly to the unprecedented tumble in liability coverage shortly after the turn of the century, as discussed in Chapter 10. It also challenges the relevance of the average policy benchmark.

For most sponsors, a portfolio dominated by equities cannot reliably defease fund obligations and might well be outpaced by a more diversified portfolio. The myth that equities are the lowest-risk vehicle for truly long-term investors has led advisers and their clients to mandate equity-heavy (hence ill-diversified!) benchmarks. The industry's craze to beat the bogey, rather than to meet the fund obligations, encourages asset managers to follow the market's animal spirits, rather than to gauge when such risks are likely to bear rewards.

IN SEARCH OF A BETTER RISK MEASURE

Long-term success requires relevant portfolio benchmarks and objectives. Most long-term investors face the following three, sometimes conflicting, objectives:

1. Defease liabilities/obligations and manage risk relative to liabilities. A shortfall relative to liabilities requires catch-up contributions. This implies modest equity risk and large interest rate sensitivity.
2. Deliver positive real returns and avoid material losses. A protracted drop in asset values is unnecessary in a world where there are always some markets with positive returns. This implies a quest for maximum Sharpe ratio and low volatility.
3. Deliver performance above peer medians. Why? A shortfall relative to peers leads to incremental funding costs, relative to peers, which weakens the competitive position of the sponsor. This requires some sensitivity to the normal mix equity-centric of our peers.

Given these three distinct objectives, many investors appear to focus almost exclusively on peer group comparisons, the least important of the three. As illustrated in Figure 4.3, this locks an investor into a portfolio, designated in medium grey at the far right, that is a poor fit with the first two, more important, objectives.

Alternatively, if we choose to immunize against the liabilities (the lighter grey circle in the upper left), we have substantial risk of shortfall in a peer group comparison and substantial volatility, against a real returns

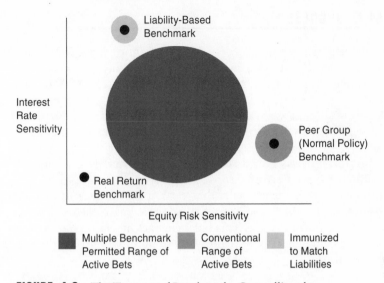

FIGURE 4.3 The Tyranny of Benchmarks Controlling the Wrong Risks
Source: Research Affiliates LLC; hypothetical example for illustrative purposes only.

benchmark. If we choose the low-volatility goal, the risk of substantial shortfalls relative to peers or relative to liabilities can be a career-ending risk. A single-minded focus on any of these three sets of objectives can leave us vulnerable to devastating risk on one of the other dimensions.

An investor should demand acceptable risk against *all three* objectives while adding value to at least two of the three measures most of the time. This expedient is less risky than status quo. It offers a better fit with liabilities than status quo, while acknowledging that many investors must not stray too far from their peer group lest a bull market puts competitors in a stronger position to serve their liabilities at a lower cost. With this blended structure, the range of possible investments is many times larger than the conventional obsession with peer groups, strengthening the ability to select attractive investments at sensible levels of risk.

While our industry focuses closely on the peer group comparison and too little on the liability mismatch, we should recognize that all three risks matter a great deal. Emphasis shall be on our ability to meet these three objectives in a consistent fashion over a long horizon. While performance can be evaluated regularly, it is also important to recognize that the whims of the capital markets can bring about extended shortfalls on *any single* metric.

In fact, this is exactly what we found when reviewing the average betas (over rolling 1-year periods, over a 10-year period, and over annual 1-year periods) of the 10 largest actively managed U.S. large cap core equity and U.S. core fixed-income strategies as of March 31, 2007, as shown in Table 5.1. (Strategies selected are based on assets under management as reported to the eVestment Alliance Database.)

A few of the managers have consistently exhibited a beta that is higher than their representative benchmark. However, most of the managers have betas that are right around 1.0 and in some cases even consistently below 1.0. In addition, almost all of the managers have correlations with the representative market index benchmark that are close to 100 percent. Is beta a relevant data point in addition to the incremental excess return for purposes of evaluating this or any other group of managers with similar investment parameters and objectives (as is the case with the group of managers in Table 5.1)? Absolutely—although, again, with the caveat that the benchmark meets the appropriate criteria.

The use of the alpha/beta methodology allows an investor to decompose an active manager's returns into the returns that resulted from taking risk and the returns that resulted from manager skill (assuming a long enough time period is available to allow the investor to distinguish skill from luck, and keeping in mind the other limitations noted in Appendix 5.1). This was the point made by the individuals who originally used the terms for purposes of evaluating active managers. Unfortunately, however, the true usefulness of the *beta* term—and therefore the relevance of the associated *alpha* term—has its limits once we step beyond the domain of traditional investment strategies with well-defined benchmarks.

KEY CHALLENGES OF ALPHA-BETA SEPARATION AND ESTIMATION

As previously defined, a benchmark portfolio should be similar to the associated actively managed portfolio from a risk standpoint in order to be most relevant for evaluating the skill of the manager. Therefore, if the benchmark does in fact have a similar level of risk and similar risk factor exposures to the investment portfolio (as proxied by a beta near 1.0, a similar level of volatility, and other risk measures where relevant), the excess returns and alpha should be roughly similar. Many traditional actively managed stock and bond strategies maintain a risk profile similar to the associated market index. In fact, it is often an explicit part of the objectives established by the client or stipulated in an investment prospectus to do so. This is why many managers and investors equate excess returns with alpha in practice. The

WHAT IS SUCCESS?

How we define investment success drives our entire approach to investing. Ben Graham was fond of saying that the essence of investment management is the management of risks, not the management of returns. Well-managed portfolios start with this precept. The management of risk presupposes that we know what risks we want to avoid. But risk itself is ambiguous. In its broadest form, it's whatever goes wrong, which we cannot know until after the fact.

Most forms of risk fall into one of three categories. An investment officer can be fired for poor returns, for lagging the performance of his peers, or for producing investment results that can't meet obligations or liabilities. Exposures must be balanced against these three broad classes of risk in the quest for investment success. This balancing act hinges on our definition of success, of eventual portfolio wealth. Accordingly, we must ask the question, what is wealth?

- Is success based on the total value of a portfolio? Hardly. A million dollars today buys much less than it did 25 years ago.
- Is it the *real* value of our portfolio? Only if we plan to spend it all today.
- Is the long-term spending that a portfolio can sustain—the annuity that our assets could procure—the best measure of success? Closer, but this ignores purchasing power once again.
- Is success best defined as the inflation-indexed real income that our assets could sustain over time? This is probably the purest definition of sucess for most investors.

Isn't it our primary goal, for most investors, individual and institutional alike, to increase the real spending that a portfolio can sustain over time, which we might call the sustainable spending? Isn't a closely related goal to avoid shocks that can jeopardize that future real spending? Consider Figure 4.4, which alters the classic risk/reward comparison to a real sustainable spending frame of reference. The return is no longer the simple return—it is the growth in the real spending stream that the portfolio can sustain.[6]

Risk is no longer the volatility of assets; it is the volatility of that real sustainable spending. Figure 4.4 includes an array of twelve asset classes, which would have been a defensible roster of available liquid asset classes 10 years ago. In this new frame of reference, TIPS replace Treasury bills as the low-risk asset class and Treasury bills actually become quite risky. Even

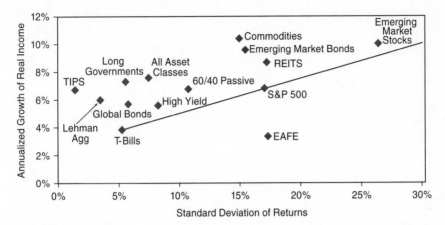

FIGURE 4.4 Annual Growth and Volatility of Real Spending Power, 10 Years Ended June 30, 2007
Source: Bloomberg.

long governments and the Lehman Aggregate are less risky than Treasury bills in this case. Figure 4.4 contains three surprises:

1. Even factoring in the bull market of the late 1990s and of the past five years, the ten-year results for the classic 60/40 stock/bond balanced portfolio is less than that of a broadly diversified multiple asset class portfolio which has far less risk. This was even after we handicapped international stocks by hedging them back into a very weak dollar. Surprisingly, the 60/40 performance is even a tad lower than the risk-minimizing TIPS portfolio!

2. When return and risk are recast in this fashion, we find that almost all asset classes have a positive incremental return relative to the classic capital markets line between Treasury bills and stocks. Only Hedged EAFE (non-U.S.-developed market stocks) fall below this capital market line. Meanwhile, commodities, REITS, and emerging markets bonds all tower above the capital markets line. To be sure, during other spans, the winners and losers would change. But, it's easy to see that many risky *but uncorrelated* asset classes will usually have a positive incremental return relative to this amended capital markets line.

3. We find that a naïve mix, equally weighting all twelve of these asset classes, offers a better ratio of return to risk (which we've redefined as the volatility of that sustainable real spending) than any markets other than the pure bond investments. We also find that, in this context, it

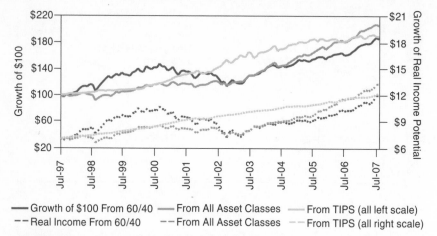

FIGURE 4.5 Growth in Assets and in Real Sustainable Spending: 60/40 Balanced, TIPS, and Naïve All Asset Classes Blend, 10 Years Ended June 30, 2007
Source: Bloomberg.

dominates the classic 60/40 portfolio. This is not to say that the naïve "all asset classes" portfolio is an optimal choice. But 60/40 is *in no way* the best we can do to defease a real spending stream.

Of course returns, and to a lesser extent risk, are exquisitely sensitive to start and end dates. This span was characterized by a monster bull market for stocks, the worst bear market since the Great Depression, and a broad multiple-asset-class bull market since then. Through all of this, TIPS, 60/40, and the naïve "all asset classes" blend earn a similar return at very different levels of risk, whether we measure the volatility of returns or the volatility of real spending power. What path did they take? We can see this in Figure 4.5.

- In the context of the past four years of the largest bull market in U.S. capital markets history, 60/40 looked brilliant for a time. As stocks unraveled, the 60/40 investor struggled, while TIPS soared. Through it all, the naïve "all asset classes" blend produced a steady—and ultimately better—return, with volatility lower than that of the 60/40 mix and barely higher than the volatility of TIPS.
- Note that the solid black 60/40 line falls, peak to trough, by only 23 percent. So why was that bear market so devastating? The dashed lower lines tell the story. Here, we convert the simple returns (the growth of $100) into the real income stream that the portfolio can sustain. At the start of this period, a $100 investment (upper lines, left scale)

would suffice to buy a $7 real income stream. By the peak of the bull market, this 60/40 portfolio could buy a $14 real income stream. By the end of the bear market, 35 percent of this spending power—over one-third!—was gone from a supposedly balanced 60/40 bond portfolio. A 23 percent bear market led to a 35 percent drop in sustainable real spending.

- It's no surprise that TIPS provide nearly straight-line growth in real spending: That's what they're designed to provide! The big surprise on this graph is how steadily the naïve "all asset classes" portfolio tracks the TIPS, without letting us down quite as badly during the bear market, with volatility in sustainable real spending which is one-third lower than the 60/40 portfolio, and yet with cumulative growth in sustainable real spending which ultimately exceeds that of the much riskier 60/40 portfolio.

- Interestingly, during most of 2005–2006, when returns for many asset classes other than stocks stalled, the fecundity of these portfolios all rose handily, very much in line with prior years. Because bond and TIPS yields were rising, the cost of buying a real inflation-indexed annuity fell by 8 percent. So even a zero return in those years would have delivered an 8 percent increase in real sustainable spending, hence an 8 percent improvement in real wealth.

CONCLUSION

What can we conclude regarding asset allocation and related investment decisions at the portfolio level from these exhibits? First, our natural focus on portfolio return and volatility, to the exclusion of sustainable spending and volatility in that sustainable spending, is likely misguided as it leads us away from a balanced assessment of investment success. Second, the power of *true* diversification should not be underestimated as a means to sustain long-term real spending power at modest risk. The classic 60/40 balanced portfolio is not *true* diversification. Indeed, one of the best-kept secrets of the investing community is that stock market return so dominates the risk of a 60/40 portfolio that a 60/40 balanced portfolio exhibits a 98 to 99 percent correlation with stocks! True diversification involves seeking out uncorrelated or lightly correlated risk factors—and not just among low-risk strategies.

In addition, just as success is not solely a function of asset growth, risk is not a singular function of asset volatility. As investors increasingly focus on the importance and benefits of diversification and their key risks—associated not so much with underperforming peers but rather with realized losses and not meeting future obligations—portable alpha has received a great deal of well-deserved attention. The portable alpha concept can be applied at the investment strategy level and also at the investment portfolio level, in both cases providing the potential for vastly improving the efficiency of the return on assets at a given level of risk.

Indeed, the recognition that asset allocation decisions and sources of alpha can be separate, independent decisions was one of the most important developments of the latter part of the twentieth century, supported in no small part by the proliferation of new instruments and trading techniques for institutional portfolios. This brought with it a sharp improvement in the opportunity for effective risk budgeting in portfolios as well, yet another very important innovation in institutional asset management in the 1990s.

A growing reliance on risk budgeting helped us to see that there are many forms of risk, some of which are pernicious and dangerous, such as liability mismatch, and some of which are relatively harmless but dangerous to a fiduciary's career, such as falling short of a peer group. But *all of them matter*. Risk budgeting is a more nuanced and subtle challenge than most investors, even today, realize.

Both risk budgeting and portable alpha are powerful tools, requiring care in order to extract the maximum benefit. It's well worth the effort. The portable alpha investment application affords investors the opportunity to improve their results, lower their portfolio risk, and reduce the mismatch between assets and liabilities. These three goals were in conflict—and could not be pursued in parallel—before the advent of portable alpha strategies. They are no longer in stark conflict, and an investor can now reasonably pursue all three goals in parallel. This is the real gift that portable alpha grants us.

CHAPTER 5

Alpha, Beta, and Alpha-Beta Separation

Sabrina Callin

Keith Ambachtsheer coined the phrase "Alpha, Beta, Bafflegab" as part of the title to his April 2006 *Ambachtsheer Letter,*[1] and then went on to suggest that it might be time to give the terms *alpha* and *beta* a rest. What was the primary reason for his recommendation that we stop using two of the key terms that underlie modern portfolio theory? The terms are seemingly being used more for purposes of marketing with the goal of selling investment strategies or products—rather than in a context that is most useful for investors. Alpha and beta appear to have become persuasive tools as much as anything, with relatively little reference to the actual definitions and original context in which the terms were used.

When you think about the now common catchphrase "pay for alpha and not beta," the idea put forth by Keith Ambachtsheer starts to resonate. Should an investor willingly pay more for uncorrelated investment returns that are derived from manager skill than for returns that result from systematic risk taking? Most definitely! The confusing part lies in the definitions of alpha and beta. If I should only pay for alpha and not beta, how do I recognize alpha and beta when I see them? Perhaps more important, how does it all relate back to my goal as an investor to achieve an optimal return on capital relative to my risk-free reference point at an acceptable level of downside risk and in consideration of other parameters that help define my investment policy?

The terms *alpha* and *beta* are derived from a regression equation whereby beta measures the sensitivity of a security or portfolio's return to the return of the market, a market index, or a set of risk factors, and alpha measures the portion of the return that is not explained by the beta (or betas) and associated market exposure. In other words, beta helps investors understand the underlying risk exposure inherent in an investment, whereas alpha is the residual return that results from skilled active management—or luck—as opposed to the return that compensates investors for assuming downside risk.

The use of the term *beta* is most commonly associated with William F. (Bill) Sharpe and his Nobel prize-winning work on the capital asset pricing model (1964),[2] as referenced in Chapter 2, whereas the term *alpha* was popularized by Michael Jensen in a paper he published in 1968 on the performance of mutual funds.[3] Importantly, the ability to accurately derive alpha as a measure of risk-adjusted excess return is entirely dependent on the use of an appropriate market benchmark or other appropriate set of risk factors for purposes of calculating the beta. Even then, *the ability to measure true alpha and active manager skill may be elusive* for all of the reasons explained in Appendix 5.1.

Today, the terms *alpha* and *beta* are used in an increasingly broad and sometimes theoretically incorrect context. The broader use of the terms is not necessarily without merit. There are plenty of examples of words where the commonly accepted definitions have evolved over time with good reason. Indeed, it is quite difficult to describe the portable alpha concept without using the relatively short word *beta* to reference market exposure. And *alpha-beta separation* does capture the essence of one of the key benefits of the portable alpha investment application—the ability to separately select desired market exposure and skilled investment managers. However, the somewhat common use and misuse of the terms can be particularly confusing and even misleading in a portable alpha and alpha-beta separation framework.

How did we get to a place where the use of the very words that seemingly help define an investment practice may result in less rather than more clarity for investors? A confluence of events, it seems, relating not just to portable alpha investment applications but also to the increased focus on hedge funds and most recently absolute return strategies. Regardless, there are key alpha, beta and alpha-beta separation concepts that are important for investors to understand when navigating the increasingly broad and complex world of portable alpha.

BETA AND ALPHA DEFINED

William F. Sharpe, Gordon J. Alexander, and Jeffery V. Bailey defined *beta* and *alpha*—and also *ex-post alpha* and the associated *benchmark portfolio*—in *Investments* (fifth edition, Prentice Hall, 1995) as follows:

> *beta coefficent* (or alternatively the *market beta*)—a relative measure of the sensitivity of an asset's return to changes in the return on the

market portfolio. Mathematically, the beta coefficient of a security is the security's covariance with the market portfolio divided by the variance of the market portfolio.

alpha—the difference between a security's expected return and its equilibrium expected return.

ex-post alpha—a portfolio's alpha calculated on an ex-post basis. Mathematically, over an evaluation interval, it is the difference between the average return on the portfolio and the average return on a benchmark portfolio.

benchmark portfolio—a portfolio against which the investment performance of an investor can be compared for the purpose of determining investment skill. A benchmark portfolio represents a relevant and feasible alternative to the investor's actual portfolio and, in particular, is similar in terms of risk exposure.

While it is still necessary to explore the meaning of alpha and beta in more detail to help put the use of the terms into a practical context, as we attempt to do here and in Appendix 5.1, a review of these definitions together with the definitions put forth in a variety of other reliable sources reveals a key truth: Alpha and beta are highly interrelated terms. To calculate alpha, it is first necessary to specify the underlying risk factor exposures. This is true in a regression context and it is also true in practice when manager returns are compared to a relevant benchmark. If the dominant risk factor exposures are not reflected in the benchmark, the so-called alpha result is not really alpha.

CAPM, ALPHA, AND BETA

According to Bill Sharpe, "The key insight of the capital asset pricing model is that higher expected returns go with the greater risk of doing badly in bad times. Beta is a measure of that. Securities or asset classes with high betas tend to do worse in bad times than those with low betas."[4]

As noted in Chapter 3, the capital asset pricing model (CAPM) is an equilibrium security pricing model that assumes that the market is perfectly efficient and all securities are appropriately priced as a result, while the Jensen's alpha equation measures the difference between the return of a portfolio and the return predicted by CAPM. The same is true of the closely related market model that was developed by Bill Sharpe around the same time as CAPM[5] but which, unlike CAPM, allowed for both an alpha term and an error term in addition to the returns that were explained by the combination of beta and the market return.

All of these are simple linear models that relate the return on a security or portfolio of securities to the return on the market, and they are effectively one and the same, once the assumption of equilibrium is relaxed to allow for returns that are not explained by a combination of the portfolio's beta and the market return (due to random chance or skill). Specifically, the formulas allow one to decompose the returns on a security or portfolio of securities into two basic components: (1) the returns that are explained by a combination of the market return and the beta and the risk-free rate; and (2) the returns that are not thus explained (the alpha component), as follows:

CAPM:

$$r_i = r_f + \beta_{im}(r_m - r_f)$$

Jensen's Measure:

$$\alpha_{pm} = r_p - [r_f + \beta_{pm}(r_m - r_f)]$$

where

r_i or r_p = return on security (i) or portfolio (p)

r_m = return on market portfolio (m)

r_f = risk-free rate

α_{pm} = intercept term

β_{im} or β_{pm} = slope term (covariance of m with security i or portfolio p divided by variance of m/i or m/p)

ALPHA AND BETA IN A PORTFOLIO EVALUATION CONTEXT

The true market portfolio is not easy to define, for the reasons highlighted in Chapter 3—and even if it were, it would not necessarily represent the right benchmark for any given investment portfolio. Rather, in practice a relevant market benchmark, as referenced in and defined by the textbook definitions of ex-post alpha and benchmark portfolio previously presented, is used in order to calculate beta and alpha.

Alpha and beta are quite useful for purposes of evaluating investment strategies with similar benchmarks and opportunity sets. To illustrate this point, consider the following example involving two portfolios, A and B, whereby each of the two investment managers may select securities from a 500-stock universe with the goal of outperforming the benchmark market index represented by the 500-stock universe.

Portfolio A exhibits a beta of 1.0, indicating that the portfolio of stocks selected by the portfolio A manager has a similar level of risk to the benchmark market index. In contrast, portfolio B exhibits a beta of 1.5, essentially indicating that portfolio B has a level of equity market risk that is approximately 1.5 times that of the market index. If both portfolios deliver an equal return, say 12.5 percent relative to a return of 10 percent from the benchmark market index and a risk-free rate of 5 percent, which portfolio has the most attractive risk-adjusted excess return or alpha? Portfolio A, of course!

Mathematically speaking, the ex-post portfolio alpha is equal to the difference between the portfolio return and the equilibrium return that is expected as a function of the portfolio's market risk and the risk-free rate, as previously explained. In this case the calculation of the ex-post alpha for the two portfolios reveals that alpha and excess return are not always one and the same:

$$\alpha_{pm} = r_p - [r_f + \beta_{pm}(r_m - r_f)]$$

Portfolio A:

2.5 percent = 12.5 percent − [5 percent + 1.0(10 percent − 5 percent)]

Portfolio B:

0 percent = 12.5 percent − [5 percent + 1.5(10 percent − 5 percent)]

In both cases, investors received total returns of 12.5 percent and excess returns of 2.5 percent, so why should an investor care about alpha as opposed to excess return (other than the investment theory that states that investors are risk-averse by nature)? The reason may not be as apparent when the market return is positive, but what if the benchmark market index return was −10 percent instead of +10 percent? In this example, all else being equal, the return on portfolio B would have been materially lower than that of portfolio A, given the much greater sensitivity of the returns of portfolio B to the benchmark market index (i.e., the higher beta). This is demonstrated by the following calculation, whereby a market return of −10 percent is substituted for a return of +10 percent and we solve for the portfolio return:

$$r_p = r_f + \beta_{pm}(r_m - r_f) + \alpha_{pm}$$

Portfolio A:

$$-7.5\% = 5\% + 1.0(-10\% - 5\%) + 2.5\%$$

Portfolio B:

$$-17.5\% = 5\% + 1.5(-10\% - 5\%) + 0 \text{ percent}$$

Most investors would agree that, while any type of loss is undesirable, a loss of 7.5 percent is strongly preferable to a loss of 17.5 percent! In addition, while the return on the portfolio of high-beta stocks in our example may be higher than that of the portfolio with a beta of 1.0 during strong equity markets (market returns greater than 10 percent), portfolio B clearly represents a less efficient investment for purposes of achieving the goal of most investors: maximizing return at a given level of risk.

THE RELEVANCE OF ALPHA VERSUS EXCESS RETURN

We have considered some statistics that attempt to demonstrate that the alpha and excess return delivered by a portfolio may or may not be the same number, even though the two terms (alpha and excess return) are often used interchangeably by investors and investment managers. We also illustrated the relevance of the distinction during a downmarket scenario. Why is this also logically the case? Beta, in this case, measures the return sensitivity of a portfolio of stocks to the return of the benchmark 500-stock market index. Manager B has selected a portfolio of high-beta stocks. In simple terms, this means that the return of the stocks in portfolio B, at least on an expected basis, should be greater than benchmark market index when it delivers a positive return and lower when it delivers a negative return.

Theoretically, a portfolio of high-beta stocks should produce a higher return relative to the market index (assuming positive market returns over time), but the higher expected return is not a function of manager B's skill—it is simply a function of the higher risk inherent in the portfolio. Investors may be willing to assume more risk for a higher expected return, but it is important that they specifically recognize that they are doing so and factor the risk into other investment decisions. For example, an investor in portfolio B should not use the benchmark market index as a proxy for the risk that the capital allocated to portfolio B is exposed to. Rather, the capital allocated to portfolio B is exposed to roughly 1.5 times the risk of the market index.

In reality, the preceding example is somewhat extreme. It is certainly not out of the realm of possibilities, but the average beta for most active stock managers who are largely restricted to holding long positions in the stocks in a representative benchmark market index—and not employing explicit stock market leverage in the portfolio via borrowing arrangements—is probably closer to 1.0 than to 1.5. The same is true of bond managers, who are generally restricted to maintaining market risk factor characteristics (duration, credit quality) similar to the representative benchmark index.

TABLE 5.1   Beta and Correlation Statistics for Largest Active Core Equity and Fixed-Income Managers (10-Year Period Ending March 31, 2007)

Active Large-Cap U.S. Equity Strategies	Average Rolling 1-Year Beta	10-Year Beta	Average Annual 1-Year Beta	Average 3-Year Correlation	10-Year Correlation
Manager A	1.29	1.20	1.29	0.92	0.91
Manager B	0.94	0.93	0.96	0.94	0.98
Manager C	0.82	0.79	0.83	0.96	0.97
Manager D	0.79	0.82	0.82	0.92	0.93
Manager E	1.10	1.07	1.08	0.96	0.96
Manager F	0.88	0.85	0.90	0.89	0.88
Manager G	0.94	0.88	0.92	0.91	0.92
Manager H	1.06	1.04	1.05	0.97	0.98
Manager I	1.04	1.02	1.03	0.98	0.95
Manager J	0.90	0.90	0.91	0.98	0.98
Average of 10 Largest Managers	0.98	0.95	0.98	0.94	0.94

Active Core U.S. Fixed-Income Strategies	Average Rolling 1-Year Beta	10-Year Beta	Average Annual 1-Year Beta	Average 3-Year Correlation	10-Year Correlation
Manager A	1.05	1.04	1.05	0.98	0.98
Manager B	0.97	0.97	0.97	0.99	0.99
Manager C	0.84	0.85	0.86	0.95	0.95
Manager D	1.09	1.11	1.11	0.97	0.97
Manager E	1.02	1.02	1.02	1.00	1.00
Manager F	0.97	0.96	0.97	0.98	0.99
Manager G	0.92	0.94	0.93	0.98	0.98
Manager H	1.00	1.00	1.00	0.99	0.99
Manager I	1.00	1.01	1.01	0.99	0.99
Manager J	1.00	1.00	1.00	0.99	0.99
Average of 10 Largest Managers	0.99	0.99	0.99	0.98	0.98

Source: Data from eVestment Alliance, compiled by PIMCO.

same holds true for portable alpha strategies *if* (and only *if*) the aggregate risk to which the capital allocated to the strategy is exposed is similar to the risk inherent in the benchmark portfolio.

The key challenge when it comes to estimating the alpha and beta—and most importantly, the inherent risks—of a portable alpha strategy actually relates to one of the key benefits of the portable alpha investment application. Unlike a situation where a manager's investment universe is constrained to either the securities in the benchmark or securities with similar risk characteristics to those in the benchmark, portable alpha strategies—generally seek alpha from an entirely different source. As a result, the potential for a significant variation in risk from the risk of the benchmark market index certainly exists.

The risk inherent in the alpha source, in some cases, may be greater than that of the benchmark market index that an investor is seeking to outperform and/or may exhibit a material positive correlation with the benchmark market index. In either case, the resulting risk profile of a combination of 100 percent of each (the aggregate risk exposure of the derivatives-based beta market exposure and the alpha strategy) will most certainly be higher than that of the associated market index. Does this mean that the beta will be higher and the alpha will be lower? Theoretically, yes. After all, alpha is supposed to measure risk-adjusted return. However, the theory relies on the appropriate specification of the related inputs.

In cases where the alpha strategy exhibits a material positive correlation with the specified beta market exposure, at least this risk factor component should be reflected in a higher beta (market benchmark sensitivity). As was the case with the second of the two stock managers in the earlier example, manager B, this means that the resulting alpha will not be equal to the excess return (it will be lower). However, as previously noted, even if an alpha strategy is uncorrelated with the specified beta market exposure, there still will be a material increase in the risk of the portable alpha strategy relative to the associated beta market benchmark if the risk in the alpha strategy is great enough. This does not mean that the alpha strategy has to be highly risky, just risky enough such that the majority of the incremental risk is not diversified away. The challenge in an alpha-beta separation framework is that, in these cases, the beta measure will not necessarily capture the additional risk.

Beta measures sensitivity and therefore works as a risk measure when a benchmark market index is used that reflects the primary risk characteristics of the investment strategy, just as an appropriate benchmark index is needed to calculate alpha. Beta does not work as a risk measure if the relevant risk factors are not included in the benchmark in the first place. Therefore investors may be understating their risk of capital loss if they use the risk associated with the beta market exposure as a proxy for the risk of the portable alpha strategy for purposes of asset allocation decisions without first verifying that the beta market is indeed a good proxy for the risk of the portable alpha strategy.

Beta and alpha may be fundamentally more difficult to calculate for purposes of evaluating portable alpha strategies due in part to the wide opportunity set availed to investors for sourcing alpha and in part to the inherent leverage afforded by the beta derivatives component. Where does this leave alpha-beta separation? The bottom line: Practice is not nearly as simple and elegant as it may sound when explained in simple terms, and this is true in spades when it comes to alpha-beta separation. There are three fundamental challenges to achieving a desirable level of alpha by independently selecting alpha and beta as follows:

1. The alpha that a strategy produces is a function of the beta (sensitivity) relative to a specific market index or set of risk factors.
2. Portable alpha implementation is complex and there may be costs, fees, and other considerations that result in a different alpha than an investor anticipates.
3. What is presented as alpha by investment management providers may or may not actually be alpha.

ALPHA IS NOT ALPHA WITHOUT BETA

One key challenge associated with alpha-beta separation relates to the simple fact that alpha, as a technical matter, cannot actually be ported from one benchmark index to another. This is because alpha cannot exist separately from an associated benchmark or beta. Investment return can exist separately, but in order to isolate the alpha associated with a given return profile, beta must also be calculated relative to an appropriate benchmark index. So, while it may be possible to isolate a manager's excess return by shorting the benchmark (most commonly using derivatives) it does not follow that an investor will receive the same alpha result when the original alpha is coupled with a different beta. This is true in part due to variations in cost and bid-ask spread associated with different derivatives contracts. In addition, the associated implementation, liquidity and operational costs can materially impact the end result, as illustrated shortly and also as described in more detail in Chapter 8.

More fundamentally, however, it is true because the betas are not the same. This does not mean that the concept behind alpha-beta separation is without merit. It simply means that while an alpha source can be obtained entirely independently from the desired beta market exposure, it is still necessary to consider the two together in order to calculate the expected beta and alpha of the portable alpha strategy. In cases where the portable alpha investment application is implemented at the portfolio or plan level, as opposed to investment strategy level, it will likewise still be necessary to consider all of the alpha strategies together with all of the beta market exposures in order to determine the true alpha relative to an appropriate market portfolio benchmark—and, more importantly, to measure the inherent risk.

Sometimes the idea is put forth that any given alpha, once identified, is a suitable alpha strategy for a portable alpha program because, by definition, alpha is uncorrelated and therefore can be combined with any given beta exposure to produce a beta-plus-alpha result. This probably comes closest to holding true if the alpha that is being ported (figuratively speaking) is originally associated with a beta market exposure that happens to be highly correlated with the beta benchmark market exposure to which it is being ported. Even then, the assumption does not hold unilaterally. The reason is very simple: While it is true that alpha is uncorrelated with the market index or risk factors used to calculate the beta in the associated regression equation, it does not follow that the resulting alpha is uncorrelated with every other risk factor or market index in existence.

Beta and alpha are dependent terms—there is really no way around that central point, and therefore the two cannot technically be separated. Beta measures sensitivity to a prespecified factor (or, in the case of multifactor regression analysis, a set of prespecified factors) and alpha explains the returns that are not explained by a combination of the return from the factor(s) and the associated beta(s).

Ultimately, for this reason and many other reasons, it is important to do your homework when it comes to selecting alpha strategies from the broad universe of possibilities to combine with beta market exposure. The two can be *sourced* separately—and that fact is indeed a profound recognition in terms of the possible alpha and diversification benefits that can accrue to investors. However, the resulting risk/return profile—including the alpha and the beta and the probability of a capital loss—will necessarily be a function of the recombined parts.

PORTING CAN BE COSTLY

Investment theory generally ignores transaction costs in the interest of illustrating key points and concepts. The same can often be said with regard to descriptions of portable alpha.

The borrowing cost associated with the beta exposure is omitted from the explanation in a surprisingly large number of cases, even though the borrowing cost is a fundamental component of the ability to obtain the desired beta market exposure without deploying a material amount of capital. The omission of the borrowing cost associated with the long derivatives-based beta market exposure from the equation may be excusable in cases where there is an equivalent short side position involved, if the borrowing rates are the same. In all other cases, however, the borrowing cost associated with the beta derivatives position(s) is a material component to understanding the expected return of a portable alpha strategy.

Cash flows and associated liquidity costs are other key components to portable alpha strategies that can be costly and are all too often overlooked. In addition, portable alpha implementation and the associated risk monitoring, exposure adjustments, and reporting are often complex. As a result, either implicit costs must be incurred on the part of the investor if these functions are performed in-house, or explicit fees must be paid to providers to perform these important functions.

To illustrate these points together with the prior point on the dependence of alpha and beta, let's take one of the common and seemingly straightforward examples that has been put forth as a potential portable alpha application: porting small cap active manager alpha to the large cap equity market. An investor has identified a small cap equity manager who consistently delivers alpha relative to the Russell 2000 U.S. small cap equity index. In order to further capitalize on this manager's stock selection skill, the investor is interested in increasing exposure to the small cap manager and then simultaneously using long S&P 500 and short Russell 2000 futures positions to bring the market exposure back into line with the levels stipulated by the policy portfolio asset allocation. Sound familiar? This example is, in concept, very similar to the pension plan example put forth in the *Investments* text referenced in Chapter 2. In this case, however, we will extend the analysis to address four of the technicalities associated with porting alpha.

1. *Liquidity costs.* One of the first questions that an investor who is considering a portable alpha strategy needs to ask is, "How will I source the liquidity needed to meet the margin or collateral calls associated with the derivatives-based market exposure?" In this case, because the investor has both a long and a short position in equity derivatives, he needs to consider the liquidity requirements of the collective exposure and recognize that the potential exists for small cap stocks to outperform large cap stocks (in fact, this has been the case historically, as illustrated in Chapter 6). When small cap stocks outperform large cap stocks, the investor will need to provide capital to meet the associated margin calls. If all of the capital allocated to the portable alpha strategy is invested with the active small cap manager, this means that the small cap equity manager will need to sell stocks to raise cash—which, of course, will involve potentially costly transactions. In addition, stock sales take three days to

settle, whereas futures margin requirements must be met on a next-day basis. Therefore, it might not even be possible to sue the stock portfolio as a source of liquidity for the futures positions. As an alternative, the investor might retain some capital (not invest all the capital in the small cap equity strategy) to meet margin calls, thereby giving up the alpha potential but avoiding trading costs and challenges associated with the three-day settlement period for stock sales. In the latter case, the implicit cost of liquidity might be best described as an opportunity cost that is a function of the capital set aside to meet liquidity needs and the expected incremental return from the alpha strategy.

2. *Implementation costs.* In this example, someone has to manage the short and long futures contract positions, which at a minimum includes making sure that exposure levels are appropriate, providing cash (daily) to each of the futures counterparties based on price changes in the derivatives contracts, deciding when to roll the current futures positions on a quarterly basis, and dealing with any associated regulatory considerations. Someone also needs to actively invest the net cash received from margin calls or raise the net cash needed for margin calls on a daily basis. Finally, consolidated risk monitoring and reporting for the portable alpha strategy together with the associated performance attribution will presumably need to be performed on an ongoing basis.

3. *Differential financing rates associated with the derivatives-based market exposure.* In the theoretical world, investors can borrow and lend at the same rate. However, in the real world, there are not only bid-ask spreads to contend with on any given security or derivatives position (differences between the price at which a security can be sold and a price at which a security can be purchased at a given point in time), but there are also very real and potentially material differences in the financing costs associated with different derivatives contracts. In the example at hand, the financing rate that is effectively received from the short Russell 2000 position may be substantially lower than the financing rate that is effectively paid for the long S&P 500 position. Currently (2007) the difference in the derivatives financing cost/revenue between long S&P 500 exposure and short Russell 2000 exposure is approximately 1.0 percent. The result? A material reduction in the realized alpha, as illustrated in Figure 5.1. Although the active small cap manager may deliver the expected 2 percent alpha after fees, the difference in the financing costs paid and received on the derivatives positions (C and F in the illustration) results in a reduction of the incremental return realized by 50 percent, for a net alpha result of 1 percent, not 2 percent, before accounting for the liquidity and implementation costs noted earlier and explained in greater detail in Chapter 8.

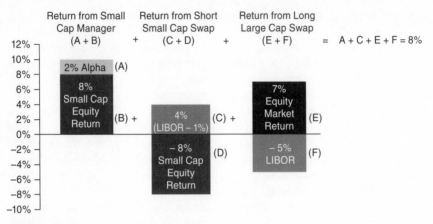

FIGURE 5.1   Example: Portable Alpha Strategy That "Puts" Small Cap Alpha to Large Cap U.S. Equities
Source: PIMCO; hypothetical example for illustrative purposes only.

4. *A different beta may yield a different alpha.* The S&P 500 and the Russell 2000 do exhibit a materially positive correlation over time. However, the two are not perfectly correlated. Therefore, when the components are combined (the actively managed small cap equity portfolio, the short Russell 2000 futures position, and the long S&P 500 futures position), the resulting alpha may differ from the alpha that was produced on a stand-alone basis by the active small cap manager relative to the Russell 2000, even ignoring the liquidity costs, implementation costs, and financing cost differences. In the case of betas that are less similar, the difference may be even more pronounced.

Chapter 8 delves into greater detail on the different costs and other considerations associated with bringing all of the component parts together in a portable alpha context and Chapter 7 provides additional relevant considerations specific to the use (and cost) of derivatives for purposes of obtaining and hedging market exposure. The key takeaway for investors from an alpha and beta standpoint is that most portable alpha strategies are not simple, from either an investment standpoint or an operational standpoint, which should not be surprising given the requisite use of both derivatives and at least one form of leverage. It therefore follows that there are associated incremental costs that may reduce the expected alpha by a material degree.

IS THE ALPHA ACTUALLY ALPHA?

Given the fact that an investor's capital is exposed to the collective risk factors of the portable alpha strategy, it is also necessary to understand and monitor the expected risk of the portable alpha strategy—not just the risk factors in the alpha strategy or the beta market exposure. One of the primary potential stumbling blocks for investors in doing so relates to the increasingly common misuse of the term *alpha.*

The broadening of the investment universe to include different types of investment strategies and tools that may in turn help improve the efficiency of an investor's portfolio (expected return on capital at a given level of investment risk) is undoubtedly positive. At the same time, there are certain challenges associated with strategies that are less well defined in terms of the underlying securities and the associated risks. In many cases there is not an obvious benchmark portfolio that can be referenced by investors to measure a manager's investment skill and to help assess and understand the inherent risks.

Some might say that the lack of an investment benchmark is a good thing, under the theory that a benchmark, accompanied by associated strict investment guidelines and tracking error constraints, may force a manager to make suboptimal investment decisions. However, the original concept behind benchmarking was not related to the volatility of excess returns relative to a benchmark index (tracking error) but rather to establishing a *benchmark* for purposes of measuring manager skill. It is certainly possible to have an appropriate investment benchmark without establishing strict benchmark relative investment guidelines and tracking error constraints. In fact, tracking error and benchmark relative guideline constraints may ultimately be counterproductive for investors as a high tracking error portfolio can actually deliver lower risk and higher returns than that of the benchmark. This is because these type of constraints may actually force a skilled manager to be less diversified and/or to take more downside risk than they otherwise would.

As the name implies, a benchmark portfolio should represent a good benchmark for purposes of measuring active manager skill or value-added. In order for this to be the case, the benchmark should be investable, should be representative of the manager's opportunity set and neutral position (expected average risk factor exposures over time), and should also exhibit similar characteristics to the actual investment portfolio, particularly with respect to risk, as noted in the definition of *benchmark portfolio* near the beginning of this chapter. Even then, it is challenging to ascertain a high degree of confidence regarding alpha for all of the reasons detailed in the appendix to this chapter. And, if an appropriate benchmark portfolio is not identified, it will be that much more difficult for an investor to evaluate the skills of an investment manager and probably not even possible to calculate alpha (at least not in a relatively straightforward way).

An article published in the *Financial Analysts Journal* in 2006 titled "The Myth of the Absolute-Return Investor," by M. Barton Waring and Laurence B. Siegel,[6] explains the same basic problem that we find in addressing the confusing use of the term *alpha* in the portable alpha investment realm as it relates to self-described absolute-return investing. The premise of their article, as the name implies, is that there is no such thing as an absolute-return investment strategy. All investment strategies are, by definition, relative-return strategies based on the original observation, put forth by Bill Sharpe, that Waring and Siegel conclude is one of the most profound insights in modern finance: that all portfolios are part beta (market component) and part alpha (nonmarket). In order to measure alpha in the first place, a strategy must be a relative-return strategy—it has to have a beta component that is based on an appropriate market benchmark, or there is no way to calculate the high levels of alpha that these types of strategies generally seek to provide.

All investment strategies that seek to provide any material amount of return over the risk-free rate must take some amount of risk exposure to do so. The exposure may be relatively constant or it may be highly variable, but it is still risk from an investor's standpoint. And, at least theoretically, the more uncertainty in terms of the likely distribution of possible outcomes—the greater the risk.

With this in mind, an interesting comparison has been put forth from time to time in a portable alpha context in support of using hedge fund and fund-of-hedge-funds strategies (and related products) as the alpha strategy within a portable alpha approach. The reason often put forth is the degree to which these strategies outperform cash on average (generally LIBOR or Treasury bills as a proxy for a money market or risk-free return), while active stock and bond managers do not outperform their respective stock and bond indexes to nearly the same degree. Therefore, the conclusion presented is that traditional stock and bond managers should be replaced with the high-alpha hedge fund or fund-of-hedge-funds managers in a portable alpha program.

Of course, there are presumably many hedge funds and funds of hedge funds available that investors may deem to be appropriate alpha sources for portable alpha strategies. Nonetheless, this comparison is not apples to apples. The stock and bond managers are compared to indexes that are presumably representative of their neutral investment position and their investment risk and otherwise meet the characteristics of a good benchmark, while the hedge fund strategies are being compared to cash! The former is a relative return comparison while the latter looks only at absolute return relative to a proxy for the risk-free rate.

It is true that cash (as proxied by LIBOR or Treasury bills) may be a common reference point used for hedge funds and funds of hedge funds, but very few if any of the strategies designed to deliver hedge fundlike returns have cashlike risk (i.e., they are not risk-free). Most investors would also agree that they are not investing in hedge funds in an effort to achieve cashlike returns—so, likewise, cash is not a suitable alternative to the chosen investment in hedge funds from an investor's standpoint.

In truth, it is probably challenging to identify an appropriate benchmark index for many of the strategies that allow the manager to invest in a very broad universe of securities and strategies and also to employ varying degrees of leverage. As such, it may only be possible to measure the return profile of these strategies in absolute-return space (i.e., relative to a cash benchmark), whereas traditional stock and bond management strategies can be measured against an appropriate market benchmark (to identify manager skill) *and* in absolute-return space (to assess the risk/return profile of the strategy).

However, it most certainly does not follow that, just because an appropriate benchmark is not identified, 100 percent of the excess return over cash is derived purely from manager skill. More importantly, from the standpoint of an investor, it does not follow that hedge fund strategies have cashlike risk and will be uncorrelated with all market risk factors.

This is all very relevant in a portable alpha context because investors must understand the risk factors associated with *both* the alpha strategy and beta market exposure in order to understand the *combination* of the two, which is ultimately what is necessary to assess the risk/return profile of a portable alpha strategy, and the appropriate category in which to place a portable alpha strategy for asset allocation and risk budgeting purposes.

To best illustrate these points, we will walk through two hypothetical case studies, both of which assume that the alpha strategy selected is a hedge fund strategy that exhibits the same risk and return attributes as the HRFI hedge fund composite index. Fortunately, one of the attributes of the portable alpha investment application is that investors have the ready ability to evaluate the historical returns of different combinations of betas and alpha strategies, even if there is no track record for the specific combination under evaluation, so long as three conditions are met:

1. Historical return data exists for both the beta and the alpha strategy (ideally an independently calculated index and an audited performance composite).

2. The beta derivatives market is reasonably liquid with relatively stable pricing so that the borrowing cost to obtain the beta exposure can be approximated, in all material respects, for purposes of the analysis.

3. Any liquidity costs associated with the need to meet margin or collateral calls and any material incremental implementation costs can be reasonably estimated.

Of course, the same caveats apply that apply to any analysis of historical returns. In addition, specific to the case studies that follow, we are using the Hedge Fund Research, Inc. (HFRI) hedge fund composite index solely to illustrate key points. As hedge funds vary substantially with respect to return, risk, and underlying risk factors, it necessarily follows that the use of a particular hedge fund or fund-of-funds strategy as the alpha strategy in a similar analysis may produce very different results. (The HFRI composite index is a commonly referenced and internationally recognized equal-weighted index comprised of over 2,000 hedge funds from the internal HFR database. Constituent funds must have either $50 million under management or a track record of greater than 12 months.)

Case Study 1

The most common market exposure that is referenced within a portable alpha context is the equity market, most specifically the S&P 500 Index. Does it make sense for the investor in our example to replace some of his large cap U.S. equity exposure with a portable alpha equity strategy that collateralizes equity derivatives with the identified hedge fund strategy?

One way to evaluate this potential option as a starting point is to construct a historical data series that assumes that an investor paid LIBOR to obtain S&P 500 exposure using futures or swaps and invested 100 percent of the capital allocated to the portable alpha strategy in the identified hedge fund strategy. Importantly, unless the hedge fund has daily or even intraday liquidity, there should be additional liquidity costs factored in that can be quite material, plus potentially material implementation costs, as referenced earlier and explored in more detail in Chapter 8. Nonetheless, sticking with our oversimplified example, what would the result have been from such an endeavour over the 10 years ended December 2006? There are many different ways to evaluate historical investment performance, but to use some of the more commonly referenced statistics across the entire time period, see Table 5.2.

As noted in Table 5.2, the average beta of 1.34 was a considerable amount above the equity market sensitivity level of 1.0 that would be

TABLE 5.2 Hedge Fund–Based Portable Alpha Equity Strategy

Back-test return	14.19%
S&P 500 return	8.4%
Beta relative to S&P 500	1.34 (range of 1.25 to 1.49 over rolling three-year periods)
Alpha relative to S&P 500	4.1%
Excess return relative to S&P 500	5.8%
Incremental (additional) volatility relative to S&P 500	5.9% (range of 3.2% to 8.8% over rolling three-year periods)
Total volatility as a percentage of S&P 500 volatility	138%
Correlation with S&P 500	97%

Source: Bloomberg, Hedge Fund Research Inc.
Statistics presented represent the 10-year period ended December 31, 2006.
Hedge fund–based portable alpha equity strategy back-test = S&P 500 return – three-month U.S. LIBOR + HFRI Hedge Fund Composite Index return.

exhibited by a passive equity index strategy, resulting in a materially different alpha than the excess return produced by the strategy (using a single-factor regression with the S&P 500 as the factor). Nonetheless, if the primary objective is attractive incremental returns, then this objective was certainly achieved with average incremental returns of almost 6 percent.

Under the category of there being no free lunch, there was also a corresponding average increase in volatility of 6 percent, representing an aggregate increase in risk, as proxied by volatility, of almost 40 percent, and not accounting for any additional risk not captured by the volatility measure.

Moving away from the statistics, other key considerations for a prospective investor may include but not be limited to the liquidity of this strategy relative to an alternative passive or active approach (passive and traditional active large cap equity strategies are generally fairly liquid) and also the ability of the investor to identify, measure, and effectively monitor the associated investment risks, which may not be best proxied solely by the S&P 500.

Case Study 2

In addition to considering the hedge fund strategy approximated by the HRFI hedge fund composite index as an alpha source for a portable alpha equity strategy, the investor may also want to consider it as an alpha source for a portable alpha *bond* strategy. In this case, the bond market exposure will be moderately more costly than the equity market exposure in the previous example, because there are not currently liquid futures available on broad bond indexes (although that may change in the near future). Other than adjusting for the differential cost component, the analysis is very similar to the preceding analysis for the potential portable alpha equity strategy.

Using the Lehman Aggregate Bond Index (LBAG) as the desired bond market exposure, we assume that this exposure was obtained at a cost of LIBOR plus 0.35 percent and that the capital allocated to the strategy was 100 percent invested in the hedge fund strategy. (The same shortcomings explained in case study 1 apply.) What would the result have been from such an endeavor over the 10 years ended December 31, 2006, using the same statistics referenced for the equity example, but measured relative to the bond market? Table 5.3 outlines this scenario.

In the case of the hypothetical portable alpha bond strategy backed with hedge fund strategy, similar to the preceding equity case study, the excess returns are very attractive. In this case, the excess returns of 6 percent literally double the return that an investor would have received from a passive bond investment.

Not surprisingly, excess returns of this magnitude are also accompanied by a material increase in risk as measured by volatility and possibly additional risks not reflected in the volatility measure. The volatility of the hypothetical portable alpha bond strategy is 222 percent of, or 2.2 times,

TABLE 5.3 Hedge Fund–Based Portable Alpha Bond Strategy

Back-test return	12.5%
LBAG return	6.2%
Beta relative to LBAG	0.86 (range of 0.5 to 1.1 over rolling three-year periods)
Alpha relative to LBAG	6.4%
Excess return relative to LBAG	6.1%
Incremental volatility relative to LBAG	4.4% (range of 1.3% to 7.9% over rolling three-year periods)
Total volatility as a percentage of LBAG volatility	223%
Correlation with LBAG	39%

Source: PIMCO, Bloomberg, Lehman Brothers, Hedge Fund Research Inc.
Statistics presented represent the 10-year period ended December 31, 2006.
Hedge fund–based portable alpha bond strategy back-test = LBAG − (three-month U.S. LIBOR + 0.35%) + HFRI Hedge Fund Composite Index return.

the volatility of the LBAG, while the absolute increase in volatility averages 4.4 percent with a range of 1.25 to 8 percent.

It follows that the beta statistic in this example (less than 1.0 on average) is a telling example of the point raised earlier that beta may not be a good proxy for risk if the market index or factor that is used to calculate the beta does not reflect of the dominant underlying risk factors of the investment strategy.

The most striking number in this example may actually be the last—a correlation of 39 percent with the associated bond market index. This, in turn, begs an important consideration specific to this example and also to portable alpha strategies more broadly: Is the portable alpha bond strategy a good proxy for bond market exposure or does the combination (in this case) of the hedge fund strategy with the derivatives-based bond market exposure fundamentally alter the risk/return profile to such a degree that it does not actually retain the key characteristics that investors typically look to their bond investments for in the first place?

Interestingly, as it turns out, this particular hypothetical portable alpha *bond* strategy is 64 percent correlated with the equity market versus only 45 percent correlated with the bond market when measured over average three-year periods, for the ten years ended December 2006. Over the entire period and also over three year periods on average, the bond risk is dominated by the hedge fund strategy risk, which in turn exhibits risk characteristics that are much more equitylike than bondlike. Is it a bond strategy or an equity strategy? In truth, while closer from a statistical standpoint to an equity strategy than a bond strategy, it actually most closely reflects the characteristics of the hedge fund strategy (the HFRI HF Composite Index), as shown in Table 5.4.

This may be a particularly important consideration within an overall asset allocation and risk budgeting context. As an example, if this type of strategy is used in place of a bond allocation in an asset allocation context, an asset allocation that was originally 60 percent equities, 30 percent bonds, and 10 percent alternatives, as shown in Figure 5.2, will be automatically transformed into an asset allocation that is effectively 60 percent equities, 30 percent hedge funds, and 10 percent alternatives, as shown in Figure 5.3. (And in this case, the hedge fund exposure exhibited equitylike characteristics resulting in a 64 percent correlation with the S&P 500.)

Clearly the potential for a portable alpha strategy to fundamentally alter the associated asset class exposure is an important matter and, where applicable, adjustments may need to be made to the overall asset allocation to make sure that the desired maximum level of downside risk is not broached and that an optimal level of diversification is maintained.

TABLE 5.4 Comparison of Hedge Fund–Based Portable Alpha Bond Strategy to Bond, Equity, and Hedge Fund Indexes

		With LBAG	With S&P 500	With HFRI HF Composite Index
Correlation	Average	45%	64%	85%
	Range	15 to 77%	35 to 87%	68 to 92%
		Relative to LBAG	Relative to S&P 500	Relative to HFRI HF Index
Volatility as % of volatility of index	Average	222%	55%	116%
	Range	132 to 363%	33 to 80%	100 to 151%

Source: PIMCO, Bloomberg, Lehman Brothers, Hedge Fund Research Inc.
Statistics presented represent rolling three-year averages, for the 10-year period ended December 31, 2006.
The back-test is calculated using monthly returns of the Lehman Brothers U.S. Aggregate Bond Index return three-month U.S. LIBOR plus 35 basis points) plus HFRi Hedge Fund Composite Index return.

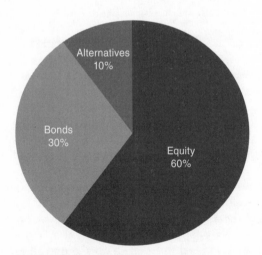

FIGURE 5.2 Approved Policy Portfolio Asset Allocation
Source: PIMCO; hypothetical example for illustrative purposes only.

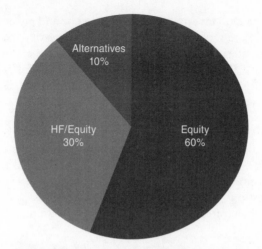

FIGURE 5.3 Resulting Asset Allocation if the Example Hedge Fund and LBAG Swap Strategy is Substituted for Bonds
Source: PIMCO; hypothetical example for illustrative purposes only.

BETA + BETA (+ BETA . . .) + ALPHA?

Is it really possible to invest in alphas separately from beta? Probably not, for all the reasons previously discussed and also the reasons noted in the appendix. This is not to say that alpha cannot be sourced separately from the desired beta market exposure—that is one of the key benefits of the portable alpha investment application. However, as noted previously, the lack of a specified market benchmark should not lead an investor to conclude that returns from a given investment strategy are alpha with no associated incremental risk or correlation with beta market exposures.

Most investment strategies that are expected to generate a material return over the risk-free rate incorporate beta or sensitivity to one or more combinations of risk factors. The challenge in an increasing number of cases lies in identifying an appropriate market benchmark, especially when the betas vary to a material degree over time and/or the risk factors are not easily quantified as may be the case with financing risk and liquidity risk as an example.

As a result, while all investment strategies, should ideally be considered on a relative-return basis (relative to an appropriate, perhaps multifactor, market benchmark in order to assess manager skill), it is not always practical to do so. However, all investment strategies can be and presumably are measured on an absolute-return basis for purposes of assessing the associated risk and return characteristics relative to the risk-free rate (i.e., the Sharpe ratio). Furthermore, as LIBOR (as a close proxy for the risk-free rate) is also the effective basis for the borrowing cost associated with the derivatives-based market exposure, it might be particularly relevant to do so in a portable alpha context.

In fact, the application of an absolute-return framework to all potential alpha sources allows an investor to move away from the casual (or even persuasive) use of the alpha and beta terms. This is because the assessment of a given investment strategy relative to LIBOR automatically leads to two important questions that investors should address as a starting point to selecting an alpha strategy for a portable alpha program:

1. What are the sources of return relative to LIBOR, the related primary risk factor and range of risk factor exposuresand the associated downside risks?
2. Is there a reasonable basis to expect that the combination and range of risk factors associated with a given alpha strategy—as managed by a specified investment manager—will result in a desirable level of returns over LIBOR in the future together with an acceptable level of downside risk?

An absolute-return framework is also a natural starting point for evaluating the risk factors in a prospective alpha strategy relative to the risk factors in the beta market exposure with which the alpha strategy will be coupled in a portable alpha context.

Opportunities abound for combinations of alpha strategies and beta market exposures that should benefit to a material degree from diversification. However, it is also true that many risk factors thought of as separate and distinct actually demonstrate a materially positive correlation. In addition, while a correlation of less than 100 percent may provide diversification in an asset allocation or policy portfolio context, a correlation of 50 percent between a potential alpha strategy and the desired beta market exposure might not provide adequate diversification in a portable alpha context unless the acknowledged goal is to have levered beta market exposure

Tables 5.5 through 5.7 provide the correlation between the returns of different bond, equity, and hedge fund indexes as a proxy for the major risk factors in each category for reference purposes with the caveat that correlations can vary substantially from one period to the next.

TABLE 5.5 Correlation between the Returns of Different Bond, Equity, and Hedge Fund Indexes, Screen 1 (10-year period ends December 31, 2006)

	HFRI Fund of Funds Composite	HFRI Fund Weighted Composite	HFRI Convertible Arbitrage Index	HFRI Distressed Securities Index	HFRI Emerging Markets	HFRI Equity Hedge Index	HFRI Equity Market Neutral Index	HFRI Equity Non-Hedge Index	HFRI Event-Driven Index	HFRI Fixed-Income (Total)	Small Cap Minus Large Cap
HFRI Fund of Funds Composite	100%	92%	49%	73%	85%	88%	65%	80%	83%	61%	50%
HFRI Fund Weighted Composite	92%	100%	40%	76%	90%	99%	55%	95%	94%	60%	57%
HFRI Convertible Arbitrage Index	49%	40%	100%	48%	32%	33%	22%	29%	38%	38%	43%
HFRI Distressed Securities Index	73%	76%	48%	100%	64%	70%	43%	68%	86%	68%	43%
HFRI Emerging Markets	85%	90%	32%	64%	100%	86%	53%	83%	80%	62%	40%
HFRI Equity Hedge Index	88%	99%	33%	70%	86%	100%	53%	96%	92%	51%	61%
HFRI Equity Market Neutral Index	65%	41%	37%	45%	41%	53%	100%	53%	43%	22%	55%

(*Continued*)

TABLE 5.5 (Continued)

	HFRI Fund of Funds Composite	HFRI Fund Weighted Composite	HFRI Convertible Arbitrage Index	HFRI Distressed Securities Index	HFRI Emerging Markets	HFRI Equity Hedge Index	HFRI Equity Market Neutral Index	HFRI Equity Non-Hedge Index	HFRI Event-Driven Index	HFRI Fixed-Income (Total)	Small Cap Minus Large Cap
HFRI Equity Non-Hedge Index	80%	95%	29%	68%	83%	96%	41%	100%	91%	51%	58%
HFRI Event-Driven Index	83%	94%	38%	86%	80%	92%	45%	91%	100%	57%	54%
HFRI Fixed-Income (Total)	61%	60%	38%	68%	62%	51%	37%	51%	57%	100%	20%
Small Cap Minus Large Cap	50%	57%	24%	43%	40%	61%	41%	58%	54%	20%	100%
MSCI World	57%	78%	10%	49%	72%	80%	21%	86%	76%	39%	21%
MSCI EAFE	72%	85%	21%	60%	82%	84%	36%	87%	79%	58%	32%
S&P 500	52%	75%	12%	50%	66%	75%	16%	85%	75%	41%	17%
Russell 2000	67%	87%	23%	61%	71%	90%	35%	95%	86%	41%	70%
MSCI EM Equities	81%	90%	23%	56%	92%	89%	50%	89%	78%	52%	38%
Short S&P 500	-52%	-75%	-12%	-50%	-66%	-75%	-16%	-85%	-75%	-41%	-17%

NASDAQ Composite	51%	76%	13%	49%	58%	78%	13%	87%	76%	30%	35%
Lehman Brothers Global Aggregate Bond	19%	7%	24%	23%	12%	−2%	13%	−2%	3%	40%	5%
Lehman Brothers Aggregate Bond	−1%	−14%	9%	−1%	1%	−21%	7%	−23%	−17%	16%	−11%
JPM Global Govt Bond Non USD	19%	8%	24%	24%	9%	1%	10%	2%	4%	41%	9%
JPM Emerging Market Bond Index	32%	41%	26%	30%	55%	34%	15%	41%	40%	37%	−2%
U.S. Treasuries	−8%	−23%	1%	−10%	−10%	−30%	6%	−32%	−27%	6%	−12%
Lehman Brothers Credit Investment Grade Index	9%	1%	19%	15%	12%	−8%	6%	−7%	0%	26%	−4%
ML U.S. High Yield Master II	49%	61%	41%	67%	59%	55%	16%	60%	71%	54%	26%
Lehman Brothers Mortgage-Backed Security Index	−3%	−17%	3%	−8%	3%	−23%	7%	−24%	−21%	12%	−19%
ML ALL U.S. Convertible Bond	71%	87%	48%	70%	69%	85%	28%	90%	88%	51%	51%

Source: Bloomberg, Hedge Fund Research Inc.

TABLE 5.6 Correlation between the Returns of Different Bond, Equity, and Hedge Fund Indexes, Screen 2 (10-year period ends December 31, 2006)

	MSCI World	MSCI EAFE	S&P 500	Russell 2000	MSCI EM Equities	Short S&P 500	NASDAQ Composite
HFRI Fund of Funds Composite	57%	72%	52%	67%	81%	−52%	51%
HFRI Fund Weighted Composite	78%	85%	75%	87%	90%	−75%	76%
HFRI Convertible Arbitrage Index	10%	21%	12%	23%	23%	−12%	13%
HFRI Distressed Securities Index	49%	60%	50%	61%	56%	−50%	49%
HFRI Emerging Markets	72%	82%	66%	71%	92%	−66%	58%
HFRI Equity Hedge Index	80%	84%	75%	90%	89%	−75%	78%
HFRI Equity Market Neutral Index	21%	36%	16%	35%	50%	−16%	13%
HFRI Equity Non-Hedge Index	86%	87%	85%	95%	89%	−85%	87%
HFRI Event-Driven Index	76%	79%	75%	86%	78%	−75%	76%
HFRI Fixed Income (Total)	39%	58%	41%	41%	52%	−41%	30%
Small Cap Minus Large Cap	21%	32%	17%	70%	38%	−17%	35%
MSCI World	100%	88%	97%	83%	81%	−97%	89%
MSCI EAFE	88%	100%	85%	80%	84%	−85%	74%
S&P 500	97%	85%	100%	82%	77%	−100%	92%
Russell 2000	83%	80%	82%	100%	78%	−82%	87%
MSCI EM Equities	81%	84%	77%	78%	100%	−77%	71%

Short S&P 500	−97%	−85%	−100%	−82%	−77%	100%	−92%
NASDAQ Composite	89%	74%	92%	87%	71%	−92%	100%
Lehman Brothers Global Aggregate Bond	−26%	10%	−15%	−8%	0%	15%	−20%
Lehman Brothers Aggregate Bond	−33%	−19%	−28%	−27%	−14%	28%	−34%
JPM Global Govt Bond Non USD	−23%	15%	−12%	−3%	0%	12%	−15%
JPM Emerging Market Bond Index	46%	44%	48%	34%	50%	−48%	35%
U.S. Treasuries	−44%	−30%	−40%	−36%	−25%	40%	−43%
Lehman Brothers Credit Investment Grade Index	−20%	−8%	−14%	−12%	−4%	14%	−19%
ML U.S. High Yield Master II	53%	50%	55%	55%	52%	−55%	51%
Lehman Brothers Mortgage-Backed Security Index	−29%	−15%	−25%	−29%	−7%	25%	−34%
ML ALL U.S. Convertible Bond	78%	75%	81%	88%	73%	−81%	84%

Source: Bloomberg, Hedge Fund Research Inc.

TABLE 5.7 Correlation between the Returns of Different Bond, Equity, and Hedge Fund Indexes, Screen 3 (10-year period ends December 31, 2006)

	Lehman Brothers Global Aggregate Bond	Lehman Brothers Aggregate Bond	JPM Global Govt Bond Non USD	JPM Emerging Market Bond Index	U.S. Treasuries	Lehman Brothers Credit Investment Grade Index	ML U.S. High Yield Master II	Lehman Brothers Mortgage-Backed Security Index	ML ALL U.S. Convertible Bond
HFRI Fund of Funds Composite	19%	−1%	19%	32%	−8%	9%	49%	−3%	71%
HFRI Fund Weighted Composite	7%	−14%	8%	41%	−23%	1%	61%	−17%	87%
HFRI Convertible Arbitrage Index	24%	9%	24%	26%	1%	19%	41%	3%	48%
HFRI Distressed Securities Index	23%	−1%	24%	30%	−10%	15%	67%	−85%	70%
HFRI Emerging Markets	12%	1%	9%	55%	−10%	12%	59%	3%	69%
HFRI Equity Hedge Index	−2%	−21%	1%	34%	−30%	−8%	55%	−23%	85%
HFRI Equity Market Neutral Index	13%	7%	10%	15%	6%	6%	16%	7%	28%
HFRI Equity Nonhedge Index	−2%	−23%	2%	41%	−32%	−7%	60%	−24%	90%
HFRI Event-Driven Index	3%	−17%	4%	40%	−27%	0%	71%	−21%	88%
HFRI Fixed Income (Total)	40%	16%	41%	37%	6%	26%	54%	12%	51%
Small Cap Minus Large Cap	5%	−11%	9%	−2%	−12%	−4%	26%	−19%	51%
MSCI World	−26%	−33%	−23%	46%	−44%	−20%	53%	−29%	78%
MSCI EAFE	10%	−19%	15%	44%	−30%	−8%	50%	−15%	75%
S&P 500	−15%	−28%	−12%	48%	−40%	−14%	55%	−25%	81%
Russell 2000	−8%	−27%	−3%	34%	−36%	−12%	55%	−29%	88%
MSCI EM Equities	0%	−14%	0%	50%	−2.5%	−4%	52%	−7%	73%

	(1)	(2)	(3)	(4)	(5)	(6)	(7)	(8)	(9)
Short S&P 500	15%	28%	12%	-48%	40%	14%	-55%	25%	-81%
NASDAQ Composite	-20%	-34%	-15%	35%	-43%	-19%	51%	-34%	84%
Lehman Brothers Global Aggregate Bond	100%	72%	97%	30%	69%	70%	9%	65%	6%
Lehman Brothers Aggregate Bond	72%	100%	54%	46%	98%	96%	11%	93%	-11%
JPM Global Govt Bond Non USD	97%	54%	100%	18%	52%	53%	2%	48%	7%
JPM Emerging Market Bond Index	30%	46%	18%	100%	33%	57%	61%	44%	48%
U.S. Treasuries	69%	98%	52%	33%	100%	91%	-2%	87%	-23%
Lehman Brothers Credit Investment Grade Index	70%	96%	53%	57%	91%	100%	31%	83%	8%
ML U.S. High Yield Master II	9%	11%	2%	61%	-2%	31%	100%	6%	75%
Lehman Brothers Mortgage-Backed Security Index	65%	93%	48%	44%	87%	83%	6%	100%	-16%
ML ALL U.S. Convertible Bond	6%	-11%	7%	48%	-23%	8%	75%	-16%	100%

Source: Bloomberg, Hedge Fund Research Inc.

CONCLUSION

One of the most important keys to successful portable alpha strategy implementation may be a true appreciation of the actual risk to which the investment capital is exposed, together with the other attributes of the investment. Unfortunately the use, or rather the misuse, of the terms *alpha* and *beta* may sometimes confuse investors in this regard by providing a false sense of comfort with respect to the underlying attributes and risks of a portable alpha strategy. The same is true of the oversimplified examples of alpha-beta separation that are put forth with respect to not just the underlying risks and actual results, but also the inherent costs and complexities.

The portable alpha investment application does allow investors to capitalize on both diversification benefits and a broader alpha opportunity set in combining a variety of potential alpha sources with different beta market exposure. However, while the lure of high levels of extra return that will help investors meet or even exceed return targets and stand out successfully relative to stipulated return goals or peer universe is undoubtedly appealing, investors must also carefully evaluate the risk exposures and, even more importantly, the downside risk characteristics before investing and on an ongoing basis.

Although the effective hurdle rate for an alpha strategy to deliver outperformance within a portable alpha context (before accounting for fees and costs) is generally a cash or money market rate (as proxied by LIBOR), it is unlikely that an alpha strategy has a similar level of risk and the other key attributes of a cashlike investment if it is expected to deliver materially positive excess returns after fees. In addition, the alpha strategy must truly be uncorrelated (and ideally negatively correlated during weak markets) with the beta market exposure *and* have a lower risk profile in order for the end result to be a similar risk profile to the underlying beta market. The alternative—a higher risk profile—is not necessarily bad, but it certainly should be acknowledged by investors and accounted for within the overall asset allocation and risk budgeting decision-making framework.

Alpha represents risk-adjusted excess returns, and the calculation of alpha depends on the use of appropriate factors to estimate beta exposure(s) or the use of a relevant benchmark that is both a reasonable substitute for and risk-equivalent to the strategy being evaluated. This holds true for all investment strategies, including potential alpha strategies for use in a portable alpha context. While an alpha-beta evaluation framework can be useful in many cases, relevant benchmarks have not yet been identified for many interesting potential alpha strategies, and it is also difficult to quantify all types of investment risk using readily available factors. Fortunately, though, most investment strategies can be decomposed into a set of primary risk factor exposure—some systematic and others variable—as explored in Chapter 6.

The most suitable combinations of alpha strategies and derivatives-based beta market exposures, if an investor decides to invest in a portable alpha approach at all, will ultimately depend on the objectives, risk tolerance, liquidity requirements, and other considerations specific to the investor. As the capital allocated to a portable alpha strategy is not exposed solely to the beta or the alpha strategy, but rather to the risk inherent in the combined alpha and beta components, understanding the collective risk and return attributes is certainly the right starting point.

APPENDIX 5.1 THE TROUBLE WITH ALPHA BY JAMIL BAZ

Why Alpha Exists—And Why It Is Elusive

To efficient marketeers, alpha is the ultimate fly in the ointment. Why? Because it is the portion of the risk premium that systematic risk factors fail to explain. In other words, alpha walks and talks like a free lunch, and free lunches are not on the menu in efficient markets.

Of course, there is more to life than efficient markets. A careful study of the topic shows that market efficiency is a vacuous concept. For example, Grossman and Stiglitz, in a paper called "On the Impossibility of Informationally Efficient Markets," argue that if investors believe in market efficiency, then markets cannot be efficient. This is because market efficiency is by definition a state of affairs where the price system is fully informative—and in that kind of world no one, including the arbitrageur and the man on the street, will have any incentive to acquire information and correct mispricings.

But, paradoxically, it is this very process of information acquisition and price discovery that makes markets more efficient. In other words, complete efficiency cannot exist because its mere existence would be self-defeating by precluding price equilibrium. At best, one can expect a market that strives toward a semblance of efficiency.

And yet this does not make the quest for alpha any easier. We argue here that, even in a world where alpha is alive and kicking, alpha is a concept fraught with subtleties. For example:

- Alpha can be a poor indicator of performance. The signal-to-noise ratio associated with alpha measurement is often low, particularly in macro-equity investing. Alpha can be more indicative of luck than skill.

- Alpha is the residual in an asset pricing equation. Sometimes it owes its existence to an omitted variable. For example, the alpha can be jump risk that has not yet materialised (e.g., liquidity risk before the summer of 1998).
- Not unlike the market efficiency paradox just described, alpha disappears once it becomes public knowledge. Examples abound: From the 1980s on, various incarnations of arbitrage in swap funding, futures basis, and convertibles all but disappeared once market players knew about them.
- Alpha can become beta: As hedge funds increase their market share, alpha-generation strategies become dominant and the risk of these strategies becomes systematic.
- Beta can become alpha. For example, if the risk factor (e.g., market to book or firm size) in a model of stock returns is not a clear risk factor to some investors, it can become alpha and be arbitraged away.

We next discuss the first two of these statements in some detail.

Alpha: Is It Skill or Noise?

To attempt an answer to this question, picture a skilled equity portfolio manager trying to beat an index. We know that the portfolio manager can beat the index by an average of 300 basis points a year. This is a high alpha. The only problem is that the 300 basis points are just an average and a lot of noise can wreck an average. There is a saying along these lines: "Statistics is the only science which tells you that, if your feet are in the freezer and your head is in the oven, you are doing well on average."

To be more explicit, if the index volatility σ_i is 20 percent, the portfolio volatility σ_p is 25 percent, and the correlation ρ between the index return and the portfolio return is 80 percent, over what horizon can the skilled portfolio manager beat the index with, say, probability 90 percent? To ask the question differently, how long will it take the portfolio manager's boss to figure out that the performance is positive with a 90 percent confidence level?

It turns out that the answer is more than 100 years—106 years to be precise. The mathematical formulation follows. If μ_p is the expected return on the portfolio and μ_i is the expected return on the index, we can define the variables:

$$\mu_r \equiv \mu_p - \mu_i + \sigma_i^2 - \sigma_i \sigma_p \rho \tag{1}$$

and

$$\sigma_r^2 \equiv \sigma_p^2 + \sigma_i^2 - 2\rho \sigma_p \sigma_i \tag{2}$$

Equation (1) defines the expected geometric return of the portfolio-to-index ratio. Equation (2) defines the variance of this ratio.

Then it can be shown that the time horizon it takes to outperform the portfolio with probability p is

$$t = \frac{\varepsilon^2 \sigma_r^2}{(\mu_r - \frac{\sigma_r^2}{2})^2} \tag{3}$$

where ε is the threshold level in a cumulative probability distribution $N(.)$ such that $N(\varepsilon) = p$. For example, for $p = 84$ percent, $\varepsilon = 1$.

We can also express the probability p of index outperformance over a time horizon t as

$$p = \frac{(\mu_r - \frac{\sigma_r^2}{2})\sqrt{t}}{\sigma_r} \tag{4}$$

Equation (4) can be tabulated to give some intuition on the horizon/confidence trade-off. See Table 5.8. This table says that it takes way longer than a career span—or for that purpose a lifespan—to judge performance.

It is also a simple matter to test the model sensitivity to its inputs. For example, for a skilled player to outperform with probability 90 percent over a one-year horizon, which is the horizon conventionally used to judge performance in the industry, the yearly expected excess return (all other

TABLE 5.8 Outperformance Horizon versus Confidence Level

Time Horizon (Years)	Probability of Outperformance (%)
1	55
2	57
5	61
10	65
25	73
50	81
100	89
106	90
200	96

Yearly expected excess returns $\mu_p - \mu_i = 300$ bps
$\sigma_i = 20$ percent $\sigma_p = 25$ percent $\rho = 80$ percent

variables being equal) needs to be between 2,000 and 2,100 basis points—an unrealistic number by any standard.

While these calculations seem to be bordering on the nihilistic, one can see why it takes so long to prove oneself in the macro-equity world—an alternative way to put it is that the signal-to-noise ratio is low. For example, under the parameters used to create Table 5.8, even though the expected alpha is 3 percent, the expected one-year information ratio is only:

$$\frac{\mu_r}{\sigma_r} = \frac{3.05\%}{15.54\%} \approx 0.2$$

In other words, the signal can be easily drowned by noise under realistic assumptions.

How does this construct translate in the fixed-income universe? It appears that fixed-income parameters are conducive to more palatable evaluation horizons. Take, for example, a credit portfolio. One can hope to generate excess returns in the order of 150 basis points a year. The typical portfolio volatility is 3 to 4 percent per year. Assuming a correlation of 95 percent between portfolio and index returns, Table 5.9 shows the horizon/confidence trade-off in a credit universe.

Assuming its parameters are realistic, Table 5.9 demonstrates two things:

1. The expected one-year information ratio is now

$$\frac{\mu_r}{\sigma_r} = \frac{1.5\%}{1.3\%} \approx 1.15$$

2. The portfolio manager will outperform the index with probability 90% over a 15-month horizon.

TABLE 5.9   Outperformance Horizon versus Confidence Level

Time Horizon (Years)	Probability of Outperformance (%)
0.25	72
0.5	79
1	88
1.24	90
1.5	92
5	99.5

Yearly expected excess returns $\mu_p - \mu_i = 150$ bps
$\sigma_i = 3.5\%$ $\sigma_p = 4\%$ $\rho = 95\%$

All of these figures need to be interpreted with caution. Parameters are all ballpark figures fraught with methodological difficulties.[7] Nevertheless, this analysis somehow frames the debate about the signal-to-noise ratio of investment performance.

Jump Masquerading as Alpha: The Case of the Missing Variable

Now, to a different kind of measurement problem. The omitted variable problem is standard in statistics. When an investor omits an explanatory variable in the asset pricing model, then coefficients attached to the remaining variables are generally biased. In a linear regression, it is a simple matter to size the bias.[8]

We argue here that the most pervasive missing variable in empirical models of asset returns is a jump variable. An example best illustrates the point.

Economists have been debating for years the so-called equity premium puzzle: The premium exhibited by equity returns relative to T-bill returns in the United States (about 6 to 7 percent a year for the past hundred years) is difficult to reconcile with reasonable rates of risk aversion by investors. It has been argued that the puzzle can be resolved once rare catastrophic events, such as the 1930s Depression or World Wars I and II, are taken into account.[9] A rare event in financial markets is referred to as a *jump event*.

Jump risk is pervasive: It is central to credit bonds, emerging market bonds, emerging market currencies, even Treasuries. As previously argued, it is also central to equity valuation.

Before we get to the heart of the topic, we describe the mathematics of a simple jump. Jump risk is generally represented as follows, where dq is a jump variable that can take one of two values:

$$dq = 0 \text{ with probability } 1 - \lambda dt$$

$$dq = -k \text{ with probability } \lambda dt$$

Think about $-k$ as a large negative return and λ as a small probability. For example, $-k$ can be thought of as of as −30 percent and λ as 1 percent. So the loss expectation on this jump process is $-k\lambda dt = -0.03dt$—that is, a yearly 3 percent equivalent. In this context, jump risk means that you can lose a lot of money very rarely.

We now posit a jump-prone asset. Its expected return is the riskless rate r. The asset offers a compensation $k\lambda dt$ for the jump risk; so the jump risk has a zero expected value since the compensation cancels the expected loss.

The asset price B follows the process:

$$\frac{dB}{B} = (r + \lambda\sigma)dt + dq$$

Think about this asset as the dollar price of an emerging market T-bill labeled in a U.S. dollar–pegged currency.

The central argument of this section is that while the true asset process is given by the preceding equation, estimating the parameters of this equation is quasi-impossible. So you may never know what kind of jump describes the asset you just bought. You may not even know there is jump risk if you never observe a jump.

How do you know whether the probability of a jump is one in a hundred years?

To answer this question, we can actually calculate, subject to the aforementioned process being the true process, the probability of guessing the right parameters from observing a data sample.

For example, if the data sample is 15 years (most emerging market assets have not been around for that long) and the true λ is 1 percent, there is an 86 percent probability that no jumps ever happens during the 15 years, a 13 percent probability that one jump happens, and a 1 percent probability of more than one jump.[10]

Table 5.10 shows the jump probabilities versus the size of the data sample.

Evidently, the smaller the sample, the more comfortable the investor will be with the asset. When the data sample is less than 100 years, it is impossible to guess the right probability. Even with a very long sample (100 or 200 years), the likelihood of guessing the right value of λ is low (37 percent and 27 percent).

When the data sample is short, say less than 50 years, the likelihood is that absence of evidence will be confused with evidence of absence. In other words, investors will overestimate their alpha. On average, in the absence

TABLE 5.10 Jump Probabilities (in Percent) as a Function of Sample (in Years) and Number of Jumps ($\lambda = 1$ percent)

	10 Years	20 Years	50 Years	100 Years	200 Years
0	90	82	61	37	14
1	9	16	30	37	27
>1	1	2	9	26	27 (2) +32(>2)

of jumps, it is tempting to think of your alpha as λk whereas it should be zero.

Worse, if more than one jump takes place over the data sample, it is very possible that trading in this specific asset be discontinued, so that the data sample is relegated to oblivion. After all, mean reversion is often about data samples that have survived rare events.

While analytically trivial, this section goes a long way toward illustrating a prevalent market attitude toward carry trading, high-yielding assets (that forgot to blow up), and other high-octane securities. As long as a trading career does not meet jumps, the views about alpha are overinflated. In these environments, excess optimism creates excess demand for risky assets, pushing expected returns ever closer to the risk-free rate. The irony is that, in the absence of jump, even the thinnest risk premium can masquerade ex-post as trading skill.

Conclusion

The existence of alpha is beyond doubt. Yet the true alpha is a riddle wrapped in a mystery, inside an enigma. Analytics can only describe it very imprecisely. At its best, alpha is probably a set of frozen cognitions acquired throughout a trading career and anchored in a deep, qualitative understanding of economics and markets.

CHAPTER 6

Global Sources of Portable Alpha, Associated Risks, and Active Management

Sabrina Callin, Alfred Murata, Don Suskind, Steve Jones, Richard Clarida, and Lisa Kim

It would most certainly take a book much larger than this one to analyze all of the rapidly expanding, global sources of alpha, associated risks, and active management techniques. As this is neither practical nor possible here, our goal in this chapter is to address this broad topic in a context that is most relevant for investors considering different portable alpha approaches, with an emphasis on the importance of identifying and measuring both the systematic and variable risk factors employed in different potential alpha strategies.

To this end, this chapter starts with a framework to help investors evaluate the different potential alpha sources on common ground by focusing on the underlying risk factors that drive returns. We then move to a discussion of different sources of available return relative to the risk-free rate, with a specific focus on the sources of return that are most commonly employed as alpha strategies today, including fixed-income, equity, and different hedge fund strategies—and also addressing the attractive risk-adjusted return benefits that are available to investors through global diversification and active currency management.

OVERVIEW BY SABRINA CALLIN
AND ALFRED MURATA

One of the most significant benefits of the portable alpha investment application is the broad universe of potential alpha sources that investors can access, independent from the desired asset class or beta market exposure. No longer are investors limited to selecting active managers within a given asset class or resigning themselves to passive index returns where reliable alpha is hard to come by. Potential alpha sources in this context are really as broad as the number of investments and investment strategies that are available and expected to deliver a return over the risk-free rate or a proxy like LIBOR. This may sound daunting at first, which is why it may be important to decompose the various types of alpha sources as a starting point.

Fortunately the returns from just about any investment strategy—including the various fixed-income, equity, and hedge fund strategies used as alpha strategies today—can be decomposed into:

- A set of systematic risk factors associated with a neutral point that reflects an active manager's average expected exposures, opportunity set, and, most importantly, the expected risk profile of the strategy.
- Tactical risk factor allocations resulting from a manager's market timing decisions, as represented by deviations in risk factor exposure around an active manager's neutral point. *Because of the potential for tactical risk factor exposure to result in higher overall risk than that associated with a manager's neutral point, it is important for investors to be aware of the maximum allowable risk factor exposures and monitor them over time.*
- Security valuation and selection by active managers to obtain desired risk factor exposure. Beyond pure fundamentally based security selection strategies, other types of security selection include but are not limited to strategies designed to capitalize on market inefficiencies, relative value opportunities, and technically and quantitatively driven security selection approaches.

With passive investment strategies, it is relatively straightforward to identify the risk factors that are expected to collectively result in performance over the risk-free rate, and to have a reasonably high degree of confidence regarding variations in risk factors over time.

With actively managed strategies it is likely more difficult to do so. However, assuming a benchmark has been identified for purposes of measuring manager skill that appropriately reflects the key characteristics and, most importantly, the risks of the associated strategy, an investor should be able to use this same benchmark as a proxy for the neutral point and risk factor exposure of the prospective alpha strategy. On an ongoing basis, of course, it is still important to measure deviations from the neutral point and also to understand the potential for deviations that may materially alter the risk factor exposure and the aggregate risk of a given strategy.

It may be more challenging to assess the risk factor exposure and the suitability of a strategy for a portable alpha program if a benchmark is not identified—especially if the strategy involves significant variation in risk factor exposure. However, even then, it may be possible to understand the likely risk factor exposure through a careful review of the primary strategy or strategies employed, the guideline parameters, the returns, and possibly the holdings. Various approaches to multifactor regression analysis or style analysis—tools that have been in use for some time for purposes of understanding the strategies and associated risks employed by active managers—may also prove insightful.

Multifactor regression analysis is essentially an extension of the single-factor regression analysis that gave us beta as a measure of the market risk and alpha as the risk-adjusted return provided by an investment. The key difference is the specification of multiple market indexes and/or risk factors rather than one. This framework allows the returns of a given strategy over a given period to be attributed to different risk factors (with the relevance and sensitivity to each risk factor defined), providing investors with important insight that may be particularly valuable in a portable alpha context. Multifactor regression analysis can be used as a means to gaining a better understanding of the risks and returns of equity strategies, bond strategies, hedge fund strategies, and undoubtedly others. This type of analysis was originally applied to equity mutual funds and more recently has been frequently applied to various hedge fund strategies.

One of the key overriding themes of this book is the importance of understanding, measuring, and monitoring the risk factors employed in the alpha strategy and making sure that they are complementary to the beta market exposure. As repeatedly noted, however, investing is much simpler in theory than in practice. Not only is it virtually impossible to come up with a finite set of risk factors, but it is also true that most risk factors are not independent and any given investment is likely to involve exposure to multiple risk factors. However, it is interesting that many asset classes and investment strategies can be broadly characterized as capturing a relatively short list of risk premiums which include but are not limited to the following:

- *Liquidity risk* is the risk that an investor will need to sell a security and suffer a loss due to transaction costs, or not even be able to complete the desired transaction. A common assumption of asset pricing models is that there are no transaction costs. While this assumption simplifies the mathematics of formulating asset pricing models, the terms *commission* and *bid-offer spread* are too commonly used to dismiss the existence of liquidity risk. Note that transaction costs are not constant, usually increasing substantially as volatility increases. Given that the likelihood of being forced to sell increases as volatility increases (which is the time at which transaction costs are greatest), liquidity risk may be dramatically underestimated. To this point, since volatility is relatively low most of the time, it follows that transaction costs are relatively low most of the time, and therefore that liquidity risk is generally estimated when volatility and transaction costs are low.

- *Commodity risk* is the risk that the value of a security could fluctuate as a function of the value of underlying commodity prices. Clearly, commodities are exposed to commodity risk. Many investments have some sensitivity to commodity prices, and some investments can even have levered exposure to commodity prices. For example, some firms have significant exposure to tar sands and will be extremely profitable if the price of oil is high or unprofitable if oil is low.

- *Equity market risk* is the risk that investments in equities will decline in value due to fluctuations in the equity market. Equity market risk is most commonly measured by the various equity market betas. Note that most market participants are implicitly thinking of equity market risk when they decompose risk into market risk and idiosyncratic risk.

- *Credit risk* is the risk that a borrower will not make good on an obligation to a lender. For example, in the fixed-income markets, credit risk is most commonly associated with the risk that the bond issuer will default on payments. Two commonly used metrics for describing credit risk are the *probability* of suffering a loss and the expected loss *severity*. Multiplying the probability of suffering a loss by the expected loss severity can give the total loss expectation. A positive credit risk premium exists if the loss expectation of an asset is more than compensated for by the extra spread (compared to risk-free assets), while a negative credit risk premium exists if the extra spread (compared to risk-free assets) is not sufficient to compensate for the asset's loss expectation. Given that most investors are risk-averse, and the fact that investing in assets that have credit risk usually results in a portfolio with greater risk, most anticipate a positive expected risk premium for investing in assets with credit risk.

- *Interest rate risk* is the risk that an investment will be impacted by fluctuations in official or market-determined interest rates. This is most commonly associated with fixed-income investments, and *duration* is the risk metric that is used to estimate price changes that will result from specified interest rate changes. There is generally a term premium that investors receive for assuming interest rate risk, as evidenced by the typically upward-sloping shape of the Treasury yield curve.

- *Vega/volatility risk* is the risk that a change in the implied volatility of a security will affect the price. Portfolios that hold options—either directly or embedded in instruments held by the portfolio—are sensitive to the implied volatilities. The value of long-term, out-of-the-money options is most sensitive to the level of implied interest-rate volatility. As an example of an embedded long-term option, fixed-rate mortgage-backed securities on 30-year mortgages give the borrower the option to prepay the mortgage at any point in time. Given that the investor is short the prepayment option, the value of such mortgage-backed securities depends on the level of implied interest rate volatility. Consequently, as the level of interest rate volatility declines, the value of the mortgage-backed security increases and vice versa.

- *Financing risk* is the risk posed by securities whose financing terms may be modified. Many securities are held by investors who manage leveraged portfolios (i.e., purchasing securities on margin). When securities are purchased on margin, the investor needs to consider the *haircut* and the *financing rate*. The haircut is the amount of collateral that an investor needs to post, while the financing rate is the interest rate the investor will pay to finance the position. Changes to the haircut or financing rate may result in a forced unwind of a position before it is desirable to do so from the standpoint of the investor. This is most commonly the case with leveraged positions during periods of associated market stress. Even investors who do not hold leveraged portfolios need to consider financing risk in investment decisions, since a change in either the haircut or financing rate may impact the desirability of such investments for leveraged investors. In general, one expects securities that are not easy to finance to be cheaper on a fundamental basis (or to have a higher financing risk premium) than securities that are easy to finance, since there is less demand from leveraged investors for hard-to-finance securities.

- *Accounting, regulatory, and tax treatment risk* is the risk caused by the potential for change in a certain accounting, regulatory, or tax treatment of a security. Tax accounting treatment is an example. Many securities are held by non-mark-to-market investors who may find certain investments that have favorable tax accounting treatment to be more attractive than similar investments that have less favorable tax accounting treatment. Consequently, investments with less favorable tax accounting treatments may be cheaper on a fundamental basis (and have a greater accounting risk premium) than investments with more favorable accounting treatments.

Of course there are risks investors can take that aren't necessarily rewarded with an expected return premium relative to the risk-free rate in exchange for the risk. For example, consider currency risk. Active, currency management may result in attractive returns over the risk-free rate. However, there is not necessarily a systematic return premium to taking currency risk. Inflation risk is another interesting risk to categorize. Most investments are exposed to inflation risk. Only inflation-protected securities do not bear this risk, and even then the hedge is only as good as the reference rate of inflation. Commodities and real estate, as an example, may not be as exposed to inflation risk as stocks and bonds, given that both are components of the inflation measures, but the link is not perfect. More importantly, any given investor's inflation reference point is likely to be different than the statistical measures that attempt to approximate inflation for a given economy as a whole.

Notably, any strategy or security that is expected to outperform the risk-free rate is likely to involve more than one risk factor. Even the most commonly referenced single-factor model—a model that measures the equity market beta of an actively managed equity strategy as a means to measure equity market risk and manager skill—was further refined into a three-factor model and also by style analysis, as noted in Chapter 3 and discussed in further detail in the next section.

Beyond traditional risk and return statistics and factor models, as discussed in the appendix to Chapter 5, value-added that may initially seem to be a result purely of manager skill may ultimately be largely a function of increasing risk in such a way that it does not show up in traditional risk measures or is not easy to quantify based on available factors that can be used in a regression context. This type of more difficult-to-detect incremental risk often involves illiquid securities, material option sales, and rare event risk—and may be especially meaningful if leverage and the associated financing risk is involved during periods of market stress. As such, and for reasons detailed in the Chapter 5, it may be important to think not necessarily in terms of alpha and beta, or even not exclusively in terms of volatility and return. Rather, perhaps it makes most sense to start by asking a few fundamental questions as part of the evaluation process of different alpha strategies:

- Why would I consider asset class and/or strategy X on a stand-alone basis outside of a portable alpha mandate? What are the key characteristics and benefits?
- What are the primary associated risk factors and active management strategies that strategy X will incorporate in order to outperform the risk-free rate? How will I measure the associated risk and component risk factors on an ongoing basis?

- What is the likely relationship between the primary risk factors contained in strategy X and the primary risk factors contained in my desired beta market exposure? Are they complementary such that diversification results in reduced downside risk—or are the returns likely to be materially positively correlated, particularly during periods of market stress?

Not surprisingly, this framework can easily be applied to the different sources of alpha that are most commonly employed in a portable alpha context—equity strategies, fixed-income strategies, and hedge fund strategies.

THE EQUITY MARKETS BY DON SUSKIND

Equity investing remains extremely popular among investors across the globe. The Investment Company Institute reports that as of the end of 2006, 48 percent of worldwide mutual fund assets were equity funds, with balanced funds, which also contain equities, representing 10 percent. According to Greenwich and Northern Trust, in the United States individuals and institutions have allocated half or more of their investable assets to equities in recent years. The case for equity investing is built on the premise that long-term expected returns are greater in equities than in more conservative investments such as bonds due to the higher embedded risk premium relative to a risk-free investment. This risk premium is intended to compensate investors for greater volatility of equity valuations and the fact that an equity holder's claim on assets is junior to that of bondholders in a bankruptcy scenario.

One way to measure the historical equity premium is to subtract the returns of a risk-free asset from equity returns. This difference has ranged anywhere from 3.5 percent to over 5 percent, depending on the length of the historical period reviewed. The future level of equity risk premium is the subject of intense debate among academics, practitioners, economists, and investors of all types. Different approaches are typically bifurcated along two primary criteria: investors' demand for returns and companies' ability to compensate equity investors. The results vary, as do surveys of experts. In most cases, the forecast equity premium is positive, as expected in order to compensate investors for assuming risk above the risk-free rate of return.

The risks embedded in equity investments have been organized in several different frameworks, typically relying on a set of factors to explain the risks and returns generated by a portfolio of stocks. For example, the Fama and French three-factor model extended CAPM's focus on equity market beta (a portfolio or stock's sensitivity to the difference between the stock market return and the return of a risk-free asset) to also measure the betas of two additional factors: (1) the difference in return between small and large stocks, and (2) the difference in return between value and growth stocks, as a means to better reflect a portfolio's risk factor exposures.[1] Some other factors that are cited in reference to equity investments include momentum, volatility, size, dividend yield, leverage, trading volume and other financial ratios, accounting figures, and characteristics of stocks.

Because of the breadth of available equity securities, the benefits of diversification may be quickly realized in equities. As an example, investing in stock markets outside of one's home country has been widely recognized as a winning strategy. The key benefit is that an internationally diversified equity investor has a broader opportunity set than one who only invests domestically. Since the correlation of stock market returns between different countries has been less than 100 percent, internationally diversified equity investors should benefit from reduced risk. Over time, researchers have argued and the markets have demonstrated that correlations between developed country equity markets may be increasing as a natural by-product of globalization, financial market deregulation, and expansion of multinational corporations, among other factors. Further, following severe market dislocations, correlations may increase, reducing the benefits of diversification. However, we can readily demonstrate the benefits of diversifying among different countries by considering the correlations of different market indexes as outlined in Table 6.1.

TABLE 6.1 Correlations of Different Equity Market Indexes (January 2002–December 2006)

	S&P 500 Total Return	FTSE 100 Total Return	DJ EURO Stoxx 50 Total Return	TOPIX Total Return	MSCI EM Net Dividend Index
S&P 500 total return	100%				
FTSE 100 total return	85%	100%			
DJ EURO Stoxx 50 total return	90%	89%	100%		
TOPIX total return	35%	41%	37%	100%	
MSCI EM Net Dividend Index	77%	70%	72%	52%	100%

Source: Bloomberg, Morgan Stanley Capital International.

Active Management in Equity Markets

Sourcing alpha from equity investment strategies is among the most familiar investment approaches on the menu today. Long-term returns from equity ownership have been very compelling, and most U.S. investors, both individuals and institutions, keep over half of their investable assets in equities as previously noted. With such large exposure to equities, investors will certainly look for ways, both conventional and pioneering, to squeeze additional returns from their equity investments. Whatever the resulting returns generated by a stock selection strategy, equity investors who hire active managers to assemble their stock portfolio will typically start with a baseline return assumption defined by the returns of the index from which their manager can select stocks. If the manager's holdings do not deviate from the stocks in the designated index, then one would expect to receive the returns of the index less management fees. This strategy, passive indexing, is perhaps the most popular equity investment strategy. Regardless, the allure of higher returns from picking the right stocks attracts droves of investment dollars.

However, as has been well documented, the preponderance of professional equity managers who rely on stock selection strategies have failed to outperform passive indexes in highly efficient markets, such as U.S. large cap equities (see Malkiel 1995). The high level of transparency for large public companies and the emphasis on eliminating the dissemination of material, nonpublic information may significantly reduce trading advantages for even the best-informed investors. In less efficient markets, such as small cap or emerging market equities, the potential for information asymmetries, likely due to limited coverage by research analysts, may avail investment managers of richer opportunities to outperform category or index returns.

The risks of selecting one stock over another may not be readily apparent. A considerable complication is that any stock contains a blend of risk factors in addition to company-specific or idiosyncratic risk, which is *inseparable* from any given stock and therefore accompanies any desired risk factor. With stocks one can't necessarily rely on factors such as the historical momentum or beta characteristics of a given stock, because the idiosyncratic risk may overwhelm other risk factors at any given point in time. For example, if a stock manager forecasted a declining stock market and decided to move her portfolio into low-beta stocks, it is uncertain whether stocks that have historically exhibited low beta will continue to exhibit a low beta going forward. Conversely, if a bond manager decided to reduce exposure to the risk of rising interest rates, the manager can decrease duration in any number of ways, such as increasing allocations to shorter-duration bonds, with relative certainty. Of course, this layer of uncertainty in stocks should result in a risk premium for which investors expect to be compensated, translating to a higher return expectation for equities over the long term.

Equity Alpha Generation Strategies

Styles and strategies for selecting the stocks that will appreciate more than their peers are varied and rely as much on art as science. Broadly speaking, approaches to stock valuation are based on fundamental, technical, or quantitative analysis. Each of these three approaches is summarized next.

With *fundamental analysis,* a manager forms a view on a specific company's value based on an intimate knowledge of that company's business prospects. In forming this view, the manager will evaluate both top-down and bottom-up factors. Top-down analysis is built on outlooks for the economy, industry, and geography in which a company competes, while bottom-up analysis looks closely at a company's financial, operating, and management capabilities in conjunction with innate competitive advantages relative to its peers. A sophisticated fundamental manager may also test a company's expected stock performance in the presence of various scenarios. By changing forecasts, introducing shocks to an industry or economic variable, the manager may develop a better sense of the range of outcomes and may more specifically assign probabilities to expected returns.

An example of a fundamentally based trading strategy is the Japan trade which was popular among global equity managers throughout the 1990s. Global equity indexes currently have 10 to 15 percent exposure to Japan. If an equity manager had a strong view that Japan was likely to grow at a slower rate than the rest of the developed world, the manager could underweight Japan, relative to the index, and outperform the index if the view ended up being correct. Global stock managers benchmarked to a global equity index throughout the late 1990s may have generated excess returns from a systematic underweight to Japan throughout the deflationary economy that characterized Japan in the late 1990s. This Japan trade may have lost viability as the Japanese economy emerged from its deflationary cycle in the early part of the 21st century.

Technical analysis involves following historical trends and patterns of a stock's price movements, among other variables, to form an expectation of the future stock price. This has also been known as *charting.* Many academics vehemently denounce the merits of technical analysis, and yet the market is full of devout technicians. One of the most direct arguments against technical analysis is the *random walk hypothesis,* established by economist Burton Malkiel in his book *A Random Walk Down Wall Street,* which argues that past price movements have no relationship with future prices. Technicians counter that the markets are driven by irrational behavior, and that certain trading strategies capitalize on nonrandom return patterns.

A technical approach to outperformance may actually relate to factors associated with the underlying equity index itself. Take, for example, the

Russell 2000. The Russell 2000 Index rebalancing occurs on the last day of June each year. Interestingly, actively managed strategies have historically posted the strongest excess return during the month of July (the month immediately after the reconstitution). Many Wall Street firms begin to speculate which stocks will add/leave the index as early as March.[2] Interestingly, March is another period of typically outsized performance for active small cap stocks (see Table 6.2). These data suggest that front-running the Russell 2000 index reconstitution may be one of the explanatory factors in understanding active small cap equity managers' outperformance of the Russell 2000.

Quantitative analysis does not require that the portfolio manager have an intimate understanding of a given company or stock's fundamental or technical characteristics. Rather, quantitative managers incorporate mathematical and computer-based statistical models to compare a range of quantifiable factors across a set of securities. The number of securities analyzed is limited only by the availability of data on those securities, and the factors used in quantitative analysis may include fundamental and technical factors. However, a key differentiation between quantitative analysis and both fundamental and technical analysis is that quantitative analysis deemphasizes, if not removes, any qualitative or judgment intervention on the part of the manager. As such, these strategies are often called *disciplined* strategies as they rely on extensive computer modeling and back-testing before implementation. Quantitative strategies are typically rules-based, in that a buy or sell decision is predicated by the output of quantitative analysis.

More recently, investors have gotten comfortable with the idea that successful managers should be able to pick losers in addition to picking winners. A natural degree of freedom that flows from this belief is granting the manager the ability to take varying levels of short positions in stocks or sectors, or long/short strategies. These strategies may range from 100 percent long to 100 percent short positions on a pair of stocks in the same industry, to long positions on a stock or stocks coupled with short positions on an industry sector or index, to varying combinations of long and short

TABLE 6.2 Average Excess Return across Managers in eVestment Small Cap Core Universe (10 Years Ended December 2006)

Jan	Feb	Mar	Apr	May	Jun	Jul	Aug	Sep	Oct	Nov	Dec
−0.43%	0.06%	0.68%	0.32%	0.25%	0.06%	0.97%	0.25%	0.22%	0.07%	−0.23%	0.12%

Source: Data from eVestment Alliance, compiled by PIMCO.
Note: The figures above span the entire universe of managers in eVestment small cap core category. As of December 31, 2006, this includes 138 products.

discretion, such as 130 percent long and 30 percent short. The equity analysis that accompanies a long/short strategy, whether fundamental, technical, or quantitative, is not necessarily new as the result of the introduction of long/short pairings. In fact, the long/short approach does not necessarily introduce new risk or return factor exposures, nor does it escape from the normal risk/return paradigms with which investors evaluate investment opportunities, aside from the theoretical potential for unlimited losses with short positions. Long/short strategies do, however, avail a manager of greater investment freedom.

THE FIXED-INCOME MARKETS BY STEVE JONES

While many investors are familiar with active equity strategies and stock selection-based approaches to adding value, many are less familiar with active fixed-income management. This section presents a discussion of fixed-income risk factors and perspective on active management, which may be particularly relevant in the context of a book on portable alpha given that a majority of assets currently invested in portable alpha strategies are specifically invested in fixed-income alpha engines, according to the 2006 Greenwich survey highlighted in Chapter 2.

Investors have traditionally looked to fixed-income portfolios as a source of incremental return with limited downside risk. Bond portfolios have typically provided a return advantage relative to "cash" or money market investments without substantially increased risk. For that reason and many others, actively managed bonds have a long history of use as a source of added return in portable alpha programs. Beyond portable alpha applications the motivations for investment in bond portfolios include income, diversification, and protection against adverse financial market conditions. Let's look at each of these motivations for fixed-income investing in more detail to understand why people invest in bonds.

Unlike many other asset classes, high-quality bond returns are generally highly predictable over longer periods of time. Most bonds provide investors with a fixed source of income via a semiannual coupon payment. The price of bonds also may change making a *total return* performance computation involving both the yield and the price return appropriate in assessing performance. However, over time, the overwhelming majority of a high-quality bond portfolio's total return is a function of the yield rather than price return component. As an example, 7.1 percent of the 7.4 percent annualized total return of the Lehman Brothers Aggregate Bond Index between 1986 and 2006 was the yield contribution to return. The remaining 0.3 percent was the price return component. Naturally, the price component of a bond portfolio's return can dominate over shorter periods. It is no surprise that the importance of yield in the return profile of bonds has caused these instruments to be so popular for purposes of capital preservation, for investors with income needs, and for those who desire more predictable return patterns.

Bonds also typically appeal to investors because of their performance characteristics in times of economic slowdown or deflation and the generally unfavorable performance of other asset classes in such environments. Even investors who think bonds are boring may find this feature of bonds particularly compelling! It is helpful to remember that ultimately the trading price of a bond depends largely on how much investors value the income that the bond provides. This is an important concept. Prevailing interest rates change and the value of a bond may change over time. Most standard bonds pay a stipulated interest rate that does not change, thus the designation fixed income instruments. However, in inflationary environments a bond's fixed income becomes less attractive because that income becomes a smaller figure in real terms. Conversely, slower economic growth usually leads to lower inflation, which makes bond income more attractive (higher in real terms). An economic slowdown is also a generally adverse environment for corporate profits and thus stock market returns, adding to the attractiveness of bond income as a source of return in this type of environment.

In fact, elaborating on this point, the diversification characteristics of bonds are actually quite powerful when thought of in a portfolio context. Diversification means simplistically not putting all of your eggs in one basket, although in practice there is a lot of consideration typically dedicated to diversification at the portfolio level. A stock market investor faces the risk that the stock market will decline sharply. To offset this risk, investors have long turned to the bond market because the performance of stocks and bonds is often noncorrelated.

As noted previously, high-quality bonds tend to do well in periods of economic slowdown, and tend to benefit from a flight-to-quality mentality during market stress environments. This was the case during October 1987 when the U.S. stock market experienced the worst-ever monthly return since World War II. Bonds rallied in this environment, as evidenced by the Lehman Brothers Aggregate (LBAG) index return of 3.6 percent for the month. Figure 6.1, which displays the rolling 12-month returns of the S&P 500 and the LBAG, shows the persistence of this negative correlation during weak equity markets. Although diversification certainly does not eliminate the risk of loss, investors look to bonds as a way to build a diversified portfolio and to reduce the risk of disappointing portfolio performance.

The fact that most bonds pay full principal at maturity is an attractive feature for investors, particularly for investors with longer time horizons.

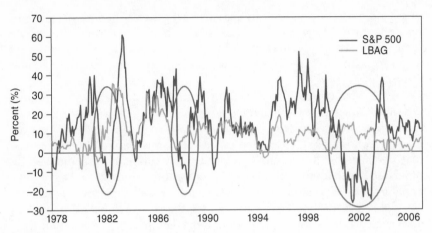

FIGURE 6.1 Rolling 12-Month Returns for the S&P 500 and the LBAG (January 1, 1978 to March 31, 2007)
Source: Standard & Poor's, Lehman Brothers.

While bond prices may be subject to volatility prior to maturity, at maturity a bondholder is paid back the initial principal value. Of course, if a bond issuer defaults on this obligation, this does not hold true. Then again, most high-quality bonds do not default. This return-of-principal characteristic of bonds causes them to be highly attractive in the eyes of investors focused on minimizing downside risk.

Investors also invest in bonds because of the lower expected volatility of returns as compared to equities, most other assets classes, and investment strategies. Stocks are much more volatile, as evidenced by a much higher standard deviation of returns and a significantly higher historical incidence and magnitude of negative total return. The reliable and low-volatility component of stock returns, the dividend yield, has been a much smaller share of total return in the past few decades. Because of their lower volatility, many investors think of bonds as an anchor to the windward in their asset allocation, providing an important damper on overall portfolio volatility and reducing downside risk.

Finally, in both a traditional investment management and also in a portable alpha context, many investors may appreciate the liquidity of a high-quality bond portfolio. This is especially true in periods of equity market stress, where bonds may be well bid as investors seek safer instruments. The liquidity characteristics of higher-quality bonds are also presumably quite important to investors who face periodic funding obligations. In a portable alpha context, alpha strategies involving actively managed bond portfolios may also benefit from a high degree of liquidity, especially as it pertains to providing liquidity for purposes of maintaining market index derivatives exposure.

For institutional investors in particular, understanding the risk and return characteristics of bond portfolios may be a source of comfort in using them in a portable alpha context. For many investors and their advisers, the risk monitoring, performance evaluation, and related due diligence associated with an actively managed bond portfolio is a fairly routine process. Despite all of the positive potential benefits commonly associated with fixed-income investments, however, there are indeed risks that investors should understand before investing in actively managed bond portfolios. Investors with a shorter time horizon may be particularly sensitive to the interest rate risk (duration) of their bond portfolio. A diversified portfolio will certainly also contain exposure to other risks, which may be influenced by factors such as credit spread risk, the risk of default, the risk of rising mortgage prepayments, volatility risk, and so forth.

Fixed-Income Instruments, Risk Factors, and Sources of Return

As is the case with most other asset classes, the overall return of a bond portfolio can largely be explained by market risk factors expressed within the portfolio. An analysis of key risk factor exposure characteristics of a bond portfolio is usually a starting point for investors performing attribution on a bond portfolio in an effort to understand returns. As an example of the result of the attribution analysis, one might find for instance that a portfolio with more duration than the index benefited from a falling rate environment to a larger degree than did the index.

Stepping back for a moment, as a starting point, recall that overall fixed-income portfolio performance can be thought of simplistically in terms of income and price return. The income and price return characteristics of fixed-income portfolios form the basis of portfolio performance. *Variations* in the price and income characteristics versus a bond market index form the basis of active decision making in traditional bond management. While it is true that the income component of bond performance provides the dominant contribution to total return performance over long periods of time, the price return does matter, especially over shorter periods of time.

In the early days of traditional fixed-income management, key market risk factors could be conveniently summarized as *duration* (interest rate risk), *yield curve, sector,* and *quality,* as a starting point. Even today, these primary elements of bond market risk exposure are among the most significant in understanding the performance of actively managed bond portfolios, although the number of risk factors has grown to include a wide variety of different types of risk and return profiles across the global fixed-income market place. Related to the concept of risk factors is a fairly unique characteristic of the bond market: the existence of *structural* or persistent return premiums associated with certain types of fixed-income instruments, sectors, and maturities.

Many of the sources of incremental return (and risk) in the fixed-income markets arise from the fact that some of the market's largest participants have different investment objectives and are restricted, or restrict themselves, in various ways. This contrasts sharply with other asset classes, especially equities, where the primary focus is on portfolio appreciation and *most investments are managed with fewer constraints.*

Case in point: U.S. money market funds. Investors who choose to invest in U.S. money market funds are presumably motivated to do so in order to secure perfect or near-perfect principal preservation and an unparalleled level of liquidity. The *clientele effect* or *market segmentation effect* of high demand for money market securities driven by the tremendous amount of money invested in U.S. money market funds results in lower yields on these instruments than would likely otherwise be the case. As a result, investors not restricted to money market investments need not assume much additional risk to receive an attractive incremental return from holding fixed-income securities outside of the money market universe. One example of this benefit is exhibited in the risk/return trade-off in the short end of the U.S. Treasury yield curve, as previously discussed in Chapter 2 and also as noted again in Figure 6.2.

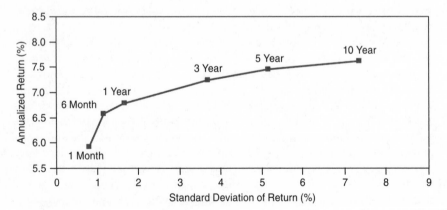

FIGURE 6.2 Annualized Return versus Risk for Various Maturities (Treasury Yield), One-Month Holding Periods January 1968 through March 2007
Source: PIMCO, Bloomberg Financial Markets.

The emergence of the corporate bond market was the beginning of the concept of a multisector bond market. Certainly the duration characteristics of any given corporate bond may be somewhat similar to similar maturity government bonds. However, corporate bonds generally have a higher risk of default and experience sensitivity to *spread risk* in secondary market trading. Spread risk means that the relative attractiveness of the bond in the market place can change due to shifts in perceived quality, general risk appetite, and so forth. As such, corporate bonds may experience favorable or unfavorable price performance in relation to risk-free points of reference. In practice, the risk-free point of reference is typically a government bond of similar duration or an interest rate swap and corporate bonds typically provide an incremental yield relative to government bonds for bearing the risk of default and not providing a government-guaranteed return of principal.

Over time the credit quality spectrum has broadened. The emergence of the high-yield fixed-income market was another important change in the fixed-income landscape. Unlike many other fixed-income risk factors, the probability of a full principal loss is much greater with high-yield bonds. In exchange for this risk, high-yield bonds have typically provided a yield well above higher-quality bonds. As a result, modeling default risk and sensitivity to changes in credit spreads is a very important component of managing this type of risk.

The invention of mortgage-backed securities was also among the most important fixed-income investment innovations in history. Even plain vanilla mortgage pass-throughs have offered alpha opportunities to traditional fixed-income managers and other investors due to the yield advantage provided by bonds in this sector. This was especially true in periods prior to the widespread use of benchmark indexes that included mortgages. Mortgages and related mortgage derivatives require much more rigorous modeling to understand their risk and return characteristics and portfolios owning mortgages are much more sensitive to factors such as convexity and volatility.

While certainly not unique to mortgages, as a similar risk exists in any callable bond, the risk in most high quality mortgages is dominated by the uncertainty of cash flows associated with prepayment risk. Prepayment risk is the risk that an investor's bond will be prepaid prior to its maturity. Prepayment risk is very common in mortgage-backed securities, because many borrowers have the opportunity to prepay their mortgage at any time without penalty. Some investors are concerned with prepayment risk in and of itself, and will not invest in securities where there is uncertainty regarding the timing of principal payments. Conversely, many investors are not particularly concerned with the fact that there is uncertainty regarding the timing of principal payments, but are concerned with the fact that the timing of principal payments is correlated with other factors that cause the bond to experience poor price performance.

For example, consider the case of an investor who purchases a fixed-coupon mortgage-backed security. If market interest rates (and mortgage rates) rise, fewer mortgagors will choose to prepay their mortgages, so the investor will be stuck in a fixed-coupon mortgage-backed security for an extended period of time. In contrast, if market interest rates (and mortgage rates) fall, many mortgagors will immediately prepay their existing mortgages as they refinance into lower-rate mortgages, and instead of observing significant price appreciation on the fixed-coupon mortgage-backed security, the investor may observe the mortgage-backed security quickly being refinanced away.

The fixed-income arena was and continues to be one of the asset classes where derivatives development has rapidly evolved. Fixed-income derivatives in and of themselves have been a profound innovation that has presented additional opportunities, as a way either to more efficiently gain exposure to underlying instruments or to establish exposures that were not practical using physical instruments. Fixed-income derivatives sometimes afford attractive financing opportunities to obtain exposures cheaper than an outright investment in physical securities. In fact, the very concept of portable alpha has its origins in the fixed-income derivatives markets.

Of course, the list of alpha strategies and related risk factors available in the fixed income and related derivatives markets continues to grow, and an exhaustive description of each is beyond the scope of this chapter. Some other examples may include exposures to real interest rates, emerging markets, and an increasingly wide array of securitized and structured instruments. Other examples include exposure to forward (as opposed to spot) yield curves, and the basis between derivatives and cash instruments. Naturally, many if not all of these factors are available in markets across the globe, suggesting an even richer opportunity set for today's global active bond manager.

Bond investors who have been in the markets for years have observed that when a product with uncertain cash flows or other unfamiliar characteristics is first introduced, the product often provides a relatively large risk premium due to the need to attract new investors to the market, as investors are not initially familiar with the product. Over time, a sufficient number of investors became familiar with the product so that it trades at a *fair* level, and eventually, such a product may trade *rich* (or with a much lower or negative risk premium) as unsophisticated investors who are not able to appropriately measure the risk enter the market.

The growing number of risk factors and attempts to add value through combining risk factors in an optimized fashion continues to change as markets evolve. Today's modern bond portfolio is global, multisector, and involves a wide array of instruments and strategy types in an effort to provide superior risk-adjusted returns.

Active Management in a Fixed-Income Portfolio Context

Active bond management has its roots in efforts to maximize the total return from fixed-income investments. In other words, the objective is to maximize both the yield and price return components of a bond portfolio generally subject to certain risk constraints. Active management in fixed-income space is widely accepted as industry standard, which differs from equities where passive approaches to investing are common. At the time of this writing, it remains difficult to successfully replicate a passive bond market index precisely in a cost-efficient manner through buying individual securities, given the sheer quantity of issues in most broad market indexes.

Proponents of passive management often believe that passive fixed-income investing is less risky because the breadth of portfolio holdings may be narrower than within an actively managed portfolio. Another argument for passive management is that the market-tracking characteristics of a passive portfolio somehow reduce risk. However, passive index strategies certainly embed many of the same factor risks (including interest rate and credit risk, for starters) that are inherent in fixed-income investing. Passive indexing also poses distinct risks and opportunity costs as well. Exceptions to the preponderance of active management may be found in specialty vehicles (such as exchange-traded funds), laddered portfolio strategies, and certain liability-driven investment approaches.

What really matters in an actively managed portfolio context is tactically allocating among key allowable risk-factor exposures and selecting securities such that the result is better performance than the benchmark. Of course, it may sometimes be difficult to distinguish between security selection and risk factor selection. Why is a cheap (higher-yielding, lower-priced) bond offered at a discount relative to like alternatives? Is it less liquid? Perhaps it trades in a more volatile fashion? Ultimately, the return of any given bond can be largely decomposed into risk factors.

In the management of bond portfolios, a common approach is to actively manage the overall interest rate risk (duration) based on forecasted movement in interest rates. In anticipation of declining interest rates an active manager may extend portfolio duration beyond that of the benchmark index because the longer the duration, the more price appreciation the portfolio will experience if rates decline. Conversely, a bond manager expecting interest rates to rise would normally reduce portfolio duration below that of a benchmark index. As rates rise, the market value of a shorter-duration portfolio should fall less than that of the longer-duration benchmark index, and vice versa in the event of falling interest rates.

Related to the duration decision, active managers commonly alter the maturity or duration composition of the portfolio. For instance, a manager anticipating a decline in shorter-term interest rates and stable longer-term rates may choose to emphasize shorter maturities to capture the associated positive price appreciation as rates fall. As another example, a manager expecting stable interest rates and who observes a particularly steep yield curve may choose to favor longer maturities with the objective of improving overall portfolio yield. Ultimately, shorter-term rates tend to be heavily influenced by central bank policy whereas longer-term rates are highly related to economic growth and inflation expectations. Because the shape of the yield curve changes based largely on the relationship between economic growth expectations, inflation, and central bank policy, active management strategies that focus on the relative value between different portions of the curve present another opportunity for adding value.

Active bond investment strategies also typically involve the management of the overall credit quality of the portfolio. For example, when economic conditions are expected to improve, an active manager might emphasize lower credit quality issues in anticipation of credit improvement associated with positive changes in the economy. In many cases, active managers attempt to take advantage of credit analysis capabilities to identify areas of the credit markets that seem likely to improve, thereby providing an incremental return as the spread risk of the issuer declines and the price of the bond appreciates amid improving credit fundamentals. In many ways the credit quality decision is also a sector decision. But corporate credit is obviously not the only sector of the fixed-income market available to an active bond manager. Active allocation decisions among governments, agencies, mortgages, and other sectors of the fixed-income markets are a fairly standard component of active bond management strategies. Each sector of the bond market has its own distinct risk and return characteristics, and may be more or less attractive at any point in time.

Of course, sector selection is ultimately about choosing among available risk factors in the fixed-income marketplace, and the relatively rapid development of the global fixed-income markets has increased the potential for value-added opportunities, as discussed in the following section.

GLOBAL DIVERSIFICATION AND CURRENCY BY RICHARD CLARIDA

International diversification, no matter what your home country, is important as a means to lower the volatility of returns for any given return objective. This diversification benefit means that a currency-hedged allocation to global bond markets is an essential part of an efficient fixed-income portfolio. Despite tighter linkages across economies in their policies and business cycles, the benefits of international diversification and associated global alpha opportunities have not diminished. The original rationale for international diversification across global bond markets was developed in the 1980s and 1990s when (1) countries pursued a wide range of monetary policies, resulting in a wide dispersion of inflation rates and inflation volatilities; (2) hedging costs were higher; and (3) a decrease in the volatility of global growth rates and related country-specific business cycles (sometimes referred to as the global "great moderation") had yet to occur and be fully incorporated into bond yields.

We begin with the observation that most government bonds in major developed countries have similar risks and react to country-specific macro developments in ways similar to U.S. Treasuries. For example, a rise in inflation or in growth prospects in a country tends to lower bond prices, while an ease in monetary policy tends to boost bond prices. Average bond yields can and do differ across countries, but this is because of differences in average inflation and growth rates.

However, differences in average bond yields across countries do not necessarily imply differences in average currency-hedged bond returns. This is because the cost of hedging to a U.S. investor is equal—to a close approximation—to the interest rate differential between the United States and the foreign bond market that prevails over the holding period for the bonds. For example, if countries with higher average bond yields also have higher average short-term interest rates (relative to the United States) then the cost of hedging currency exposure to invest in these foreign bonds can and often does offset the foreign yield advantage. Thus, on an ex-ante basis, a portfolio of foreign government bonds issued by major developed countries hedged back into dollars should be expected to produce roughly the same total return as a portfolio containing U.S. Treasuries. The average hedged return in foreign and U.S. government bonds will not be identical, to the extent that a home bias by U.S. investors persists (which it does) and U.S. investors are risk-averse (which they are).

This reasoning suggests that a currency-hedged diversified portfolio of government bonds should produce similar average returns to a passively held U.S. Treasury portfolio, but with possibly lower volatility. Volatility will be lower for a currency-hedged portfolio of government bonds if there is some country-specific return volatility that can be diversified away. This is important, if true, because it is possible to obtain superior returns at lower volatility by investing on a currency-hedged basis across global bond markets.

To assess the evidence, we look at data on foreign government bond returns hedged back into dollars for the period 1990 to 2006. We divide the sample roughly in half, looking at subsamples of 1990–1998 and 1999–2006. It is interesting to look at the two subsamples separately for several reasons. For example, the birth of the euro and of the European Central Bank in 1999 is an important regime change that might be expected to have altered the risk and return profile to global bond investing. Also, because of the common shocks of a global tech bust and equity sell-off, countries' business cycles of 2000–2002 shared a substantial common component, which might have diminished the benefits of international diversification. Finally, as more and more countries pursue inflation-targeting strategies with similar inflation targets and similar inflation outcomes, country-specific inflation risk is substantially reduced and, it might be argued, so are the benefits of international diversification.

Consider data on monthly total returns on U.S. Treasuries (Citigroup U.S. Treasury Index) and a hedged portfolio of foreign government bonds (JP Morgan Government Bonds ex-U.S. Hedged). Over the sample 1990–1998, the total return on the Citigroup U.S. Treasury Index was 8.6 percent a year, while the total return on the JP Morgan Government Bonds ex-U.S. Hedged Index was 9.0 percent per year. Thus the average realized excess return on the JP Morgan Index over the Citigroup U.S. Treasury Index was about 40 basis points a year between 1990 and 1998.

What about the risks of investing in these two portfolios? The realized volatility of the hedged foreign bond portfolio during 1990–1998 was 3.6 percent per year, while the realized volatility of investing in the Treasury index during this period was 4.3 percent. The lower realized volatility of the foreign bond portfolio resulted from the fact that foreign bond markets were typically (but certainly not always) less volatile than U.S. bond markets. But it also results from the fact that the foreign bond portfolio contains different countries' bonds, so it is already benefiting from diversification.

We also look at risk/reward ratios. Over the period 1990–1998, the yield on one-month LIBOR averaged 5.4 percent. Thus, over the 1990–1998 period, the realized risk/reward ratio on the passive Treasury investment was about 0.7 while the realized risk/reward ratio on the passive investment in the portfolio of foreign bonds was 1.0. Thus, perhaps because of home bias, U.S. investors on average during 1990–1998 received a somewhat higher return with a somewhat lower volatility by holding a currency-hedged portfolio of foreign government bonds.

Now let's look at the realized return and risk during 1990–1998 on various blends of U.S. and foreign government bonds. See Figure 6.3. A picture is indeed worth a thousand words. During 1990–1998, adding currency-hedged foreign bonds to a portfolio of U.S. Treasuries produced a portfolio with lower volatility and a similar return.

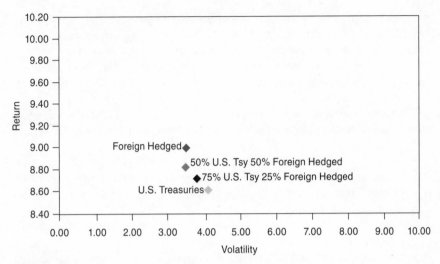

FIGURE 6.3 Realized Risk and Reward to Global Bond Diversification, 1990–1998
Source: Bloomberg Financial Markets.

Was this fortuitous? Has the convergence of monetary policies across countries and the moderation of national business cycles altered these relationships? In particular, have the benefits of international diversification been eliminated by the great moderation and the spread of Taylor rules across the globe? (By way of background, the Taylor rule is a formulaic approach that suggests an appropriate amount for central bank policy rate changes that should be undertaken in relation to deviation between both actual and potential GDP and inflation.) We next consider the issues and the evidence.

Are There Still Benefits to International Diversification?

It is frequently observed that the global bond market is more tightly integrated now than in the past. We see evidence of this integration all around us. In the major markets, we saw elevated correlations in government bond yields in 2006. These tight linkages are also evident if we look at real yields on inflation-indexed bonds issued by most of these countries, real yields that filter out the effects of country-specific inflation differences that are embedded in nominal bond yields. While there is no doubt that home bias remains a fact of life in international investing—so that, for example, an investor in the U.S. does not view an investment in a (currency-hedged) European government bond to be equivalent to an investment in a Treasury of the same maturity—there appear to be important secular forces at work reducing home bias and encouraging investors to increase international diversification.

What are these forces? While the list of potential candidates is long, it is reasonable to expect that the most important and most likely to endure are the following:

- A convergence among countries in the goals, inflation-targeting strategies, and average outcomes pursued by their central banks in the conduct of monetary policy.
- A resulting reduction in inflation volatility and thus country-specific inflation risks to international investing.
- A reduction in cross-border hedging costs to international diversification associated with greater market liquidity and a closer convergence in short-term interest rates.
- A decrease in the volatility of global growth rates and thus country-specific business cycles and possibly interest rate risk, a phenomenon sometimes referred to as the "great moderation."

Now, to some extent there is a common, global component to cross-country business cycles, and this global component will tend to make bond returns in different countries positively correlated (which they certainly are in practice). But at least historically, not all interest rate changes are a consequence solely of a global business cycle; country-specific factors have been very important. As a result, and as we documented earlier, the benefits of international diversification during the 1990s were substantial. However, if there has in fact been a great moderation in business cycles across the globe, this reduction in business cycle risk around the world will have tended to reduce country-specific interest rate risk, and thus to encourage international diversification. Moreover, as more and more countries run more or less the same style of inflation-targeting monetary policy (with more or less the same targets), this will also tend to influence international diversification. The argument then is that as more investors seek to diversify globally, and as the country-specific risks to interest rates diminish, the benefits of diversification will decline and the available alpha derived from diversification across global fixed-income markets will disappear. Let's look at the evidence.

Over the sample 1999–2006, the total return on the Citigroup U.S. Treasury Index was 5.10 percent a year, while the total return on the JP Morgan Government Bonds ex-U.S. Hedged index was 5.20 percent a year.

Thus, between 1999 and 2006, the average realized excess return of JP Morgan Index over the Citigroup U.S. Treasury index was shaved down from 40 basis points to 10 basis points a year, perhaps as a result of a fall in home bias. See Figure 6.4.

What about the risks of investing in these two portfolios? The realized volatility of the hedged foreign bond portfolio during 1990–1998 was 2.5 percent per year, while the realized volatility of investing in the Treasury index during this period was 4.7 percent. Thus, while the volatility in the U.S. Treasury returns was approximately the same over 1999–2006 as it was in 1990–1998, the realized volatility of investing in a currency-hedged portfolio of foreign government bonds was substantially lower than in the earlier period. This was no doubt due, at least in part, to the Economic and Monetary Union (EMU) and the creation of a euro-denominated market for European sovereigns. Over the period 1999–2006, the yield on one-month LIBOR averaged 3.6 percent and thus the realized information ratio on the Treasury investment fell to 0.3, while the realized information ratio on the investment in the portfolio of foreign bonds fell to 0.6. While home bias has probably narrowed, realized and most likely ex-ante information ratios on investing in global government bonds continue to exceed those obtained by limiting one's investments to Treasuries.

What about the benefits of international diversification? Some have argued that as the integration of global bond markets has advanced, the

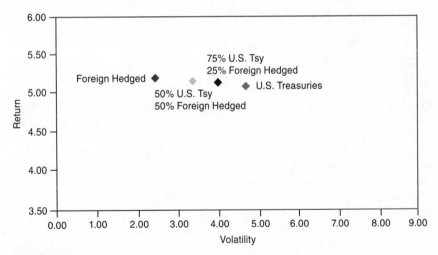

FIGURE 6.4 Realized Risk and Reward to Global Bond Diversification, 1999–2006
Source: Bloomberg Financial Markets.

diversification benefits of international diversification may have diminished. This is because the same factors that are driving global bond market integration (countries are running similar, successful monetary policies and business cycle volatility appears to have waned) might also be reducing country-specific interest rate risk and thus the potential benefits of diversification. A case can be made either way in theory, but in practice, the data is clear. As can be seen in Figure 6.4, notwithstanding the forces that have tended to increase the linkages in global bond markets and thus lower average returns, risk premiums, and home bias, the benefits of international diversification during this decade have remained.

Although past performance is no guarantee of future returns, it may be reasonable to anticipate that these diversification benefits will persist in the foreseeable future. This is for two reasons. There remains a significant country-specific component of international business cycles. The beta of a particular country's GDP growth on U.S. GDP growth is usually estimated (with a substantial residual) to be less than 1.0, to be time varying, and to differ from cycle to cycle. This reflects the reality that local and regional business cycles have been and will likely continue to be important influences on bond returns across different local markets. Also, there have been important differences across countries in their monetary policy reaction functions—for example, in the parameters of their Taylor rules. There is empirical evidence that confirms this is the case. Thus, even if countries' business cycles are tightly correlated, their monetary policies and bond returns are likely to be less so.

Examples of Alpha Sources in Global Fixed-Income Markets

We have seen that while government bond returns, risk premiums, and home bias have declined in recent years, the benefits of international diversification have not diminished. Thus, even in this brave new world in which countries are running similar, successful monetary policies and business cycle volatility appears to have waned as part of a great moderation, the benefits of international diversification have persisted and are likely to remain going forward. Because of country-specific differences in business cycles and monetary policies that produce the benefits of international diversification, these same factors should create opportunities to generate risk-adjusted excess returns relative to a country and even global benchmarks. In other words, precisely *because* there remain country-specific differences in business cycles and monetary policies that produce benefits of international diversification, these same differences in business cycles and monetary policies will create opportunities to generate risk-adjusted excess returns relative to a country or even to global benchmarks. The benefits of international diversification remain, as do the opportunities to profit from the factors that create them. Here are some examples of global alpha opportunities that PIMCO has identified in recent years and that we believe, going forward, may continue to offer favorable risk/reward profiles. We consider both currency-hedged opportunities as well as structural alpha opportunities in the currency markets themselves.

Front-End Forward Swap Curve   Historically, a long position in the front end of the forward U.S. dollar swap curve, especially the fifth Eurodollar futures contract, has offered a good risk/reward ratio. The structural support for this trade derives from the fact that a demand for liquidity by investors seeking cashlike investments drives a wedge between the required return on the fifth contract, maturing in 13 to 15 months, and the lower required return on LIBOR investments maturing in one to 12 months. Thus, a large constituency for U.S. dollar liquidity creates a reward, on average, for those investors willing to lend just beyond the one-year maturity date. It is natural to ask if this same structural alpha has been available in the European money market futures (Euribor) markets. If so, this would be a valuable source of alpha to a U.S. investor because the performance of Euribor futures is not always highly correlated with the returns to a long position in the Eurodollar curve.

Here is the evidence. As Table 6.3 shows, using the front-end Euribor contracts consistently adds positive excess returns over 5- and 10-year swaps. It is also clear that, as in the United States, the sweet spot on the Euribor curve appears to be with the fifth contract. This is true over rolling 2-, 5-, and 10-year periods. In Table 6.3, the investment in each point on the front end of the Euribor curve is made in proportions that bring its duration in line with the alternative investment in 5- or 10-year swaps.

The Cash/Futures Basis   Given their use as a liquid, short-hedging instrument, bond futures contracts tend to trade cheap relative to the underlying government security. In other words, the repurchase rate embedded in a cash loan collateralized by a government bond tends to be less than the interbank rate at which the cash can be re-lent. This structural cheapness provides an opportunity to switch into futures and out of the underlying bonds when the basis widens. As Figure 6.5 illustrates, this opportunity has been available in other markets. Over long periods of time, the structural cheapness of futures has the potential to generate alpha without increasing portfolio volatility.

The CDS/Cash Basis   Credit default swaps (CDS) take exposure to the credit spread of a corporate bond. Although the cash and CDS markets tend to

TABLE 6.3 Taking Advantage of Front-End Roll Down in a European Context

| | | Average Excess Returns of Euribor over 5-Year and 10-Year Swaps (bps per year) | | | | | |
| | | Average Excess Returns over 5-Year Swap (bps) | | | | | |
	Security	2 years	3 years	4 years	5 years	7 years	10 years
Using the front-end	ER1	−13	−12	−5	−12	−6	−10
contracts, Euribor	ER2	−6	−7	1	−6	15	−7
consistently adds	ER3	3	5	6	−1	19	−1
positive excess	ER4	9	11	11	4	25	4
returns over 5-	ER5	11	14	11	6	25	6
and 10-year	ER6	9	12	10	6	25	6
swaps	ER7	6	9	8	5	24	5
	ER8	2	6	7	5	24	4
High ex-post information ratios		Average Excess Returns Over 10-Year Swap (bps)					
No observed periods	Security	2 years	3 years	4 years	5 years	7 years	10 years
of negative excess	ER1	6	−6	−3	−8	−3	−7
returns	ER2	1	0	3	−2	18	−3
	ER3	10	11	9	3	22	3
	ER4	16	18	14	8	28	8
	ER5	18	20	14	10	27	10
	ER6	16	18	13	10	28	10
	ER7	13	15	11	10	26	9
	ER8	9	12	10	10	27	8

Source: PIMCO, Bloomberg Financial Markets

move together, sometimes the credit spread of the CDS may differ from that of the underlying bond by a material and profitable amount. There are opportunities, especially in Europe, to take advantage of the basis between the CDS and cash markets for individual names. With this strategy, PIMCO buys the cheaper of the CDS and cash bond, believing that the credit spreads between CDS and the bond will converge over time. (See Figure 6.6.)

Alpha Opportunities in Currency Markets Up to this point, we have considered opportunities in global fixed-income markets that are hedged for currency exposure. In other words, the dollar return of these strategies in Europe and Japan markets depends on the movement in interest rates or spreads in these markets, not on the dollar exchange rate with the local currency of the bond. It is important to understand that *it is possible to generate*

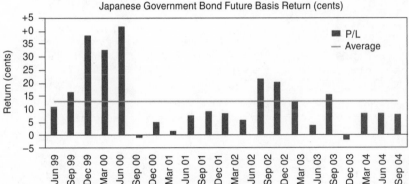

- Given their use as a liquid short hedging instrument, futures contracts tend to trade chronically cheap.

- PIMCO attempts to capture this structural cheapness by switching into futures and out of cash Treasuries when the basis widens.

- Over long periods of time, the structural cheapness of futures has the potential to add modestly to alpha but without increasing portfolio volatility.

FIGURE 6.5 Global Structural Alpha Strategy—Holding Cheap Futures in Japanese Government Bonds
Source: Bloomberg Financial Markets.

alpha in global fixed-income markets without taking on currency risk. However, it is also the case that there are alpha opportunities in the currency markets themselves. Although the returns on opportunities in currency markets tend to be more volatile than the returns in fixed-income markets, there are strategies that historically have produced good information ratios.

One such strategy is the *forward bias* basket: buying a portfolio of high-yielding currencies and funding this portfolio with a basket of low-yielding

- Credit default swaps (CDS) take exposure to the credit spread of a bond.
- Sometimes the credit spread of the CDS may differ from that of the underlying bond.
- Hence the CDS may be more expensive or cheaper than the bond.
- We buy the cheapest believing that the credit spreads between the CDS and the bond will converge over time.

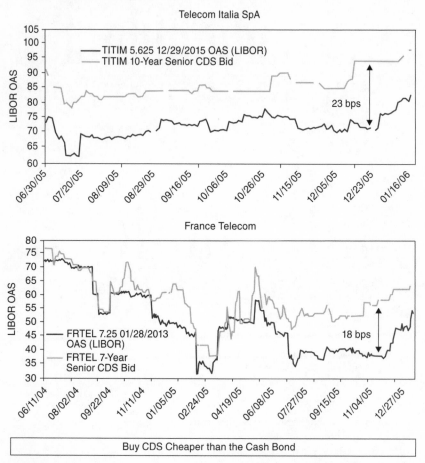

FIGURE 6.6 Taking Advantage of Credit Spread between a Bond and Its CDS
Source: Lehman Brothers.

currencies. This strategy relies on the historical tendency, at least among G10 countries, for the currencies of high-yielding countries to appreciate relative to the currencies of low-yielding currencies. As shown in Figure 6.7, this strategy, while more volatile than the others discussed thus far, has produced alpha on average over the past 15 years.

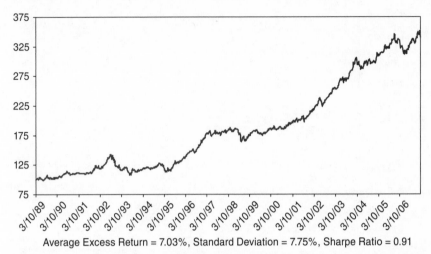

Average Excess Return = 7.03%, Standard Deviation = 7.75%, Sharpe Ratio = 0.91

FIGURE 6.7 Historical Cumulative Returns on Forward Bias Currency Basket
Source: Bloomberg Financial Markets.

The opportunities for adding value to portfolios by investing across global fixed-income markets continues to grow. The examples just presented of alpha strategies available in global markets are a representative, but by no means an exhaustive, list of these opportunities. In particular, curve and duration opportunities to invest globally almost constantly arise as countries' business and monetary policy cycles are rarely perfectly in synch.

HEDGE FUNDS STRATEGIES BY LISA KIM

Hedge funds have gained the spotlight in recent years as the industry has experienced significant growth. According to HFRI, assets under management have grown 46-fold since 1990[3] with total estimated assets at $1.8 trillion at the end of September 2007, as shown in Figure 6.8, and well north of $2 trillion according to Hedgefund.net. In tandem with the surging asset growth has been the sheer increase in the volume of new funds entering the industry and the turnover of these new funds. As of September 2007, there were more than 9,000 hedge funds, of which over 3,500 had been launched in the past two years and 1,500 have closed their doors.[4]

The growth of the hedge fund industry has been spurred by demand across a wide range of investors. Formerly the exclusive domain of ultra high-net-worth individuals, the investor base for hedge funds has expanded dramatically. Institutional investors seeking higher returns have turned to

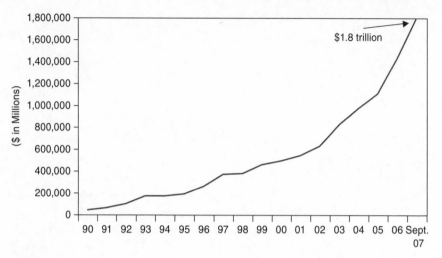

FIGURE 6.8 HFRI Weighted Composite Asset Size 1990 thru Q3 2007
Source: Hedge Fund Research Inc.

alternative investment vehicles as a source of attractive returns and diversification, and the investor base now includes public and private pension plans, charities, foundations, and endowments, and other accredited investors. College and university endowments have steadily increased their allocation into hedge funds, with the average allocation increasing from 2.2 percent in 1997 to 9.6 percent in 2006.[5]

Hedge funds, like other alternative asset classes including real estate, commodities, and venture capital, are often cited as providing diversification benefits, return enhancements, and lower volatility than other risky asset classes or investments. The investment strategies they employ cover all global capital markets. With broader investment discretion, many hedge funds and funds of hedge funds offer a larger set of risk and return combinations than traditional long-only equity and bond investment strategies, ideally resulting in superior risk-adjusted returns in both bull and bear markets. Another benefit that many associate with hedge funds is the idea that hedge funds are likely to attract the brightest minds in the investment industry, given the fact that the associated fee structures and therefore potential compensation (typically a 1 to 2 percent base management fee plus a performance fee of 20 percent of the investment gains) are much higher than those charged elsewhere in the asset management industry. In addition, the investment vehicles are generally less constrained from a regulatory and disclosure standpoint than are public investment vehicles.

But what is it about hedge fund investments and strategies that provide these characteristics, if at all? Do they really provide positive returns in all market environments? The fact that hedge funds are not effectively required to be fully invested in the stock market at all times (as is the case with most equity strategies) creates the potential for a substantially reduced downside during weak equity markets—if the hedge fund manager is, in fact, not exposed to risk factors that are highly correlated with the equity markets. Decomposing hedge funds' performance to find their sources of returns has been a widely debated topic and is one that we touch on.

Hedge funds is a commonly used term to describe lightly regulated pooled investments that may have very little in common with each other. They cover a large variety of investment strategies and are not limited to long-only strategies. The common thread that ties them together is the full degrees of investment discretion and also the required use of a broker/dealer as part of the investment fund structure due to the inherent leverage. Hedge funds are free from the constraints imposed by the Investment Company Act of 1940, which limits the extent of short selling, company holding concentration, the use of leverage, and the ability to hold shares of other investment companies. They are also not required to publicly disclose their strategies or performance. In essence, the lack of such trading restrictions allows hedge funds to employ nontraditional trading techniques such as short selling, the use of various forms of leverage, and the extensive use of derivatives.

Along with the additional discretion hedge funds enjoy comes the additional complexity in understanding risks related to their diverse and often complex investment strategies. Conventional risk measures such as volatility and value at risk (VaR) are widely known to have built-in limitations with respect to quantifying potentially extreme losses in hedge fund strategies. The primary limitation cited is that these types of risk measures only capture potential losses under a specified normal or regular distribution of probable outcomes and under generally static environments. Risk models using measures like sigmas, confidence intervals, and variances fall short in assigning the likelihood of rare events, as they rest on quantifying risk in a world of mean-variance outcomes. To address this shortcoming, variations of VaR have been proposed to better capture the skewness and nonnormal distribution of hedge fund strategies' returns. Modified VaR calculations that take into account the higher moments and co-moments of non-normal distributions help cover unique aspects of hedge fund risk measurement. In addition, risk management solutions such as stress testing, scenario analysis, and more complex modeling of distribution tails with extreme value theory have all been utilized as a framework for more effective risk management of hedge funds.

It is generally accepted that there are systematic risk exposures that contribute to the returns of hedge funds. Many academic writings and practitioner studies have addressed the issue of disentangling hedge fund returns derived from multiple market and/or risk factor exposures from decisions made by an investment manager that are risk-neutral. We performed a similar exercise as a means to better understand the primary risk factors inherent in different hedge fund strategies for purposes of evaluating hedge fund strategies as potential alpha strategies within a portable alpha context. Specifically, we developed a brief list of risk factors found in fixed-income, equity, and other markets with the goal of creating a representation of the wide range of investment strategies across global capital markets. Specifically, the following 10 data sets were selected as being broadly representative of typical hedge fund market risk factor exposures:

- U.S. large cap equity: S&P 500 Index.
- Convertible bonds: Merrill Lynch All U.S. Convertible Securities Index.
- U.S. interest rate risk: U.S. 1-3 Year Government Index.
- Emerging market equity: MSCI Emerging Market Equities.
- U.S. small cap risk: Spread between Russell 2000 and S&P 500 Index.
- Investment grade credit risk: Lehman U.S. Credit Bond Index.
- Mortgage risk: Lehman GNMA Mortgage Index.
- High-yield bond risk: Lehman U.S. Universal High Yield Corporate.
- Emerging market bond risk: JPM EMBI+ Composite.
- Commodities: DJ AIG Spot Commodity Index.

Using these factors as independent variables we generated linear, stepwise regressions against various hedge fund universes. The hedge fund universes evaluated include the HFRI Hedge Fund Weighted Composite, Hedge Fund of Funds Index, and the individual style categories as represented by HFRI Hedge Fund and CS/Tremont indexes. Our multifactor linear regression was based on the five-year period ended December 2006 for each hedge fund strategy's monthly excess returns over three-month LIBOR. We derived statistically significant beta coefficients for each factor in order to determine the factor weights and an R-squared (based solely on the explanatory factors previously listed) for each universe of underlying funds. We defined betas to be statistically significant at the 95 percent confidence interval, corresponding to a t-statistic of approximately 2.0. A summary of the results of our regressions is shown in Table 6.4.

We found that in the most recent five-year period, hedge fund returns, on average, have been driven largely by systematic exposure to market factors in some combination proxied by the universes listed in this table, in many cases. The returns of the HFRI Weighted Composite, which represents a broad

TABLE 6.4 Hedge Fund Factor-Based Regression Analysis (Five Years Ended December 31, 2006)

Factors	U.S. Equity	Convertible Bonds	Govt Bonds	Emerging Market Equity	R2K-SP500	IG Credit	Mortgage	High-Yield	Emerging Market Bonds	Commodity	R-squared
				Beta Coefficient							
Fund of Funds	—	—	—	0.138	0.102	—	—	—	—	—	0.70
Weighted Composite	—	0.221	—	0.146	0.093	—	—	—	—	—	0.92
Convertible Arbitrage	(0.199)	0.469	—	—	—	—	—	—	—	—	0.48
Distressed	—	0.283	—	—	—	—	—	0.286	—	—	0.62
Emerging Markets	—	—	—	0.441	—	0.287	—	—	(0.106)	—	0.86
Equity Hedge	(0.067)	0.242	—	0.188	0.152	—	(0.276)	—	—	—	0.93
Equity Market-Neutral	—	—	—	0.076	0.050	—	—	—	—	—	0.42
Equity Non-Hedge	0.287	0.387	—	0.188	0.275	—	—	—	—	—	0.97
Event-Driven	—	0.288	—	0.095	0.096	—	—	0.182	—	—	0.86
Fixed-Income Arbitrage	—	—	0.427	—	—	—	(0.299)	—	—	—	0.18
Global Macro	(0.327)	0.273	—	0.213	—	—	—	—	—	—	0.55
Merger Arbitrage	—	0.159	—	0.055	0.073	—	—	—	—	0.106	0.66
Multistrategy	—	0.254	—	—	—	—	—	—	—	0.059	0.54
Managed Futures	—	—	2.251	—	—	—	—	—	—	0.340	0.22

Source: HFRI for all except for multistrategy and managed futures; source for those is CS/Tremont.
Note: Nonsignificant betas have been set to zero.

universe of hedge fund managers, were more than 90 percent explained by a handful of market risks, including convertible bonds, emerging market equity risk, and a U.S. small cap equity risk premium.

Far from a homogeneous asset class, the hedge fund universe is broadly classified by the various strategies and approaches. This large opportunity set can be broken down into different categories based on the primary investment strategies that are employed, the fundamental systematic risk factors they access, and/or techniques employed to assess individual strategies as potential alpha sources within a portable alpha context. More specifically, the breakdown of hedge fund strategies into underlying risk factors may be useful in understanding how these risks may be correlated with the risk factors in potential beta market exposures.

Convertible Arbitrage

This strategy seeks to find value and exploit inefficiencies in the convertible bond market by trading in convertible securities and hedging out some piece of the underlying exposure inherent in convertible bonds. The three main risk characteristics embedded in convertible bonds are *credit risk premium, volatility risk,* and *equity risk.* Convertible arbitrage hedge funds will seek to find mispricings in any of these components while employing various hedging strategies, although by far the most common is a delta-neutral hedge on the equity risk leg. This entails selling short the underlying stock to neutralize exposure to the equity risk. The net resulting market exposure is a long position in the undervalued convertible debt, a long volatility position through being short the equity, and long exposure to the credit risk premium associated with corporate bonds.

The return of convertible bonds is derived from two main areas: income and long volatility. Income comes from the coupon payments on the bond component and the interest collected from the short position in the underlying equity. (*Note:* Income is reduced by the cost of borrowing to open the short equity position and by net dividends paid to the long holder of the equity position). The long volatility comes from the equity option characteristic embedded in the the convertible bond, with the higher delta associated with the convert being more equitylike and a lower delta being more bondlike, which is associated with the variability in the value of the conversion option.

Various studies have reviewed convertible arbitrage hedge fund performance in an attempt to better understand the underlying risk factors. For example, Hutchinson and Gallagher (2004) found a positive correlation between portfolios constructed of long convertible bonds and short underlying common stock with the HFRI and CSFB Tremont Convertible

Arbitrage Indexes.[6] Similarly, Argarwal et al (2004) extracted the common risk factors in the Japanese convertible bond market, documenting two risk factors—positive carry (interest) and volatility arbitrage—as statistically significant explanatory variables in capturing the risk/return characteristics of convertible bond arbitrage strategies.[7] We were not surprised to find in our own regression analysis that the HFRI Convertible Bond universe displayed a statistically significant negative beta coefficient with U.S. equities and positive beta coefficient with the broad convertible bond index, given the typical strategies employed in convertible arbitrage.

Managed Futures (Trend-Following)

This strategy is used by professional investment managers known as commodity trading advisers (CTAs), who trade across a global spectrum of futures and options for the purpose of capturing momentum-driven price movements. These trading programs attempt to profit from large directional moves in prices across a range of asset classes, resulting in returns that exhibit a nonlinear, long-volatility characteristic. With the continuous financial innovation in instruments and investment strategies, the investment opportunity set for CTAs varies far and wide and includes commodities, currencies, interest rates, bonds, stocks, and more.

Managed futures strategies encompass both statistical, rules-based, technically driven investment styles and fundamental, dynamic, discretionary investment styles. The common thread underlying these very different styles is the trend-following nature that drives the return stream. The trend-following and momentum-driven nature of these strategies results in a nonlinear distribution of returns. Fung and Hsieh (2001) attempted to replicate the trend-following return stream through a combination of look-back type options on publicly traded stocks, bonds, and commodity markets to capture the directionally driven, long-volatility orientation of trend-following strategies.[8] The payoff of a look-back straddle would replicate the investor who, in theory, bought a look-back call and exercised the option at the lowest price of the underlying security over the life of the option. The investor would also own a look-back put and conversely, exercises the put option to sell at the highest price of the underlying security over the life of the option. In other words, he bought the asset at the ex-post lowest price over the historic life of the option and sold at the ex-post highest price over that same period. The investor would have had perfect hindsight to maximize that *buy low, sell high* return payoff. Fung and Hsieh's portfolio of various look-back straddles resulted in return characteristics of a trend follower, establishing a strong correlation to the returns of trend following commodity trading advisers.

Not surprisingly, our regression analysis suggests a positive, statistically significant relationship between the returns of the managed futures hedge fund universe and the changes in commodity prices generally. Our analysis also suggests a positive relationship with the returns from bonds which contain interest-rate-risk. However, the combined R-squared of the regression of the managed futures hedge fund universe against the independent variables (factors) we selected was 22 percent, one of the two lowest we evaluated by a wide margin.

Equity Long/Short (Equity Hedge)

The first known hedge fund strategy was an equity long/short strategy created by Alfred Winslow Jones in 1949. His fund used leverage, short sales, and performance-based incentive fees, all hallmark features of hedge fund advisers today. Jones invested in combinations of long and short equity positions, with the shorts to hedge his stock portfolio against drops in stock prices, without any constraints on a net neutral dollar position (i.e., without a requirement to be equity market exposure).

Today the equity long/short strategy claims the largest share of assets in the broader hedge fund universe, comprising 30 percent of the total market.[9] Investment managers in this category typically hold both long and short equity positions; however, the strategy tends to exhibit a net long bias over time. The net long exposure reflects the broader appreciation of equity market valuations over long periods of time (long/short equity managers attempt to deliver positive returns by dynamically adjusting their long and short exposures to varying degrees as they deem appropriate). Managers may invest in a wide array of stocks, but they tend to specialize in a sector, a specific style orientation, or a geographic market focus.

Various studies have shown that the performance of equity long/short strategies, on average, can be almost entirely explained by a set of finite market risk factors. For example, our representative series came up with a set of factors whereby the beta coefficients (sensitivity to each of the factors) explained over 90 percent of the returns over the past five years. One of the factors that has shown significant explanatory power in the various studies is the small cap risk premium, which seems a logical result given that over the long term, small cap stocks have outperformed large cap stocks. A simple comparison of the performance between the small cap and large cap universes shows that during the past 10 years, the Russell 2000 Index outperformed the S&P 500 by 4.25 percent on a rolling three-year basis, with 5.62 percent incremental volatility, and a Sharpe ratio of 0.32 versus 0.19 for the S&P 500, as shown in Figure 6.9.

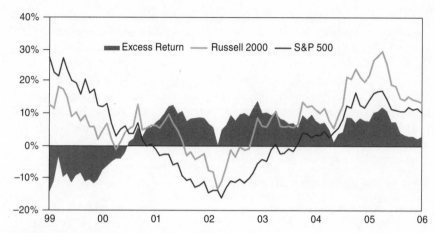

FIGURE 6.9 Rolling Three-Year Returns of Russell 2000 versus S&P 500, 10-Year Period Ended December 31, 2006
Source: Russell, Standard & Poor's.

Long/short equity hedge funds have the flexibility to employ short sales plus the use of leverage to isolate this small cap risk premium. Frequently, the ability to sell short is accompanied by the freedom to invest in both small cap and large cap stocks. Fung and Hsieh (2004) show empirically that equity long/short hedge funds carry persistent exposure to two risk factors: the excess returns of the equity market over cash, and the spread between small cap and large cap stocks.[10]

Equity Market-Neutral

Equity market-neutral strategies employ long and short equity positions while attempting to keep their overall equity market risk close to zero. These managers generate positive returns primarily through successful stock selection abilities and should not benefit from rising equity markets or be negatively impacted by weak equity markets. In theory, their returns are uncorrelated to the broader equity or fixed-income markets. Industry and certain style exposures are also minimized in many approaches.

The excess return produced by a strategy which is truly market-neutral would be the closest to the traditional alpha measure derived when regressing a stock manager's returns against a representative benchmark index. One would expect that this excess return would not have a meaningful correlation or beta with a given market index. As such, the majority of market-neutral equity strategy returns should not be explained by the existence of systematic market risk factor exposures.

However, a regression of the HFRI Equity Market Neutral index resulted in an R-squared of 0.42. The three factors that bore statistical significance included emerging market equities, the small cap risk premium, and the S&P 500, with positive betas to the first two of these and a negative beta to the third as shown in Figure 6.4. Other studies have also found equity market-neutral hedge fund strategies to exhibit some degree of exposures to equity market risk, for example Patton (2004) found that between one-fourth and one-third of market-neutral funds demonstrate some significant exposure to equity market risk.[11]

Distressed Securities Investing

This strategy invests in stocks, bonds, or any other financial claim to a company that is believed to be in, or expected to move into, financial trouble. In general, the market has discounted the various layers of the company's debt and equity based on the anticipated valuation decline, whether warranted or not. Distressed securities investors opportunistically buy some component of the company's capital structure at a steep discount. These assets are often considered the trash that no one else will touch, because the likelihood of par redemption or equity appreciation is slim. These managers must possess skill and expertise in corporate turnarounds, restructurings, liquidation assessments, and fundamental valuations. Their active management is directly linked to the ability to accurately assess and effectuate the potential future appreciation of discounted assets.

Such investment strategies tend to exhibit a low correlation to the broader equity and fixed-income markets. This is primarily due to two reasons. The first is that the performance of distressed securities is largely dependent on the resultant endogenous events unfolding after the company-specific financial trouble. The price action on these securities reflects valuation arising from idiosyncratic conditions and deemed to be uncorrelated with the broader market. The second is that distressed securities tend to be very illiquid, hard-to-price securities; thus volatility in broader markets may not influence the volatility of a distress fund's holdings. This second phenomenon may also serve to understate the actual risk of distressed assets simply due to frictional markets for those assets.

Asness et al (2001) and De Souza and Gokcan (2004) documented a high degree of serial correlation in most hedge fund strategy monthly returns, meaning that the returns of one period were correlated to returns of prior periods, in theory due to reduced price discovery from illiquid markets, thus understating the actual volatility and correlation with traditional asset classes.[12] Additionally, Asness found that lagging the equity market performance stream by one, two, and three months resulted in statistically significant beta coefficients and a higher model R-squared than by just using a single-factor contemporaneous performance stream of the S&P 500. Our analysis on the HFRI Distressed Securities universe suggests a positive return sensitivity to both convertible bonds and high-yield bonds and a negative relationship with emerging market bonds, with an overall model R-squared of 62 percent.

Merger Arbitrage

Also known as risk arbitrage, a merger arbitrage investment strategy attempts to profit from a positive spread between investments in a possible corporate merger or takeover/acquisition as noted in Chapter 3. When a company announces a merger or acquisition, the potential target company's stock price will rise, but generally by less than the full offering price. The market tends to place a discount on the target company's offered value due to the risk of the deal not closing, which is partly dependent on the length of time until closing.

Some investors consider merger arbitrage strategies to be equity market neutral (net equity exposure of zero). However, even if merger arbitrage strategies tend to have a net dollar equity exposure of zero, the largest risk in these strategies, deal break, tends to be sensitive to broader market conditions. Aside from the idiosyncratic risk of a specific merger transaction falling apart, merger/acquisition activity in general is highly dependent on the strength of the overall equity market. Weak stock markets will tend to reduce the number of deals closing as well as the number of deals out to market. Interestingly, our regression analysis didn't find a strong relationship to equities except for a small, but statistically significant relationship to emerging market equities and the small cap premium. Both are intuitively appropriate explanatory factors, as one might expect merger arbitrage activity to spike in times of global economic strength, which would typically be accompanied by outsized strength in emerging markets and smaller stocks. Our regression analysis also resulted in a positive significant relationship to convertible bonds which is logical given that convertibles tend to perform well in rising equity markets while offering downside protection via the conversion factor during weak equity markets.

Mitchell and Pulvino's (2000) research in dynamic trading strategies modeled the returns of a merger arbitrage strategy using 4,750 merger transactions during 1963 to 1998.[13] They simulated a simple rules-based strategy that invests in each announced merger deal, with a prespecified entry and exit rule. The resulting performance of their constructed strategy was very similar to the returns of merger arbitrage hedge funds. Moreover, they showed that merger arbitrage strategies exhibit a nonlinear return profile, where returns are fairly uncorrelated to equity markets in flat to bull markets but strongly correlated to equities in falling equity markets. The return payoff was very similar to the returns obtained through short put options on the stock market, affirming that merger arbitrage strategies present an optionlike nonlinear return profile.

Fixed-Income Arbitrage

Fixed-income arbitrage hedge funds attempt to exploit valuation differentials between fixed-income securities. They may combine the underlying risk factors in the bond universe in different ways than traditional active fixed-income managers. However, the underlying risk factors employed are still the same—they just may be highly leveraged and represent both long and short risk exposures that change over time. Various risk exposures are employed, including interest rate, liquidity, credit, term structure, and yield curve risks. Common types of trades include cash versus futures basis, yield curve spreads, Treasury versus credit spreads, and cross-market spreads and curves. Successful active management relies on identifying and exploiting pricing anomalies, valuation inconsistencies, and other relative-value bottom-up type trades and strategies.

Our factor regression assigned one factor exposure, short maturity government bonds, with a beta coefficient of 0.43 and the lowest R-squared value to the HFRI Fixed-Income Arbitrage index out of all the hedge fund strategies at 18 percent. This is fairly consistent with the findings of Duarte et al (2005), where they delineate the positive risk-adjusted excess returns and positive skew in the return distribution of various fixed-income arbitrage strategies.[14] In other words, broad factor-based approaches to explaining the return profile of fixed-income arbitrage strategies appear less instructive than for other types of hedge fund strategies.

Equity Non-Hedge

Non-hedged equity hedge funds typically involve long positions in equities and may involve leverage to enhance returns. These strategies generally use short sales in an attempt to extract relative value or to tactically reduce market risk. The use of short sales may or may not be continuously applied in overall portfolio strategy. Unlike equity long/short or equity market-neutral, funds in this category do not always have a hedge in place and do not always engage in short sales. In addition to equities, these funds may use a wide variety of equity derivatives and may also have assets invested in other types of securities.

The return profile of a universe of funds employing equity non-hedge strategies is explained robustly by our basic regression model. A full 97 percent of the variability of returns was accounted for by positive beta coefficients in the various equity and equitylike factors we utilized, including U.S. equities, emerging market equities, the U.S. small cap premium (S&P 500, Russell 2000), and convertible bonds.

Emerging Markets

Funds in the emerging markets category establish positions in equities or fixed-income instruments of issuers in emerging market nations. Some funds specialize in specific regions, countries, or asset classes. Investments may be primarily long or may involve a combination of long and short positions.

Some of the risks in emerging markets include volatile growth rates, high inflation, uncertain exchange rates, and, in some cases, political uncertainty. Other risks include regulatory restrictions on foreign capital, lower credit quality, and the potential for periods of sharp economic decline. Funds focused on emerging markets will often look for potential inefficiencies in associated market prices and undervalued assets. In our regression analysis on emerging market specialist hedge funds, the betas for both emerging market equities and the credit markets were materially positive, explaining approximately 86 percent of the variability of returns over the test period.

Event-Driven

The event-driven style of hedge fund investing essentially seeks to anticipate and capitalize on corporate events including but not limited to mergers, acquisitions, bankruptcy, share buy-backs, and spin-offs. The investment focus of such funds is the likely effect on security prices due to a corporate event as opposed to fundamental or credit analysis. Typical instruments utilized by these funds include long and short stock positions, fixed-income securities, and options. Leverage may be used by some strategies. Fund managers may hedge against market risk by engaging in option strategies.

Similar to our findings on merger arbitrage, the event-driven universe of hedge funds also displayed a positive relationship (beta) with higher-risk components of the equity market, including emerging market equities and the small cap premium, and also with convertible bonds. Unlike merger arbitrage, the universe displayed a positive relationship with high-yield bonds and a negative relationship with the mortgage market generally, with the preceding positive and negative betas explaining 86 percent of variability of returns over our test period.

Global Macro

Global macro hedge funds seek to generate attractive risk-adjusted returns through opportunistic investing across major asset classes, sectors, and geographic regions based on top-down global macroeconomic considerations. Their investment discretion covers equities, fixed-income, currencies, and commodities while employing a broad array of instruments and ideas.

Global macro managers are generally focused on interest rate/growth trends, foreign exchange fluctuations, and the political climate with respect to international and government policy factors. Their investment strategies can be either directional in nature or relative-value structured positions. In either case, profit opportunities exist from perceived pricing dislocations or relative misvaluations that are expected to return to some state of equilibrium. And while it is the case for nearly all successful investment managers, timing and risk management are particularly important in the global macro arena given the potentially destabilizing combination of extended leverage, directionality, and endurance of market disequilibria.

Global macro hedge fund strategies are among the most well-known types of hedge fund strategies, given the high-profile headlines of certain fund managers. George Soros is one of the most notable figures, gaining instant notoriety on his historic currency bet against the British pound in 1992, which allegedly produced a profit in excess of $1 billion. Soros's investment thesis was based on what he termed *dynamic disequilibrium,* forecasting correctly that the Bank of England would not be able to support the British pound against the European currencies as mandated in the Bretton Woods Agreement. He believed a post–Cold War reunification of Germany would invariably lead to inflationary pressures, strengthening the German mark and eventually forcing the Bank of England to withdraw from the European Exchange Rate Mechanism vehicle, allowing the pound to devalue. On September 16, 1992, the British pound fell precipitously and Soros was dubbed "the man who broke the Bank of England."

Since then, hedge funds became associated with leveraged speculation and potential destabilizing forces on global financial markets. In reality, less than 5 percent of total assets of the broader hedge fund universe are dedicated to the global macro investment strategy. Moreover, the broader top-down macroeconomic and global political analysis that global macro managers draw heavily upon are the same broader conditions and forecasts that fixed-income, equity, and other asset class investment managers analyze. As already mentioned, the investment mandate for global macro managers covers a wide investment opportunity platform with both directional and relative-value positions, and fundamental as well as quantitative-driven analysis.

When applied to the global macro hedge fund category, our regression model showed statistically significant relationships with equities (negative), commodities, convertibles, and emerging market equities (all positive), explaining approximately 55 percent of the variability of returns over the test period.

Multistrategy

The final major category of hedge funds we reviewed is the multistrategy category. Multistrategy funds look for opportunities to add value from investing in different strategies and adjusting fund investment decisions among a wide variety of markets and investment approaches. Unlike many hedge funds with expertise in one specific discipline, multistrategy hedge funds look to implement more than one type of hedge fund strategy at a time or rotate among different strategies based upon perceived opportunities. Many funds of funds pursue a multistrategy approach in constructing an optimal blend of hedge funds based on market conditions and other considerations. A similar concept is applied in multistrategy hedge funds although, in contrast to funds of funds, they employ their own portfolio managers and traders, who execute a variety of different investment strategies.

Given the tactical, rotational, and disparate approaches used in this universe, it is not surprising that our regression model for this universe yielded a statistically significant relationship with only 2 of the 10 factors we included in the analysis (convertibles and commodities).

CONCLUSION

The ability to select from a broad range of strategies that provide attractive incremental return relative to the risk-free rate—and ideally also attractive after-fee excess returns relative to a given beta market exposure—is a central benefit of the portable alpha investment application. The asset class or sector decision and the alpha decision are no longer necessarily linked, and the associated benefits for investors can be quite compelling. Almost all investments and investment strategies that are not limited to money market instruments are presumably expected to generate excess returns over money market rates and therefore may provide an attractive source of alpha within a portable alpha strategy. In this sense the selection of an alpha strategy is very similar to investing in general, where the goal is to achieve an optimal return for risk assumed over the risk-free rate, and investment choices are governed by an investor's risk tolerance, liquidity needs, and other considerations.

The key difference in terms of the selection of a suitable alpha strategy in a portable alpha context relative to investing more broadly is the leverage aspect. It is generally the case that each unit of capital invested in a portable alpha strategy is exposed to two sets of risk factors: the risk factors associated with the beta market exposure and the risk factors associated with the alpha strategy. Therefore, diversification is not only key to the optimization of the associated risk-adjusted return, but it might also be argued that it is critical from a risk management standpoint.

The inherent leverage associated with portable alpha does not necessarily result in increased downside risk. In some cases the opposite actually may be true. Indeed, the diversification benefits afforded by the portable alpha investment application can be quite powerful. However, it is important for prospective investors to understand not only the types of strategies and risk factors that an alpha strategy manager is employing to generate returns over money market rates, but also the correlation of the associated risk factor exposures with the risk factors in the beta market exposure. Of course, a prerequisite to measuring or even assessing likely correlations between the two in different market environments is a thorough understanding of the primary underlying risk exposures or factors associated with a given alpha strategy in addition to other relevant characteristics.

A wide range of investments and investment strategies are employed as alpha sources in portable alpha strategies, including a variety of approaches that are categorized by investors as bond strategies, equity strategies, and hedge fund strategies. Investment benchmarks that are reflective of the general characteristics of an investment strategy—most importantly the primary risk factor exposures—are likely to serve as a good proxy for the average expected risk factor exposure for purposes of many potential alpha strategies. In the case of a number of other potential alpha strategies, however, investment benchmarks are not specified. Rather, the returns are reviewed relative to the risk-free rate only, rather than relative to the risk-free rate to assess the return per unit of risk and also relative to a benchmark for purposes of measuring investment manager value-added or skill. There is also not likely to be a readily specified benchmark in cases involving active strategies plus separate hedges to remove undesirable market exposure. Regardless, most investment strategies that are expected to outperform a risk-free rate by a material amount will almost certainly involve risk. This is true whether or not hedges are involved—unless all risk factors are perfectly hedged, in which case a materially positive return over the risk-free rate is not a highly likely outcome.

In addition to equity market beta, as proxied not only by a broad market index but also by emerging market indexes, small cap indexes, and even the difference between equity market styles (small cap versus large cap, value versus growth), many different investment strategies also exhibit sensitivity or beta to various forms of interest rate risk, credit risk, commodity risk, liquidity risk, vega/volatility risk, and so forth. Different strategies may also involve varying degrees of liquidity risk; accounting, tax, and regulatory treatment risk; and financing risk, among other risk factors. The ultimate key from a portable alpha investor's standpoint when selecting from the vast universe of possible alpha sources is to understand the associated risk factors and potential range of risk factors and how these risk factors are likely to complement (or not) the desired beta market exposure.

CHAPTER 7

Derivatives-Based Beta Management

Jim Keller and Mihir Worah

In this chapter our goal is to give the reader a good sense of the risks and costs associated with derivatives-based beta management. Some people will tell you that you shouldn't pay for beta. After all what is the skill in simply executing and rolling futures or swaps? Perhaps this is the same group that lives in a world where markets are assumed to be frictionless and continuous, transaction costs are assumed to be zero, and markets are perfectly competitive with many buyers and sellers who are small compared to the size of the overall market. None of these assumptions hold in the real world, and hopefully we will be able to dispel the notions that gaining and managing indexlike exposure via the derivatives market is simple or that the management of derivative-based market exposure should be free. Beta management, like alpha strategy management or indeed any investment management assignment, is a risk-transfer arrangement that carries with it risks—risks that (hopefully) are managed using specialized skills and systems that do not come for free.

SECURITIES LENDING AS A FORM OF LOW-RISK PORTABLE ALPHA

Where might the concept of free beta management come from? One possibility is best illustrated using the following example. Assume there is a fictional plan sponsor (PS) that hires an investment manager (IM) to manage a portfolio benchmarked to the Lehman Brothers Aggregate Index (LBAG). Let's say this PS has a securities lending arrangement with its trustee bank such that the bank always lends out any available securities whenever it can reinvest the proceeds at a profit (taking into account transaction costs). In this example, the trustee bank will typically lend out any securities it can at LIBOR less 25 basis points (bps), and (safely) reinvest the cash or proceeds from the loan at LIBOR less 15 bps or better.

In this example, the PS has entered into an agreement where the trustee bank offers exposure to this subset of the account—the amount being lent out—without having to physically own the securities. In other words, the PS is getting the market exposure (beta) associated with those securities being lent out, without having to physically own the securities for a period of time. The PS is effectively *renting* someone else's balance sheet by simply parking the securities somewhere else for a period of time. This frees up the proceeds to be invested in other investments, hopefully generating alpha over the borrowing cost (i.e., the cost for renting someone else's balance sheet).

The makeup of the greater portfolio in this example is entirely outside the trustee's control. Sometimes the IM may hold a great deal of Treasuries, agencies, and mortgages, in which case a large percentage of the assets might actually be warehoused on someone else's balance sheet. At other times, the portfolio might be almost entirely made up of illiquid assets for which there is no interest in the collateral market. Exogenous factors are simply out of the trustee's control; it takes what portfolio it is given and works with it.

The trustee, however, is given complete control in coordinating which securities to lend out, where to invest the excess cash, and when. The extent to which the trustee utilizes discretion changes with the nature of the portfolio, the demand for borrowed assets, and the supply of investment vehicles.

Most important, the trustee has some risk tolerance that governs how much risk it is willing to accept. For example, the agreement between the PS and the trustee may state that if the trustee enters into securities lending operations with the portfolio, the profits will be split but the trustee is completely responsible for any *risks gone bad,* or losses. This type of arrangement necessitates a very conservative approach. The Trustee only engages in securities lending when it is effectively a sure thing. This is perhaps the most primitive form of portable alpha or alpha-beta separation. The plan has completely delegated the responsibility to manage this securities lending strategy to a third party under the condition that the plan takes no risk. As we know from basic finance, if you don't take much risk, you can't expect outsized rewards! This simple example is, then, the crux of the misconception that beta management should be free, vastly underrepresenting the complexity and cost.

From these humble beginnings, where an investor parks a portion of his portfolio on somebody else's balance sheet, it is easy to see how, with a little imagination and a greater risk tolerance, an investor might take this simple concept and stretch it along all the various axes. Why not lend out most of the securities in your portfolio? In fact, let's reduce the uncertainty in the amount of the portfolio you can lend out by simply holding the index. Taken one step further, why not lend *all* of it out? And then take the proceeds and give them to a skillful manager who can outperform cash (the borrowing rate) by a relatively large margin most of the time? This last proposition is portable alpha as it is currently understood. The more risk you are willing to take, the greater the potential rewards (and the greater likelihood of a negative scenario).

In this chapter, we tackle what it means to gain exposure without owning the assets. When is it easy and when is it difficult? What are the market-based risks? What are the operational risks? Where is the skill? Along with an introduction to the nuts and bolts of derivatives-based beta management, what we hope to illustrate is that if beta management is to be risk free, it requires a combination of complete coordination between the borrowing and lending aspects, as well as strict controls over the risks taken on the asset side of the equation. Once these preconditions are relaxed or *separated,* as in alpha-beta separation, risks can and do escalate in a hurry, as do the corresponding management costs.

FUTURES

Most of the proposed solutions to this problem—gaining exposure to an asset class without owning the assets—employ the use of derivatives. Derivatives are complex financial instruments whose value is derived from some other market or asset. Futures are in some ways the simplest, so we start there. We begin with a dissection of the risks involved in running a basic futures position, then expand the analysis to the swaps market. Once we have an understanding of the risks that need to be managed, we take a fresh look at the job of managing beta from a portfolio viewpoint and introduce the various skills that can be employed to increase performance, decrease cost, and minimize risk.

As an aside, try transacting futures in your brokerage account with Charles Schwab or E-Trade. Probably not possible: You must open an account with an approved futures broker. Even then, before you are able to buy or sell a single contract, you must read and sign off on a series of documents roughly the size of the Manhattan Yellow Pages, all designed to warn you of the risks you are about to undertake. This should be the first warning that all is not simple when broadening the tool set to include derivatives.

Let's use an example to define some of the terms necessary in understanding how futures work. We will use Treasury futures as our example,

and expand on the related factors that are important from a portable alpha
standpoint as mentioned in Chapter 2. Rest assured that these basic fundamentals are all relevant when we move on to the over-the-counter swaps
market. (See Table 7.1 for these values in other relevant securities.)

Ten-year note futures contract. Each contract has a face value at maturity of roughly $100,000.

Delivery. Futures can be financially settled (based on the price of the
referenced underlying at expiration) or physically settled (requiring
the delivery of the referenced underlying at expiration). Treasury
note futures are always physically settled. There are a number of
deliverable cash Treasury notes that can be delivered to settle the
contract: essentially any 10-year Treasury note with current maturity between 6.5 years and 10.0 years.

TABLE 7.1 Examples of Futures Contract

	Primary Exchange	Contract Notional	Initial Margin	Variation Margin
U.S. 10-year	CBOT	100,000	$878	$650
U.S. 30-year	CBOT	100,000	$1,350	$1,000
EURO Bond-Future (10-Year)	EUREX	100,000	EUR 1,750	EUR 1,400
Japan (JGB)-Future (10-year)	TSE	100,000,000	JPY 850,000	JPY 680,000
Euro$	CME	1,000,000	$743	$550
S&P 500	CME	250 × Index	$17,500	$14,000
Russell 2000	CME	500 × Index	$20,000	$16,000
Euro-Stoxx 50	EUREX	10 × Index	EUR 4,106	EUR 3,285
TOPIX	TSE	10,000 × Index	JPY 737,500	JPY 590,000
Crude oil	NYM	1,000 U.S. Barrels	$4,050	$3,000
Gold	CMX	100 Fine Troy oz.	$2,700	$2,000
Copper	CMX	25,000 lbs	5,738	$4,250

Source: Futures exchanges.
CBOT = Chicago Board of Trade
EUREX = EUREX
CME = Chicago Mercantile Exchange
TSE = Tokyo Stock Exchange
NYM = New York Mercantile Exchange
CMX = Commodity Exchange, Inc.

Initial margin. This is the amount of money that must be provided to the broker up front for every long or short contract—in this example, $878 per contract. This is the capital requirement associated with financing Treasury note exposure.

Maintenance margin. In this example, the maintenance margin is $650 per contract. Should the futures position move against you such that your assets held on margin falls below $650 per contract, you must contribute additional cash into the account to bring it back up to the initial margin amount of $878. This is known as a margin call.

Margin call. The notice that you must pledge additional assets within a preset time period in order to continue to hold your futures position, or face a voluntary or forced liquidation.

Forced liquidation. Should an account fail to answer a margin call both (a) in time and (b) with the necessary funds, the brokerage firm has no choice but to liquidate the position for the account at the next available market level.

In this example, one could theoretically buy 100 10-year Treasury note futures contracts with about $100,000 in a margin account. The portfolio would be very highly leveraged with only $100,000 in capital and $10,000,000 of 10-year Treasury exposure, leading to a duration of approximately 600 years! A mere 15 basis point increase in 10-year Treasury yields would completely wipe out the entire account. The possibility that leveraged derivatives positions lead to large losses is one of the reasons derivatives get a bad rap. It is important when using derivatives to monitor and maintain leverage at the desired level.

The clearinghouse. Futures contracts rely on a centralized clearinghouse. Whenever a long position is opened, someone else opens an equal-sized short position. Rather than the two end users paying each other their gains and losses, they simply pay the clearinghouse, which is responsible for debiting and crediting all member firms' (futures commission merchants, or FCM) accounts. All participants except explicit members of the exchange operate through FCMs, who essentially act as a buffer between individual participants and the centralized clearinghouse.

Counterparty risk. Credit, or counterparty risk, is essentially the risk that a broker or FCM will goes out of business, and that an account or position is greater than the insurance that covers it. Note that in actuality the market-based credit risk is just one day's movement in a position. Because all futures positions are settled up daily, the true exposure is the amount the position made during the trading day. Moreover, most major Wall Street firms that are also FCMs have a clear legal segregation of assets. Creditors of the firm in its other business lines have no recourse to the assets it holds in its FCM line of business. Note that this low credit risk is a strong competitive advantage futures have versus over-the-counter derivatives like swaps (which we address next). A second business risk, often overlooked, could be that the broker decides to exit the futures business. Firms enter and exit lines of business all the time. The risk then is more of an operational risk in that investors may be left without desired exposure during the transition period, as they line up positions with another broker. This is not insignificant, nor should it be overlooked. As with all aspects of derivatives, these details *require* management.

Liquidity and volatility risk. This is the risk undertaken while holding any security or asset. The value of the asset is only worth what someone else is willing to pay, regardless of when an investor wants or needs to liquidate it. While it may sometimes seem that we live in a world of endless liquidity, this is not always the case. For example, today's condo market in Miami, San Diego, and Las Vegas may not have buyers at prices anywhere close to yesterday's market. Another twist is that some futures contracts have daily price limits. It is not unusual to see some agricultural commodities limit up or limit down for consecutive days, where no trade takes place. For example, in 2004, at the height of the mad cow disease fears, the live cattle futures contract was locked limit-down on consecutive days. This obviously creates a very uncomfortable situation if investors are trying to remove their exposure and the market is going against them. The 10-year Treasury futures contract does not have a limit, but that is of no solace if the value gaps 5 to 10 percentage against holders when there is seemingly no bid in sight for their positions.

Summary

The basics of futures entail a complicated system where leverage is managed through a combination of margin accounts and the threat of forced liquidation. Furthermore, there is a large incentive for every FCM and every individual investor to do their own due diligence on the creditworthiness of counterparties, as well as their commitment to the futures business. Finally, the fallacy of constant liquidity is clearly at play. Investors are at the mercy of the marketplace, especially when they need to liquidate contracts in order to free up margin account assets for use elsewhere. These are crucial concepts that anyone entering into derivative agreements must be aware of and manage. They come up time and time again. Most importantly, there is nothing simple about managing them!

SWAPS

Once we clearly understand the futures market, swaps are simple. With swaps, there is no centralized clearinghouse and each contract is an individual contract between two counterparties. The contract takes the place of the clearing entity and typically spells out, often in agonizing detail, the relationship between two parties in terms of the risks we laid out earlier—margin flow, forced liquidation, and credit events. Because of the complexity involved in the contract, counterparties find it worthwhile to negotiate International Swap Dealers Association (ISDA) Master Agreements, designed to act as the governing document for all swaps executed between them.

Note a key difference between swaps and futures: while we mark swaps to market every day, cash flows are exchanged typically only once every one to six months on prenegotiated swap reset dates. This may be attractive from an operational standpoint if managed in-house, since there are fewer cash flows to deal with. However, it does create increased counterparty risk as the market value of swap positions fluctuates both positively and negatively as the market moves. Because of this, counterparties typically negotiate terms for collateral transfers in the ISDA Master in order to minimize counterparty credit risk, making swaps look more like futures in terms of frequency of cash flow.

Total Return Swap (TRS)

A total return swap (TRS), or total rate of return swap, is a contract whereby a broker/dealer agrees to pay a client the total rate of return on an asset or index during a period, while receiving a financing rate of LIBOR plus or minus some spread.

In Figure 7.1, if the TRS were on the Russell 3000 index, the client would receive the same return as if he held the stock index in exchange for paying a financing rate. This is a clear example in which the client is just renting the broker/dealer's balance sheet. The financing rate will fluctuate based upon the market's desire to be short the Russell 3000, the cost of funding the hedge position, and the desire of institutions to rent out their balance sheets.

It is very important to understand that *banks' and brokers' balance sheets can both expand and contract.* The supply of capital available to affect beta strategies can be reduced or even shut off! If an investor is asking a

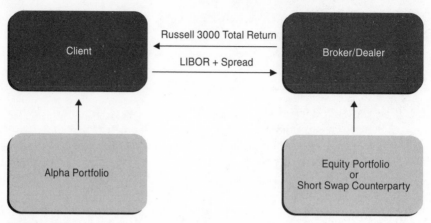

FIGURE 7.1   How Does a Long Equity Swap Position Work?
Source: PIMCO.

bank to expand its balance sheet by warehousing the investor's risk position on it, the bank will charge the marginal cost associated with that balance sheet expansion. Thus the cost of renting out balance sheets can go up. Moreover, during periods of stress, when banks are forced to reduce their balance sheets dramatically, there may be no financing rate high enough to entice the bank to continue to offer its balance sheet for rent. It's really no different than renting an apartment, where the renter stays in the apartment at the pleasure of the landlord. By choosing to rent instead of own a home, the renter gives up any claims on future rights (not to mention costs) to occupy the abode beyond the lease. Anyone who has ever been forced to move (living in a world absent renters' rights) can attest that the unwanted transition is typically very costly in terms of time, money, and perhaps most importantly, disruption.

Interest Rate Swaps

One area of potential confusion in the swaps market lies in the difference between an interest rate swap and a total rate of return swap.

An interest rate swap (IRS) is in many ways much simpler to understand than a total return swap. Any textbook will tell you that an interest rate swap is an agreement between party A and party B, where (as an example) party A agrees to pay party B a fixed interest rate for, let's say, five years, and in return, party A will receive LIBOR (see Figure 7.2).

Payments will be made twice a year, similar to the coupon on a bond. In fact, the similarities to owning a bond go well beyond the payment

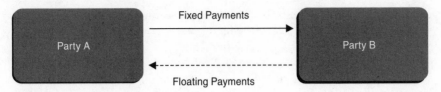

FIGURE 7.2 Interest Rate Swap Diagram
Source: PIMCO.

mechanisms. If you deconstruct a five-year IRS, you will find that the economics of party B's position are almost identical to a situation where party B bought a five-year bond from party A and simultaneously agreed to finance the purchase for the entire period. Rather than rolling over repurchase agreements (discussed next) daily or monthly, party B has decided to lock in a floating-rate financing arrangement for the entire life of the bond. In this way, we can see that a five-year IRS has many of the same characteristics as owning a five-year bond. It has a coupon, duration, market value, and so forth. Moreover, it has the benefit of being entirely customizable in terms of its start and end date, and it is fungible among various counterparties. And, with the help of an ISDA Master Agreement, investors can minimize credit or counterparty risk via mutual collateral agreements. Now you can begin to see why the market for generic IRS derivatives has exploded the way it has over the past 15 years (see Figure 7.3).

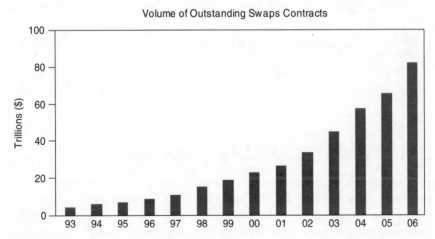

FIGURE 7.3 Growth of Swap Market
Data source: The Options Clearing Corporation (OCC) as of December 31, 2006.

Repurchase agreements (repos) are short-term financing transactions whereby the owner of a security sells the security to a third party and, at the same time, agrees to repurchase the security at a later date. A financing cost is incurred by the original owner of the security and earned by the third party during the holding period, while any coupon, dividend, or principal repayments associated with the security on repo accrue to the original owner.

Both interest rate swaps and total return swaps can be helpful tools (in addition to futures and cash-plus-repo transactions) in the quest to gain market exposure while employing limited amounts of capital. Total return swaps are customizable with respect to their reference index, reset frequency, payment frequency, and so forth, which is an advantage. However, this customization comes at a sizeable cost. Ideally, the marketplace for risk transfer includes many buyers and many sellers. In this way we reduce the cost of transferring risk and increase the likelihood we will be able to maintain this risk in the future. However, aside from the S&P 500, *very few indexes* truly have a well-developed *two-way* market for total return swaps.

It should be noted here that having a liquid TRS market in an index is often a reflection of how easy it is to replicate that index using futures (since that is often what the counterparty will do). This is not to say you cannot induce or coerce a counterparty to enter into a swap on an index that is more difficult to replicate, like the Lehman Long Government Credit Index. However, it can be very costly. The cost will be up front in terms of a higher balance sheet rental fee and there will be a wider bid-ask spread to exit or adjust exposure. The cost will also fluctuate with each renegotiation, creating further uncertainty over any fragile plan structure.

Finally, there is an implicit cost of disruption should the counterparty ever decide to exit this line of business. At that time, there is no guarantee of finding another counterparty at a reasonable or even economically feasible level. For all these reasons, TRS may present some material challenges for ongoing maintenance of market exposure in alpha-beta separation strategies. As such, investors should, of course, recognize and plan around the unavoidable risks that have been detailed here.

BETA MANAGEMENT: BASIS RISK

Having covered futures and swaps—the basic tools of beta management—we now turn to the issue of skill. So where is the skill? How much skill does it take to buy and sell futures or swaps? Why shouldn't beta management be free? This is reminiscent of a decision to join some friends parachuting for the first time a few years ago. When we got to the site we learned that there would be a four-hour school or tutorial required prior to the big jump. The obvious question at the time was, "How could it possibly take four hours to learn how to jump out of an airplane?" The obvious answer was that we didn't spend four hours learning how to jump, but rather four hours learning what to do if something goes wrong. Because, rest assured, if you keep jumping out of airplanes long enough, something will eventually go wrong!

There are many professions, products, and services that are similar in nature to learning how to jump out of an airplane, such as that of a security guard or an airline pilot. Household fire alarms and flashlights as well as AAA motor club and life insurance also provide a suitable analogy. A security guard is not paid based on his ability to do the crossword puzzle; security guards are paid for their ability to react. And there are clearly quality differences among all of these examples and many more that can be presented.

The management of derivatives-based market exposure is similar. Skill comes into play, not just in the ability to execute an order, but in the daily management of the position and process and the ability to react during periods of stress. In this section we give examples of how skillful beta management can play a meaningful role when strategies face market risk and operational risk, and how it can minimize operational and legal costs.

The difference between a derivative price and its cash market equivalent is called *basis*. The volatility of the basis exists in virtually every derivative contract and is typically referred to as *basis risk*. Much like jumping out of an airplane, investors can choose to either manage the basis risk or take their chances.

For example, take the S&P 500 futures contract, one of the longest-standing, most liquid, and most straightforward ways to finance broad equity exposure. It might surprise investors that there can be considerable basis risk between S&P 500 futures and the underlying cash stock market. First of all, a major component of the basis is the aggregate dividend rate of the stocks. More precisely, it is the future dividend rate. This is the size of the dividend that would have been earned as of the futures contract maturity date, had you held stocks instead of futures. Typically, the dividend rate is fairly stable but it can change very quickly, as we show shortly in an example. Companies can start competitively increasing their dividends very rapidly. Similarly, turnover in the makeup of the S&P 500 (stocks leave and enter the index every month) can further exacerbate the difference between what the dividend was last quarter and what it will be next quarter. While it may be difficult to come up with dramatically better estimates of future dividends than the rest of the market, recognizing the uncertainty and managing the risk can be crucial to rolling from one calendar to the next at the most attractive levels (i.e., maintaining the lowest borrowing or repo rate on the position).

Second, the repo rate for the S&P 500 is not stable, even when discounting dividend uncertainty. Repo rates fluctuate based on supply and demand for synthetic futures positions as well as supply and demand for the underlying collateral, in this case a basket of stocks. As in most markets, there are times when the supply and demand curves shift and do not intersect—in other words, the market fails to clear. The most recent occurrence of this was during the lead-up to Y2K. Heightened uncertainty surrounding the bank settlement system and adequate computerized record keeping meant that there was a dramatic reduction in the pool of capital available for short-term collateralized loans. The implied repo (financing) rate for the S&P 500 futures contract reached levels of LIBOR plus 100 basis points and greater, in order to move from December 1999 to March 2000 contracts. Once again, a skilled manager who understands and follows the dynamics in the underlying cash and collateral markets can respond more quickly to these events than a manager who blindly takes whatever the market is offering.

Finally, we would say that a skilled manager can tell the difference between a temporary market dislocation that causes a sudden drop or spike in repo rates, and an event or change that is expected to be more permanent. In this case, the risk is that the S&P 500 ceases to be the benchmark that it once was. Either a generalized shift toward a different index or the sudden demise or takeover of Standard and Poor's could result in a dramatic and permanent change in the supply and demand for synthetic exposure to the S&P 500 stock index. Managing this process requires recognition of what is going on and a recommendation to the client on how to best react among the vast laundry list of possible risk transfers that can make a dramatic difference in both liquidity and the total cost of continuing to run an obsolete strategy.

EXAMPLES OF PROACTIVE BETA MANAGEMENT

In the following examples, we expand on some that we have already mentioned and also offer new ones that illustrate the market intelligence and skill that is often needed to optimally manage derivatives-based beta exposure. We use examples from the equities market, which has long been a popular beta source in portable alpha strategies, followed by some examples from commodities, an increasingly popular beta source.

Equities

Despite the fact that equity derivatives have been used in various portable alpha applications for at least two decades, derivatives-based equity beta management is far from simple. Rather, as previously noted there are important complexities and other considerations that must be carefully weighed by investors and beta management providers. Here we give a few examples of intelligent derivatives based equity index beta management.

Dividend Risk   As mentioned earlier, purchasing and rolling S&P 500 futures involves accurately predicting expected dividends in order to correctly value the basis between futures and cash. Two examples illustrate the importance of doing this:

1. The Jobs and Growth Tax Relief Reconciliation Act of 2003. This law decreed that dividends would be taxed as capital gains rather than income as they had been in the past. Not surprisingly, investor demand for high-dividend stocks increased and there was a corresponding and notable increase in the trend rate of S&P 500 dividend payouts. However, Wall Street estimates consistently lagged actual dividend payouts for the first few quarters after the tax law change. Investors who calculated S&P 500 futures fair value using Wall Street estimates for expected dividends consistently paid too much for their futures as a result. At the same time, the TRS market was still trading in line with the futures market, although there is no dividend uncertainty associated with total return swaps. Given this situation, an alert beta manager would have compared the relative cost of futures versus swaps and decided whether to move exposure from futures, which were mispricing expected dividends, to TRS, which have no dividend risk.
2. In July 2004, Microsoft announced a one-time dividend of $3.00 per share and increased its regular dividend. Markets initially thought this one-time dividend would be treated as a regular dividend, which would imply that December 2004 S&P 500 futures were too rich by almost $2.00. Almost $2 billion of the December 2004 S&P contract traded in the overnight session at extremely cheap/incorrect levels, until the market got clarity about how S&P would treat the dividend (as a one-time special dividend, meaning that the index price adjusted, but the relative valuation of cash versus futures basis didn't change). Realizing that the market was mispricing the dividends would have allowed an alert indexer to purchase (roll) futures at a significant discount to fair value.

Financing Rate Risk   The best example of financing rate risk (often commonly referred to as repo risk) is the Y2K liquidity crunch during the December 1999–March 2000 futures roll to which we referred earlier. The implied financing or repo rate got to LIBOR plus 100 basis points versus a previous average of LIBOR plus 10 basis points. The alert beta manager would have had to make a decision as to whether to maintain equity exposure via the futures market by rolling the futures positions. For example, unless one were confident that the alpha strategy would beat cash rates by over 100 basis points, it might have made sense to purchase and hold a basket of S&P 500 stocks instead of maintaining the futures position until equilibrium returned to the futures market. A purchase of physical securities requires enough cash to cover the entire beta exposure, and would require action from the investor if alpha and beta portfolios were not being managed in a coordinated fashion.

Rebalancing Risk Indexes rebalance as companies get added and deleted, and floats of companies in the index increase and decrease based on share issuance and buybacks. Simple replication via the purchase of a cash basket means that managers have to stay on top of this, and decide on proactive trading. The Russell family of indexes is particularly closely watched in this regard since the rebalance date and rebalance rules are very transparent. Still, historical studies show such things as outperformance of names entering the index versus those leaving. An alert indexer has to make the decision whether to be a price taker and rebalance at whatever price the market dictates, or to be proactive and move ahead of the market.

Commodities

Commodities are an increasingly popular beta that is replicated though the use of derivatives in a portable alpha context. Key considerations specific to commodity derivatives are presented as follows together with a few examples of intelligent derivatives based commodity index beta management.

Rebalancing Similar to the issues described with equity derivatives, the major commodity indexes (SP-GSCI or DJ-AIG) reset the weights allocated to different commodities that make up the index in a fairly predictable way every January. As a beta manager of a commodity index portfolio, one could be a price taker and dutifully rebalance the portfolio on the days specified at whatever price the market demanded. As is often the case, other market participants, anticipating this rebalancing, could push up the prices of the commodities whose weights were expected to increase or sell those that were decreasing, thus forcing the purely passive investor to transact at noneconomic prices. Alternatively, the active beta manager will have a model that predicts the turnover, and make a decision regarding the most opportune time to rebalance.

Limit Moves Several commodities, notably agricultural products, have pre-specified price or percentage bands in which the futures can trade on a given day, as in the cattle example discussed earlier. Obtaining or removing beta exposure on a day where one or more commodities have stopped trading due to limit moves requires active decision making. For example, an investor could decide to obtain exposure in the OTC or swap market for those commodities, using indications from where the options market is trading, as well as overseas listed markets in similar commodities, to calculate a fair value price for the commodities that are not trading any more due to limit moves. Alternatively, one could decide to trade at the first nonlimit markets in the subsequent days.

Delisting of Commodity Contract　In January 2007 the NYMEX delisted the original gasoline contract (HU), which required delivery of reformulated gasoline containing the carcinogen MTBE. This was replaced by a new contract (XB) that required delivery of gasoline not containing MTBE and was ready for blending with ethanol. These two contracts traded side by side throughout 2006, with liquidity and open interest transitioning from the old (HU) contract to the new (XB) contract. Both major commodity indexes (SP-GSCI and DJ-AIG) made changes in anticipation of the upcoming demise and dwindling liquidity in the HU contract. The Dow Jones AIG replaced HU with a similar quantity of XB, and the SP-GSCI reduced the weight of gasoline, with XB replacing HU for the reduced weights. Once again, the alert indexer would have to replicate these changes in a cost-effective manner at a minimum, and hopefully determine the price at which to execute rather than having the market dictate it to him.

The overriding message we have tried to convey in these examples of market price risk is that beta management is simple only if one is content to be a price taker and a believer of the hypothesis that the market is always perfectly efficient and perfectly priced. However, a skillful beta manager will seek to save significant amounts of money by reacting to market developments in a timely fashion and finding the cheapest instruments to implement the beta exposure.

Even in a market as large and generally efficient as the S&P 500 futures market, decisions regarding the timing of the futures contract roll can lead to a lower or higher financing cost relative to other market participants. Figure 7.4 shows the incremental financing cost paid, relative to the average, to roll S&P 500 futures exposure dating back to the first quarter of 1998. The incremental cost paid or saved (greater or less than the average) is broken down into quartiles, with the grey bar representing the richest (highest cost paid) quartile. Interestingly, the range of financing costs incurred in the S&P 500 futures market appears to be commonly at least 20 basis points—a number that may be much greater in the case of derivatives markets with lower liquidity. As a result, there may be a payoff in the form of cost savings

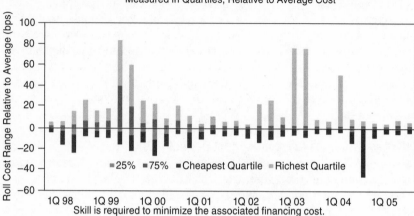

Historical S&P 500 Futures Calendar Roll Costs Paid by Market Participants, Measured in Quartiles, Relative to Average Cost

Skill is required to minimize the associated financing cost.

Skill and resources are also important for cash flow management, maintaining appropriate market exposure, and operational risk control.

FIGURE 7.4 The Cost of Maintaining Desired Beta Using Derivatives Varies across Market Participants
Source: Merrill Lynch.

for a market participant willing to invest the time and effort to monitor and analyze the futures roll on an ongoing basis.

BETA MANAGEMENT: OPERATIONAL RISK

It is naïve to think that adding derivatives and leverage, sometimes a great deal of both, to an investment plan comes without additional risks. In addition to the obvious investment risk, one area where the increased risk has a very real and tangible cost comes in the form of operational risk: namely credit, collateral, and coordination.

Credit risk goes hand in hand with derivatives-based beta management. It can and should be minimized, but it cannot be removed entirely. At the end of the day, a counterparty has promised economic gains and losses associated with a given market exposure, and until the wire transfers clear, there is credit risk. Even a futures market with FCMs and centralized clearinghouses have a nonzero amount of credit risk. A prudent derivatives manager creates a system of dynamic credit management whereby a pool of approved counterparties is reviewed continuously. Credit quality is not a fixed variable and can fluctuate over time, and therefore counterparty management should likewise take into account changes in credit quality. Should the entire pool of counterparties experience declining credit quality, a quality derivatives manager should stand prepared to demand extra collateral up front, shift to futures, or enter into off-market transactions in order to further minimize counterparty risk.

Collateral management is the primary tool used to minimize credit risk in OTC swaps. Margin calls or calls for collateral are a form of marking the position to market and ensuring that cash or cash equivalents are set aside in order to make good on contractual promises. Collateral management is not a passive exercise. Highly volatile markets can require daily collateral flows back and forth between counterparties. Trending markets can require very large amounts of cash be raised, converted into collateral form and delivered to counterparties, often within a few hours. Even in the staid world of fixed income, these amounts can be quite large. We've seen multiple occurrences over the past 20 years where Treasury futures can drop by more than 8 to 10 percent in less than a month. Applying that kind of move to an overlay portfolio with 25 years duration (as is increasingly common in the interest rate swap-based liability-driven investing strategies as outlined in Chapter 10), investors might need to come up with roughly 25 percent of the notional amount of the plan in short order—enough to disrupt the asset allocation of even the most sophisticated plans, typically at the most inopportune time.

So what do skillful beta managers do? To invoke the skydiving metaphor, they need to plan on the parachute not working properly by requiring adequate liquid collateral on hand in case the client cannot respond quickly enough, to avoid being stopped out of the position at the worst time. A skillful beta manager will likewise conduct periodic credit fire drills that make sure everything is in place and the machinery is well oiled in case a counterparty unexpectedly gets into trouble. As in any crisis management situation, it is typically actions in the first few minutes or hours that are critical to avoiding negative outcomes.

RECOMMENDATIONS

We've focused on two of the most obvious risks associated with derivatives-based beta management: market risk and operational/collateral management risk. So what's an investor to do? As with any risk, investors have basically three options: Choose to ignore it, manage it internally, or outsource it to an external manager. Choosing to ignore the risk is a legitimate option, but self-managed or externally managed insurance is preferable to being ignorant of the risk. Let's see how these options apply to the risks we have covered so far.

1. *Ignore.* Ignoring the risks is not as absurd as it sounds at first blush. If, for example, a defined benefit pension plan is small relative to the overall company size, it may be generally well funded and might be covered by an understanding with the firm's management structure that insures against major risks. This is a plausible arrangement but, needless to say, very few plans or investors fit this mold and even fewer are reading a book like this.
2. *Manage the risk internally.* The more complicated a plan becomes, the more important the coordination between all the moving parts. At some point, complexity and coordination rise to a level where it is advantageous to manage the risk internally. Once a firm decides that the alpha-beta separation may be permanently managed internally, or via multiple external managers providing separate alpha and beta components, it may be prudent to build the capabilities in-house. This structure requires an investment in people and infrastructure. A common error is to build and maintain adequate infrastructure to handle three- or four-standard-deviation events (recall that three-standard-deviation events happen every year, while four-standard-deviation events happen every 40 years).The costs related to this option can often begin to compare in scale with the decision to buy insurance, which leads most firms to seriously consider outsourcing as a superior solution.
3. *Outsource.* Firms outsource tasks because they can get higher-quality service and lower prices. Certain tasks lend themselves to outsourcing. It is rare that a company finds it cost productive to run its own fire department, for example, with the possible exception of Disney World. The vast majority of firms will find it in their best interest to hire expertise in managing certain risks for them. The pricing differential will likely reflect the difference in quality between managing the risks we have been discussing or simply acting as an agent in helping a plan acquire exposure.

If outsourcing is deemed the best situation for a given investor, a quality derivatives-based beta manager will provide the following services:

- *Basis risk.* The hired manager analyzes, monitors, and minimizes basis risk between the derivatives positions and the underlying exposure. It attempts to minimize the cost of exposure through traditional money management tools, managing the maturity or duration of exposure, utilizing various ways of gaining exposure, and of course trying to time the market for financing positions where appropriate.

- *Credit risk.* The outside firm will manage counterparty risk, monitor credit quality, dynamically add and remove credits from the assignment, and work to diversify credit risk. In many indexes, this will include working with additional counterparties in order to improve liquidity in the appropriate market.

- *Collateral management.* The hired manager will minimize the absolute value of credit risk through efficient collateral management policies and processes.

- *Coordination.* The firm will minimize the risk of forced liquidation through adequate liquidity planning. This includes minimum initial collateral or cash accounts used to manage the derivatives depending on the volatility of the underlying instruments. Obviously, gaining exposure to a low volatility index such as the Merrill 1–3 Year Treasury Index should require far less up-front cash than the S&P 500 index or a portfolio of 30-year swaps. Moreover, the form of the collateral matters. If the collateral itself is volatile as in a long-duration portfolio, the manager should require more cash than if the collateral were in Treasury bills. Finally, in order to insure against truly disastrous scenarios, managers should have access to additional funds on a same-day basis in order to avoid forced liquidations during periods of dramatically reduced volatility.

CONCLUSION

If market exposure were truly a free good—in other words, if gaining beta market exposure using derivatives offered no possibility of value-added— then there would be no reason for investors to outsource. Plans could simply, easily, manage the beta themselves.

Of course, this is not the case. The mere desire for plans to hire managers to handle beta for them tells us that there is a nonzero cost associated with the service. As we have seen, even the most rudimentary beta management tools require a significant investment in education alone. Maintaining dedicated beta management staff, whose sole purpose is to maintain and improve upon existing liquidity conditions, minimize the cost of rolling exposure forward, all while minimizing the hidden costs associated with credit disruption risks, requires significant skill and an investment. If investors are simply looking for a beta manager that is willing to take them up in a plane and push them out the open door, they will no doubt find this at a substantial discount to the best-of-breed beta managers. At the end of the day, beta management is not that different from alpha management. Both require a willingness and expertise in assuming and managing risk. You get what you pay for.

Portable alpha is a powerful strategy for investors and plan sponsors to contemplate, but it is not for everyone. It goes without saying that any strategy entailing the use of leverage and derivatives should be thoroughly understood at all levels of the investment organization and carefully contemplated in the investment policy. The risks to the strategy should be fully disclosed, and the plan sponsor should work with trusted advisers to minimize those risks. If necessary, the scale and scope of an overlay strategy should be modified such that any temporary dislocations in the strategy don't send the entire plan into chaos for a period.

Finally, the alpha-beta strategy should entail some concept of flexibility. The costs of leverage clearly fluctuate with short-term interest rates. When short rates are higher, you are pay a higher financing rate and renting a third-party balance sheet is more expensive. Plans should look at alpha-beta separation dynamically as a function of cost, and models should reflect this. Essentially, the separation of alpha and beta allows a plan to borrow money in order to invest in alternative risk factors and strategies designed to generate alpha and ideally to diversify risk. It works out great when the borrowing rate is 5 percent and there is a broad range of investment strategies available that are expected to return 10 percent. However, the plan must be aware of any deterioration in the strategy should conditions change.

In other words, *a plan that uses leverage needs to manage the leverage* by increasing it when terms and conditions are favorable and scaling back when conditions don't look so good. Bottom line: Leverage needs to become part of the asset allocation and investment policy decision, and should not be taken lightly. This is true in general and most certainly is true in the context of portable alpha strategies.

CHAPTER 8

Portable Alpha Implementation

Sabrina Callin

Given the extraordinary increase in interest in portable alpha strategies, it's not surprising that the number of providers launching portable alpha products and related implementation services has grown dramatically in recent years. A greater number of options is generally valuable, and this holds true for investors interested in accessing the potential benefits of the portable alpha investment application. However, given the inherent complexity of portable alpha implementation, navigating the intricacies of different approaches can be intimidating, if not outright daunting, to investors who must dissect the operational risks and costs in addition to the investment risks of different strategies. Of course the detail behind different portable alpha implementation approaches varies from provider to provider and from investor to investor. Nonetheless, in analyzing the different ways that investors and practitioners are combining distinct alpha sources with various beta market exposures, there appear to be four basic elements associated with the implementation of most programs, as depicted in Figure 8.1:

1. The alpha strategy investment.
2. The derivatives-based market (beta) exposure.
3. Liquidity for margin or collateral calls.
4. Consolidated risk management, risk monitoring, and reporting.

In addition, most of the approaches offered by providers and employed by investors fall into one of three categories: fully integrated, completely segregated, and something in between that we call *semibundled* for purposes of our analysis. Each approach has advantages and disadvantages, and it is essential that investors understand the complexities, costs, risks, and risk controls associated with a given approach before investing. The

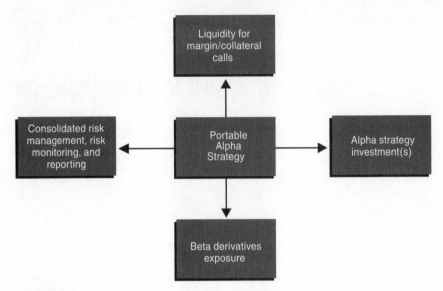

FIGURE 8.1 Most Portable Alpha Approaches Involve Four Basic Elements
Source: PIMCO.

cost component may be particularly relevant when investors consider the trade-off between investment risk—which is necessarily tied to gross-of-fee return—and expected after-fee return.

THE ALPHA STRATEGY

We have already spent a considerable amount of time focused on the alpha strategy in the preceding chapters. This is not surprising, since the alpha strategy (or set of strategies) is the headline component of most portable alpha programs. More fundamentally, the vast majority—and in many cases all—of the investor's capital that is allocated to a given portable alpha strategy is invested in the alpha strategy. Therefore the return on this capital is likely the key determinant of whether a portable alpha strategy is successful in generating incremental return for the investor. Likewise, risks and other characteristics associated with the alpha strategy are relevant—together with the derivatives-based market exposure or beta component—for purposes of evaluating a prospective portable alpha investment relative to other options and classifying the portable alpha strategy within an asset allocation and risk budgeting context, as already described in previous chapters.

THE DERIVATIVES-BASED MARKET EXPOSURE (BETA)

Despite the fact that people often downplay the relevance of the beta component of portable alpha strategies, the derivatives-based market exposure serves as the fundamental building block to any portable alpha approach. Derivatives provide investors with the ability to obtain market exposure without a capital commitment, thereby enabling investors to allocate all or the majority of their capital to the alpha strategy. Although the derivatives component is largely if not entirely unfunded, the associated market exposure is just as real and sometimes more important than the alpha strategy in terms of the associated risk and return. It follows that effective derivatives management is an essential part of a successful portable alpha program.

As a starting point, the derivatives instruments to gain the desired market exposure must be selected. This typically involves a comparison of the relative financing and implementation costs of futures and swaps, which change over time and expire regularly. In addition, the notional market exposure must be constantly monitored and adjusted to make sure it is appropriately sized and collateral for the derivative-based market exposure must be maintained.

The bottom line: Managing and maintaining derivatives-based market exposure is not a simple task, as reviewed in Chapter 7, and introduces an important element of complexity to portable alpha implementation that must be addressed by investors and/or their investment management service providers.

LIQUIDITY FOR MARGIN OR COLLATERAL CALLS

Liquidity for margin or collateral calls associated with derivatives-based beta market exposure is a critically important element of portable alpha implementation, and also a relatively unique element compared to traditional investment strategies. This is not to say that liquidity isn't always a relevant investment consideration, but liquidity requirements are generally a function of the *investor's* needs, whereas derivatives require liquidity for the *investment's* needs. Furthermore, if liquidity is not available when it is required, the result will likely be a quick liquidation of the desired market exposure altogether. This can be quite inconvenient or even outright disastrous if the (liquidated) market exposure is a key component of an investor's carefully designed asset allocation, or when the market exposure is removed just before a market rally. Therefore, investors and providers must carefully monitor the liquidity element of a portable alpha strategy.

Certain types of alpha strategies have a high degree of inherent liquidity. In these cases, liquidity management may be a relatively straightforward process involving the establishment and maintenance of an appropriate minimum level of highly liquid securities that can be sold for same-day or next-day settlement to meet margin or collateral calls. Other types of alpha strategies have limited liquidity. In some cases cash flows are explicitly restricted to month-end or quarter-end periods and often require significant advance notice. It may also be the case that the investment manager reserves the right to restrict liquidity altogether (so clients cannot access their funds) for extended periods of time. In other cases, the alpha strategy may have limited liquidity due to the nature of the underlying investments. Regardless, if the alpha strategy is not inherently liquid—or in some cases even if it is liquid but it is managed separately from the beta market exposure—the investor will be required to accommodate the ongoing liquidity needs of the portable alpha program through some type of separate arrangement.

In most cases where the investor does not have ready access to the capital invested in the alpha strategy, some portion of the capital allocated to the portable alpha program must be set aside as an immediate source of liquidity to collateralize the derivatives-based market exposure. Managers specializing in the derivatives-based market exposure element of portable alpha strategies (often called *overlay managers*) generally require investors to provide them with an initial allocation of capital and to maintain a stipulated minimum level of capital to support the potential margin and collateral cash flow requirements. Investors who manage the derivatives themselves must establish similar liquidity provisions. The minimum amount of liquid capital necessary is a function of the volatility and downside risk potential of the beta market, the investor's ability to borrow additional capital from other sources with relatively short notice, the cash flow terms of the derivatives contracts, and the risk management practices and policies of the manager and investor.

For an equity futures-based portable alpha strategy as an example, an investor might determine that an appropriate amount of immediately available liquidity is approximately 20 percent of the value of the notional derivatives exposure, based on an analysis of historical volatility and short-term declines in the equity market. In the case of a 20 percent market decline (as experienced on October 19, 1987, in the S&P 500), a margin call of about 20 percent would be required the following day and potentially the same day, in order to maintain the futures exposure. In the event that the alpha strategy does not provide this type of liquidity, and/or the beta derivatives (overlay) manager does not have immediate access to the alpha strategy for purposes of meeting margin calls, appropriate liquidity provisions must be made.

Liquidity requirements associated with portable alpha strategies where the beta and the alpha strategy are managed by different managers or the alpha strategy is not inherently liquid do not come without a cost.

The opportunity cost of setting aside 20 percent of the capital allocated to the portable alpha strategy and holding it in cash can be calculated as 20 percent times the difference between the expected return on the alpha strategy and the return on cash (typically slightly less than LIBOR). As illustrated in Table 8.1, if the expected return on the alpha strategy is 5 percent over LIBOR and the cash return equals LIBOR, the drag on the total return of the portable alpha strategy will be equal to 1 percent relative to a portable alpha strategy that does not require a separate liquidity provision, all else equal. This is a fairly significant opportunity cost by most any measure.

Even if a portable alpha strategy includes adequate cash reserves to meet worst-case-scenario margin or collateral calls over short periods of time, there still should be a contingency plan for sourcing additional funds

TABLE 8.1 Liquidity Requirements to Maintain Beta Exposure May Reduce Returns

	Additional Liquidity Provision Not Required	Additional Liquidity Provision Required
Desired beta market return	8 percent	8 percent
Derivatives financing cost (LIBOR)	−5 percent	−5 percent
Hypothetical alpha strategy return contribution	10 percent (100 percent × 10 percent)	8 percent (80 percent × 10 percent)
Cash collateral return	N/A	1 percent (20 percent × 5 percent)
Total return	13 percent	12 percent

Source: PIMCO, hypothetical example for illustrative purposes only.
Hypothetical mathematical example assumes:
- Desired market beta return: 8 percent.
- Derivatives financing cost: 5 percent.
- Alpha strategy return: 10 percent.
- Derivative-based beta overlay manager collateral requirement = 20 percent of notional exposure.
- Overlay manager provides LIBOR return on cash collateral.

if needed. In portable alpha strategies involving illiquid alpha strategies, this backup contingency may be an externally sourced line of credit with an explicit maintenance cost in addition to the financing cost if it is actually tapped.

During the equity market crash of October 1987 as an example, the S&P 500 fell over 30 percent in a five-day period. As a result, an investor who retained 20 percent of the capital allocated to a portable alpha strategy in cash to meet margin calls would have used all of the ready liquidity within a matter of days. If the remainder of the capital allocated to the portable alpha strategy was invested in an illiquid alpha strategy, the investor would have had to borrow additional funds to meet margin calls thereby avoiding liquidation of the equity derivatives positions.

While October 1987 may be an atypical example, over the course of the 19 years for which daily S&P 500 index returns are available, there have been 152 10-day periods and 303 20-day periods where the S&P 500 declined by over 5 percent to levels sometimes exceeding a decline of 15 percent. This is illustrated in Figure 8.2. Therefore, investors should plan accordingly when

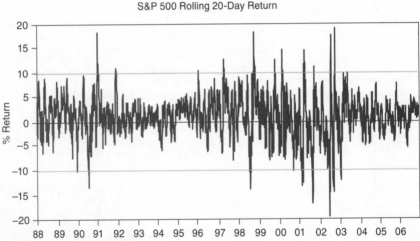

- Worst-ever five-day S&P 500 market decline: over 30% in week leading up to and including "Black Monday" (October 19, 1987).

- Over past 18 years (December 31, 1987 to December 31, 2006):
  - 152 10-day periods where the S&P 500 declined 5–15%+
  - 303 20-day periods where the S&P 500 declined 5–15%+

FIGURE 8.2   Adequate Liquidity in Collateral Portfolio May Be Critical
Source: Standard & Poor's.

it comes to maintaining an appropriate amount of readily available liquidity for equity and other types of derivatives-based beta market exposure in a portable alpha context.

An alternative for many organizations or investors to establishing an external line of credit may be to explicitly or implicitly establish an internal line of credit. With larger institutional investors this credit line can be extended by a parent company at relatively attractive rates. In other cases an investor may literally construct his own line of credit. An example of the latter case would be a an investor who plans to borrow funds internally from a different, more liquid, investment pool as needed to provide liquidity to the portable alpha program—for example, a short- or medium-term bond portfolio.

In the case of internally established lines of credit, the investor or fiduciary may want to consider both disclosing and accounting for this effective borrowing arrangement as part of the overall investment policy. To illustrate the relevance of this point, consider a circumstance in which a significant decline in the equity market causes an investor to make a series of material withdrawals from his bond portfolio to meet margin calls associated with unfunded equity derivatives positions. The result is a decrease in allocation to bonds relative to the stipulated asset allocation or policy portfolio level at what may be the worst possible time (since bonds often benefit from both a flight to quality and a decline in interest rates during equity market sell-offs).

Consider an investor in a portable alpha strategy that collateralized equity derivatives with a hedge fund (quarterly liquidity) that was required to provide 8 percent to an S&P 500 swap counterparty following the equity market sell-off in November 2000. Since this investor would not have had access to the capital allocated to the hedge fund for at least another month, the required capital might have been borrowed from the investor's bond portfolio with the idea that it would be replenished one month later. In this case the cost of the loan from the bond portfolio would be equal to the total return on the bond market or actively managed bond strategy over the life of the loan. In December 2000—this cost was close to 2 percent (over 24 percent, annualized!) on the 8 percent borrowed—and the total realized cost to the portable alpha strategy was 2 percent times 8 percent, or 16 basis points. Looking at this another way, the borrowing cost of about 2 percent is equal to the return on capital that the investor would have realized had he not temporarily allocated the capital from the bond strategy to the portable alpha equity strategy during the month of December in order to meet obligations associated with the equity derivatives.

Importantly, as the preceding example illustrates, in cases where potential liquidity needs are intended to be met by internal borrowing arrangements, it may also be appropriate from an accounting standpoint to deduct the forgone return on the borrowed assets from the portable alpha strategy.

In the preceding example, the bond allocation would then likewise be credited with a return to best reflect results from the different investments—the bond portfolio and the portable alpha portfolio.

Note that all three solutions for sourcing liquidity outside of the portable alpha capital allocation are roughly economically equivalent. Whether the borrowing cost is explicitly charged (by an external lender or a parent company) or is incurred as a function of a temporary redeployment of capital, the resulting cost is clearly associated solely with the portable alpha strategy or program and should be accounted for accordingly.

A different type of borrowing arrangement involves customized total return swaps tailored by broker/dealers such that the liquidity element is less of an issue—at a cost. To put this into context, consider that the most common total return swap arrangements—where the investor receives the total return of a beta market index or reference point (see Figure 8.3) in exchange for paying a LIBOR-based financing rate—are structured with the following two objectives from the standpoint of the investor:

1. Minimize counterparty risk.
2. Minimize the financing cost.

Both goals can generally be accomplished by negotiating swap terms that involve cash flows that occur with a reasonable degree of frequency with potential collateral calls in between cash flow dates in the event that the liability on either side (payable or receivable) exceeds a stipulated dollar amount.

The relevant counterparty risk from an investor's standpoint is unpaid receivables, which accrue when the associated beta market appreciates. However, the counterparty may require similar provisions in order to minimize their counterparty risk, and therefore the financing cost charged to the investor.

In contrast to more familiar total return swap contracts, customized swaps and similar borrowing arrangements being sold for portable alpha implementation may also involve a third and fourth objective that may

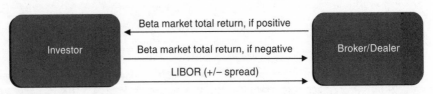

FIGURE 8.3   Swap Cash Flow Diagram
Source: PIMCO.

actually be more important to the buyers of these swaps than the two mentioned previously:

- Scheduling the cash flows to occur only at prespecified dates that coincide with points in time when the investor or provider has the ability to invest or withdraw funds from the alpha strategy.
- Scheduling the cash flows to occur with a prespecified time lag between the time that the amount of the next scheduled cash flow is determined and the time that the cash flow actually takes place.

For example, the terms of cash flows might be set for quarter-end only with the amount of the cash flow determined 30 days prior to quarter-end, in contrast to the terms of normal total return swaps where cash flows occur monthly a few days after month end with the cash flow amount determined based on month-end values. This means that, while the maximum counterparty risk that a broker/dealer bears in a normal total return swap arrangement (with monthly resets) is one month of negative market return, the maximum amount of counterparty risk that a broker/dealer bears with the above described arrangement is four months of negative market movement. In the case of the equity market in particular, the magnitude of the capital at risk has the potential to be quite large over a four-month period relative to a one-month period. Of course, in this example—and with most if not all of these type of arrangements—the swap provider (the broker/dealer) will charge a higher cost to compensate for the potentially greater counterparty risk and term. As such, effectively these types of arrangements are simply a different form of borrowing arrangement with an associated cost that is tied directly to the relative illiquidity of the alpha strategy.

CONSOLIDATED RISK MANAGEMENT, MONITORING, AND REPORTING

The final and possibly most overlooked element of a portable alpha approach is consolidated risk management, monitoring and reporting. It is a requisite element to successful portable alpha implementation when the alpha and beta are managed separately. While the same is also true with integrated portable alpha strategies, in these cases it may not generally thought of as a separate element but rather as a natural component of the manager's investment management and reporting process.

While alpha-beta separation sounds great in theory—and may be great in practice—consolidation of the components is essential for an accurate assessment of the returon as well as risk exposures of the capital invested.

This is not unlike consolidated financial reporting for corporations. Investors who have an equity stake and lenders who have loaned the corporation money need to be able to assess the future growth prospects and financial heath of the organization taken as a whole.

Enron is a perfect case study to illustrate the magnitude of potentially negative ramifications for stock owners and lenders if the financial condition of a corporation as a whole is not adequately assessed and disclosed. The same logic follows for portable alpha strategies. The capital allocated by investors to a portable alpha strategy is exposed to the investment risks of the collective components. It may be possible to separate the management of the alpha strategy and the derivatives-based market exposure, similar to a corporation separating the management of different business units. However, doing so does not relieve investors and fiduciaries of their responsibility to measure, monitor, and report the consolidated risk and return on the capital allocated to the portable alpha strategy.

Consolidated historical performance reporting may be relatively straightforward, although it is important for investors to incorporate all of the associated costs of a portable alpha strategy in order to most accurately report and evaluate the results, as previously discussed. However, consolidated risk measurement and reporting may be much easier said than done if the management of the alpha strategy is physically separated from the derivatives-based market exposure. In order to accurately assess the risk to the investor's capital, the investor or a manager will need to have a reasonably deep understanding of the risk factor exposure in the alpha strategy in addition to the beta exposure, and will likely need to make associated correlation assumptions and employ stress test scenarios.

Another area of consolidated measurement, monitoring, and reporting that may be an important consideration for portable alpha implementation is the ongoing net asset value of the investment for purposes of making appropriate associated alpha strategy risk factor and liquidity adjustments. If the beta derivative positions are held in the same portfolio as the assets associated with the alpha strategy, the market value of the derivatives exposure will be automatically reflected in the market value of the portable alpha investment, assuming a mark-to-market accounting approach is employed. From a risk management perspective, this means that the associated risk factors will be measured based on the market value of the portable alpha strategy. However, if the alpha strategy and the beta derivatives exposure are managed separately, the alpha strategy manager does not have automatic insight regarding any material changes in the value of the derivatives market exposure, and vice versa. The end result, if the investor or a provider does not provide this insight to the individual alpha strategy and beta derivatives managers on an on-going basis, may be leveraged market exposure and/or leveraged alpha strategy exposure, whereby the net asset value of the portable alpha strategy is materially below one or both components.

Consider a situation where an investor allocates $100 million to a portable alpha strategy. The next day, the beta market falls by 15 percent and the alpha strategy simultaneously declines in value by 10 percent, but there are no associated cash flows as may be the case when the beta exposure is obtained using certain types of swaps. In this example, the net asset value of the portable alpha strategy is $75 million ($100 million initial investment minus $10 million decline in the alpha strategy minus $15 million liability associated with the swap position). If there is no consolidated net asset value monitoring and reporting and therefore no attempt on the part of the investor or the managers to make adjustments, the investor will have $90 million of risk factor exposure associated with the alpha strategy plus an additional $85 million of risk factor exposure associated with the beta market, even though the net asset value of the portable alpha investment is only $75 million!—as shown in Table 8.2. Thus, in effect, the portfolio has moved from a position where the total risk factor exposure was 200 percent of the value of the capital ($100 million of alpha strategy risk factor exposure and $100 million of beta market risk factor exposure) to a position where the risk factor

TABLE 8.2 Example of Impact of Derivatives-Based Beta and Alpha Strategy on Portable Alpha Strategy

	Derivatives-Based Beta Exposure	Alpha Strategy	Portable Alpha Strategy Net Asset Value
Day 0	Value = Ø	Value = $100,000,000	Value = $100,000,000
	(Market exposure = $100,000,000)		(plus $100,000,000 of off-balance-sheet derivatives-based market exposure)
Day 1	Beta market falls by 15 percent	Alpha strategy declines in value by 10 percent	Portable alpha strategy net asset value declines by 25 percent
	Value = $15,000,000	Value = $90,000,000	Value = $75,000,000
	(Market exposure = $85,000,000)		(plus $85,000,000 of off-balance-sheet derivatives-based market exposure)

Source: PIMCO; hypothetical example for illustrative purposes only.

exposure is 233 percent (($85 million + $90million)/$75million) due solely to market movement, not as a result of an intentional decision to increase the risk exposure of the capital allocated to the portable alpha strategy.

If the alpha strategy and beta market continue to decline, the potential for a very negative outcome becomes painfully apparent, helping demonstrate the potentially critical importance of consolidated risk measurement and management.

For portable alpha implementation, as previously noted, most approaches fall into one of three categories—integrated, semibundled, or segregated—and the four previously described elements serve as a useful basis for understanding the different approaches, as described in the next section.

INTEGRATED APPROACHES

In a truly integrated portable alpha strategy, one manager manages all four elements in—as the name implies—an integrated fashion, as illustrated in Figure 8.4.

The prerequisite for integrated portable alpha strategy management is an asset manager—or, in the case of in-house management, investment staff— with the skill and willingness to manage all of the different elements. This approach may be the most straightforward from an investor's standpoint, as the responsibility for the success of the portable alpha strategy lies squarely

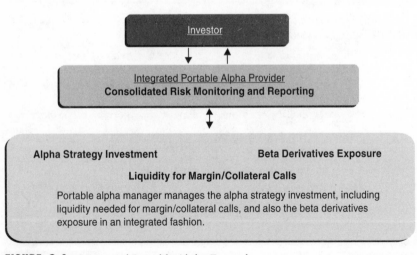

FIGURE 8.4   Integrated Portable Alpha Example
Source: PIMCO.

with one manager, similar to traditional investment mandates. This means that one manager is ultimately responsible for delivering an attractive return profile, after all fees and costs, relative to the most appropriate market reference point (typically the market exposure represented in the investor's asset allocation). This specifically means that the manager is motivated to:

- Deliver an attractive risk-adjusted return on the capital invested in the alpha strategy.
- Invest in market risk factor exposures that are complementary to the market risk exposures captured by the beta derivatives exposure.
- Minimize the financing cost associated with the derivatives exposure.
- Optimally invest and provide liquidity for cash flows.
- Adjust risk factor exposures for changes in the net asset value of the portable alpha investment.
- Maintain appropriate levels of minimum liquidity within the alpha strategy to meet potential margin or collateral calls.

As a result, the manager's incentives are directly aligned with the investor's ultimate goal (an optimal risk-adjusted return on the capital allocated to the portable alpha strategy). In approaches where the different elements are separated, it may be much more difficult to manage all of the components in a cohesive fashion. For this reason, integrated approaches may have the opportunity to employ the tightest operational and investment risk controls among the three types of approaches and are also likely to be the most cost efficient. This is especially true when implicit costs to the investor (time and effort) are considered in addition to the explicit costs incurred and fees paid to providers.

However, the major drawback to the integrated approach is that the alpha strategy and beta derivatives exposure are limited to the offerings of integrated portable alpha providers or to investors who have the in-house skills and resources to effectively manage an integrated portable alpha strategy. Fortunately, given all the interest on the part of investors, an increasing number of investment managers are offering integrated portable alpha strategies.

SEGREGATED APPROACHES

In a segregated approach, all four elements are separately managed and the investor generally plays a key role in terms of the ongoing implementation, as illustrated in Figure 8.5.

In addition to selecting and overseeing the alpha strategy investment and separately selecting and overseeing (or managing in-house) the beta derivatives exposure manager, the investor is responsible for maintaining liquidity

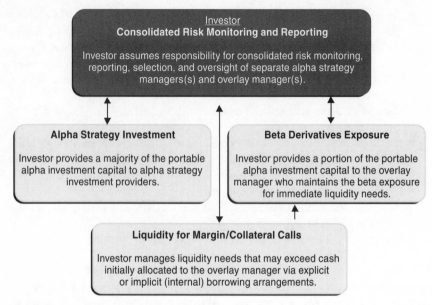

FIGURE 8.5 Segregated Portable Alpha Example
Source: PIMCO.

that cannot be readily offered by the alpha strategy, as well as directing cash flows between the alpha strategy manager and beta derivatives manager as needed. Unless the investor hires a third party to provide consolidated risk monitoring and reporting, the investor is also responsible for monitoring the aggregate risk factor exposures of the portable alpha strategy, directing adjustments as needed, and providing consolidated performance reporting for the portable alpha strategy.

The segregated approach clearly offers investors the greatest flexibility in terms of selecting different alpha sources and pairing them with different beta derivatives exposure, which is a definite benefit. However, there is typically also a significant time commitment and associated cost to the investor, and appropriate risk controls and communication are critical.

SEMIBUNDLED APPROACHES

The third category, the semibundled approach, offers investors the ability to work with one central provider who in turn oversees and/or manages the four elements, as illustrated in Figure 8.6.

The elements are still segregated as a technical matter, although the central provider bundles them for the benefit of the client, in some cases

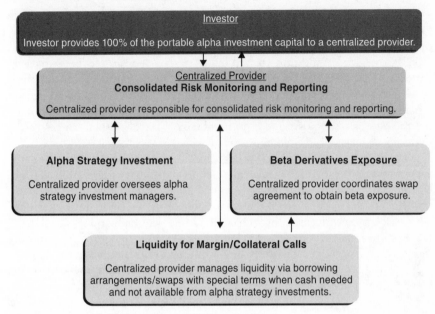

FIGURE 8.6 Semibundled Portable Alpha Example
Source: PIMCO.

actually creating a unique fund that houses the beta derivatives, any other borrowing arrangements (i.e., lines of credit, etc.), and the alpha strategy or strategies. Housing the first three elements in one fund may also allow for more straightforward consolidated risk monitoring and reporting for the portable alpha strategy. Currently, this approach is offered by managers with direct oversight of the alpha strategies, as is the case with a fund of hedge funds provider who offers portable alpha strategies. This type of service may also be offered by providers who do not have a preexisting direct relationship with the alpha strategy managers.

As an example, an investor may invest in a portable alpha strategy with the fund of hedge funds provider that is designed to provide a return of x percent after fees and costs with an incremental volatility of y percent (in addition to the market benchmark risk). The investor allocates his capital to the fund of hedge funds provider, who in turn selects the underlying combination of hedge fund alpha strategies, invests the capital with the hedge fund providers, and separately negotiates swap terms and potential line-of-credit terms to provide for and manage the liquidity element. The fund of hedge funds provider also directs cash flows between the underlying hedge fund providers and the derivatives counterparties, and provides the consolidated risk measurement, monitoring, and reporting to investors.

Alternatively, the investor, not the centralized provider, may select the alpha strategies for inclusion in the fund. In both cases, the centralized provider may actively hedge undesirable beta market exposure from the alpha strategies in addition to making sure that the desired beta market exposure is maintained at appropriate levels. This may be a crucial step from a risk control standpoint when combinations of independent alpha strategies are employed within a portable alpha context, given the potential for the aggregate exposure to a particular risk factor or beta to result in undesirable levels of levered exposure.

The key benefits of this approach may be the potential for access to a greater number of alpha strategies relative to what is available via integrated approaches, and also the centralized oversight that simplifies the implementation process from the standpoint of the investor. However, the costs associated with this approach can be somewhat high and the legal documentation may be complex. This is not to say that the costs are without merit, of course. Given the individual and collective complexity of certain types of alpha strategies and portable alpha implementation, investors may be very happy to pay the higher costs.

COMPARING AND CONTRASTING DIFFERENT APPROACHES

As illustrated in Table 8.3, integrated, semibundled, and segregated portable alpha strategies might be described as sitting on a continuum where integrated strategies are likely to have the lowest costs, the tightest operational and investment risk controls, but also the least flexibility in terms of potential alpha/beta combinations. At the other end of the continuum are segregated

TABLE 8.3 Continuum of Costs, Risks, and Flexibility for Different Portable Alpha Approaches

	Integrated Strategies	Semibundled Strategies	Segregated Strategies
Explicit and implicit costs	Low	Moderate	High
Operational and investment risk	Low	Moderate	High
Flexibility to provide different alphas and betas	Low	Moderate	High

Source: PIMCO.

strategies that are likely to have higher costs (implicit and explicit), higher potential operational risk and unintended investment risk, but also a much greater degree of flexibility with respect to different alpha/beta combinations. The semibundled approach, not surprisingly, sits somewhere in the middle—although investors should be aware that the explicit fees (management fees plus borrowing costs, etc.) of these approaches can also be quite high.

IMPLEMENTATION COSTS

Perhaps the most important benefit to using a framework for reviewing different approaches to portable alpha relates to the ability to navigate what can be a relatively complex set of terms, fees, costs, and borrowing arrangements. The costs paid to different providers may be entirely justified, given the end result and the skill level required. It also may be necessary to incur borrowing costs in order to capture potentially attractive risk premiums associated with less liquid alpha strategies. In addition, there may be requisite legal fees, administrative and other costs that are unavoidable when it comes to more complicated structures to allow for leveraged transactions—all of which may allow investors to access desirable return profiles that would not otherwise be possible.

Ultimately, however, investors need to keep in mind one simple fact: There is a fundamental relationship between investment risk and investment return. This is not to say that all strategies that have the same investment risk will produce the same return, and it is true that diversification can improve return at a given level of risk or reduce risk at a given level of return, but there are limits.

To this point, consider a fund of hedge funds semi-bundled portable alpha example where 100 percent of the capital allocated to the portable alpha strategy is invested in underlying hedge funds with limited liquidity. In this case, it will likely be necessary to incur additional borrowing costs above LIBOR to maintain the beta derivatives exposure. These additional costs may be incurred in a variety of forms as described previously and can vary, but for purposes of this example we assume that LIBOR is 5 percent and the additional borrowing costs above LIBOR are 0.5 percent. We also assume that the fund of hedge funds manager charges a fixed fee of 1 percent and the underlying hedge fund managers are paid a fixed fee of 2 percent plus a performance fee of 20 percent of returns over LIBOR.

As detailed in Table 8.4, the total fees and costs associated with this example portable alpha strategy are equal to 8.5 percent plus the performance fee that is paid to the underlying hedge fund managers. Solving for the

TABLE 8.4 Fund of Hedge Fund Semi-Bundled Portable Alpha Strategy Example

Objective: Net of fee/cost return of 4 percent over equity or bond market index

Costs and Fees
   2.0% Fixed fee paid to underlying hedge fund managers
   1.0% Fixed fee paid to fund of hedge fund manager
   5.0% LIBOR-based swap cost
   0.5% Borrowing/liquidity cost above "normal" LIBOR-based swap cost
   8.5% Fees/costs + hedge fund performance fee

+ 20% performance fee paid to underlying hedge fund managers on returns over
   LIBOR (5% in this example)

Solve for net of fees/cost return of 4 percent whereby X = required return from
   hedge fund managers:
   $X - ((0.2 * (X-5\%)) + 8.5\%) = 4\%$
      $X = 0.2X + 11.5\%$
   $.8X = 11.5\%$
      $X = 14.375\%$ or a return of 9.375% over LIBOR, in this example

required gross of fee/cost return that is required from the underlying hedge fund managers in order for the portable alpha strategy to deliver a return over the beta market return after fees and costs of 4 percent, we find that the hedge fund managers must deliver a return between 9 and 10 percent *above* LIBOR or between 14 and 15 percent, assuming a LIBOR of 5 percent.

Even if the expected volatility of an alpha strategy as put forth by the investment management provider appears to be relatively low, there is no getting around the idea that an expected return of 9 to 10 percent over LIBOR most likely involves some material amount of risk in exchange for the expected return premium. This is not to say that the associated investment result will not be attractive. Rather, the main point is that investors should reference the expected gross-of-fee and cost return as a starting point to evaluating the associated investment risks.

EVALUATING PORTABLE ALPHA IMPLEMENTATION APPROACHES

Portable alpha implementation is not a simple task. This is true of the simplest approach due to the use of derivatives and at least one form of leverage, and it is true in spades with the more complex approaches. However, there are some very basic reference points that may be useful to investors for purposes of understanding and evaluating different structures. Specific points that investors may want to evaluate initially, and on an ongoing basis, include but are not limited to the following:

- The effective borrowing cost paid to own the beta market exposure using derivatives.
- The risk controls, processes, and procedures for maintaining adequate liquidity, together with any related borrowing costs or potential borrowing costs.
- Accounting and risk management practices to make sure that the risk exposure is at appropriate levels relative to the net asset value of the strategy.
- The expected risk profile of the strategy and the actual risk profile at any point in time, including any magnified downside risk potential associated with leveraged positions and exposures.
- The expected and actual return on the capital allocated to the strategy (in many cases, relative to the desired market exposure benchmark).
- The fees paid to all associated providers.
- Internal staff time and resources allocated to associated risk monitoring, reporting, and any other related responsibilities.

CONCLUSION

The details associated with any given individual approach to portable alpha implementation will likely vary, and not every approach will neatly incorporate only the four elements described or fall into the three categories noted. In particular, investment approaches involving multiple derivatives-based market exposures and multiple alpha strategies with aggregate risk reporting and monitoring at the investment plan level, not the investment strategy or asset class level, will deviate to at least some degree from what has been described thus far. However, even then, the key considerations may still be similar.

Regardless, we hope that the preceding description of the different primary elements of portable alpha implementation, including the alpha strategy, the beta derivatives exposure, the liquidity for margin or collateral calls, and the consolidated risk management, monitoring, and reporting, together with the broad characterizations of different approaches, serves as a helpful framework for investors who are evaluating different approaches.

APPENDIX 8.1 SEGREGATED PORTABLE ALPHA CASE STUDY BY BRUCE BRITTAIN

To date, the more complex types of portable alpha strategy have been adopted mostly at larger firms with sufficient internal resources to manage the various moving parts. The segregated approach has plenty of positive aspects, but it also has elements that might increase fees, expose the portfolio to investments whose market stress characteristics are unclear, and commit capital to dead-weight cash collateral.

The following is a hypothetical case study for implementation of a complex portable alpha strategy and its purpose is to highlight an extreme example of the issues that might arise when the alpha strategy and the beta derivatives exposure are managed in a segregated manner. In this example, the investor replaced an active equity manager that was in charge of a $100 million equity allocation. The investment was then shifted into a portable alpha portfolio composed of $100 million worth of passive equity market beta, achieved via an investment in S&P 500 futures contracts. The investor is seeking alpha from combined investments in a hedge fund-of-funds and an individual hedge fund. Figure 8.7 shows how the portfolio might be structured. The equity portable alpha structure involves assumptions and estimates related to the cost of holding cash collateral, maintaining lines of credit, and supporting internal management.

The elements listed in Figure 8.7 are the building blocks of a portfolio structure whose internal frictions can absorb as much as 100 basis points of the return generated by the stylized alpha transport strategy—not taking into account the investment management fees charged by the alpha strategy managers. Another significant consideration is whether the assumptions of contained volatility and low correlation among the building blocks can be justified. Investors who adopt the segregated approach typically confront the following uncertainties posed by this type of portable alpha structure.

1. *Correlation assumptions.* Track record, transparency, logic, and consistency of performance are all factors that investors consider when evaluating alpha sources. Hedge funds, as a group, can be challenging in this regard. Without direct access to portfolio holdings over extended periods of time, the investor may find it impossible to verify the hedge fund manager's style, proclivity to change style, and willingness to tolerate out-sized risks at particular points in time. Investors will thus find it difficult to judge whether the manager's returns will continue to demonstrate desirable correlation characteristics. Not that transparency of portfolio holdings is any panacea! Systemic deleveraging events of the sort that occurred in 1994, 1998 and 2007 cannot be forecast from the holdings of individual mangers. Systemic risks don't appear in individual manager portfolio holdings, but they can dramatically impact manager results. They appear only after the fact and as a surprisingly high degree of correlation among investment strategies. The feature is particularly evident among hedge funds.

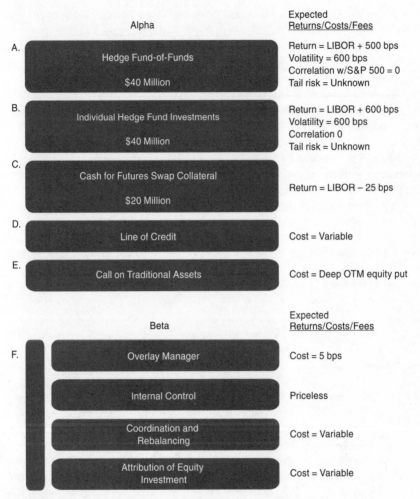

FIGURE 8.7 A Hypothetical Segregated Alpha Transport Structure
Source: PIMCO.

2. *Volatility assumptions.* Volatility and correlation statistics are all derived from the same basic return data. So for the same reasons that
correlation assumptions may be questionable, so may volatility assumptions.

A Worst-Case Scenario

Stress-testing is common in the hedge fund arena so we thought it might
be worthwhile presenting the results of a stressed portable alpha strategy.

We stress the structure with several simultaneous adverse events—a sharp drop in the value of the equity markets, a sharp increase in the correlation of hedge fund and equity returns, the triggering of intra-day margin calls on equity futures exchanges and a perverse, late-day rebound in the equity markets. This highlights some of the risks and uncertainties inherent to the more complex types of unbundled portfolio structures. The stress test begins with two elements; neither is highly likely but neither is outside the realm of possibility. The first element of the stress test is a 25 percent decline in the stock index amid chaotic trading conditions. The second is that the hedge fund investment expresses a latent or hidden dependence on the equity markets and falls 10 percent in value, violating the correlation assumptions that the investor made when entering the structure.

Those two occurrences initiate a series of events. At first, amid chaotic market conditions, futures exchanges initiate hourly margin calls on outstanding contracts, as they did during the stock crash of 1987. These calls require the investor to deliver collateral on an hour's notice, a demand that might not be able to be met. Operational issues might keep the investor from exercising the next line of defense, the line of credit, in a timely fashion. If this were to happen, the exchange would liquidate the futures contracts, leaving the investor with no equity exposure. Later in the day, the stock market rallies back 10 percent to end the session down 15 percent. The investor does not benefit from this rally because the equity futures contracts have been liquidated.

Taking stock at the end of the day, the CIO notes that the portable alpha portfolio has lost 25 percent of its initial value from the decline in equity futures and another 10 percent of its initial value from the decline in the value of its hedge fund holdings. The CIO also notes that stocks are down 15 percent. At first blush, the portable alpha construct appeared elegantly to combine two uncorrelated positions with a high likelihood of producing returns superior to equities. In the cold light of day, the structure amounted to two (leveraged!) bets on the stock market and a package of serious operational flaws.

CHAPTER 9

The Real Holy Grail: Risk Measurement and Management

Vineer Bhansali

The basic principles underlying portable alpha should be clear at this stage of the book. Instead of allocating investable cash to traditional investment mandates that incorporate systematic market exposure (beta) and, in cases of actively managed strategies, manager security selection and market timing decisions (potential alpha), the portable alpha investment application takes advantage of financial market tools and engineering in an effort to achieve an improved return profile. Market exposure is replicated using derivatives of some sort, while cash is invested in an alpha strategy, which ideally should be complementary to the derivatives-based market exposure. So every portable alpha program inherently uses leverage.

Of course, in addition to the leverage associated with all portable alpha investment applications, in some cases the underlying alpha strategy also incorporates leverage as well as strategies involving illiquid, infrequently traded securities, a material degree of optionality, and/or rare event risk—all of which are not typically reflected in traditional volatility-based risk measures. The end result may be attractive incremental returns, but the real Holy Grail for investors lies in a thorough ongoing understanding of the sources of return and associated risks—including the potential downside of and correlation among key risk factors across different market environments.

Leverage magnifies the returns and, insofar as risk is connected to the likelihood of negative returns, leverage may also increase risk. Portable alpha as a concept is often explained to investors with the underlying assumption of perfect, frictionless markets. However, the presence of leverage also magnifies the possible adverse impact of market frictions and, in extreme cases, may make the whole portable alpha program impractical. Mapping the connection between leverage and risk is not straightforward. Actually, the situation is even worse: There is no unique leverage measure that applies to all market classes; hence it is next to impossible to use one definition of leverage as a stand-alone risk management metric. In this chapter we discuss the limitations of some alternative approaches to the measurement of leverage.

IDENTIFYING RISKS: ALPHA, BETA, AND LEVERAGE

The hallmark of a good portable alpha program is one that digs deeper to understand and control the risks to the factors that determine the performance of both the alpha strategy and derivatives-based beta exposure components. As described in detail in Chapters 5 and 6, true alpha is generally derived from security selection and/or market timing. Alpha is the residual return that is not explained by the risk associated with a given investment strategy. Only market risks command risk premiums; pure alphas do not depend on market factors, and hence do not carry risk premiums. When people talk about alpha, they often refer to value-added from harvesting security-specific mispricing. However, exposure to different market betas is also an active decision for reaping the risk premiums from a specific source of market risk.

Investors know intuitively that the expected return from a source of market exposure that is positively correlated to the economy is greater than the expected return from a source of market exposure that is negatively correlated to the economy. So equitylike market exposures provide a positive expected excess return, relative to risk-free bond-like market exposures. One simple reason for this is that in aggregate, investors prefer insurance like quality of assets that outperform when the economy is not doing well. We think of Treasury bonds as protecting us during economic downturns, and we are willing to accept a lower yield for them. However, these assumptions and the cost of the insurance are highly variable and nonconstant, and the definition of risk-free assets as benchmarks will necessarily vary by investor type as discussed in Chapter 3.

The basic point is that the expected excess return from market sources is not only proportional to the risk embedded in the market sources, but also to the risk aversion of the representative marginal investor. Since both volatility and risk aversion are highly dynamic, a portable alpha program will only succeed if the asset allocation to the market sources is done with its suitability in mind. This analysis of risk is relevant not only for the derivatives-based beta component in portable alpha investments but also for the alpha strategy, for all of the reasons highlighted in Chapters 5 and 6.

One immediate question that arises is the decomposition of the expected returns from the alpha strategy into pure alpha and risk factor exposures. As described in Chapter 6, a variety of different research reports have shown that a material portion of the returns of various hedge fund styles can be explained by a relative short list of market risk factor exposures and/or relatively simple trading strategies. In other cases, investment strategies are highly specialized and involve esoteric risks that may not be readily replicated through liquid securities and derivatives. Or the investment manager might be taking market risks in a highly refined way, where the result of dynamic risk management gives the appearance of no market risk. Adverse selection bias could also be at work: Investors who have the skill and ability to deliver pure alpha are not likely to explain in detail how they do it. However, we do have to allow for the existence of real skill—or value-added beyond the expected return that an investor may expect to receive in exchange for assuming the associated investment risks of a particular strategy. Regardless, we still need methods and frameworks to evaluate the risks of portable alpha investments, including the underlying alpha strategies, on some uniform footing.

Apart from the sources of return and risk specifically associated with the alpha strategy, the combination of market exposures through derivatives and the simultaneous investment of cash into the alpha strategy creates leverage. Leverage creates risk because adverse market movements can lead to a forced unwind of positions. One way to measure this leverage is to simply count the notionals and sum them up. However, this methodology, while suitable for accounting purposes, does not achieve any profound risk-management purpose. For instance, a position in first-month money market futures contract (such as the Eurodollar contract traded on the CME) creates a notional position of $1 million per contract, but is arguably much less risky than a much smaller notional size position in bond futures contracts.

One way to connect leverage to risk for a fixed-income portfolio is to normalize the leverage weight by the duration of the securities. So a Eurodollar contract with 0.25 years of duration would contribute one-sixteenth of the duration of a Treasury derivative with an eight-year duration. However, though better than a notional leverage calculation, even this measure of leverage simply mixes risk and leverage in a more intuitive but eventually ad hoc fashion.

Another way to measure the risk from leverage is to measure the ability of the margin account that collateralizes the position to be rolled over in periods of market stress. However, there is no ex-ante way of knowing what requirements margin counterparties will impose in periods of stress. Since many leveraged positions in fixed income are created via the repo/repurchase market, knowing the risks from leverage requires a knowledge of the term repo rates for the instruments that are being leveraged, as well as the probability paths of their evolution. This is a hard task.

Many alpha strategy providers claim that a portion of their investment strategy is based on the idea that they are *sellers of liquidity* to the market.

In other words, they claim to provide a service to the market in exchange for which their investors receive compensation. Long Term Capital Management had very large bond/old bond spread positions, where they sold the on-the-run liquid bond and hedged the associated primary factor risks (duration, etc.) using older bonds. Other hedge fund sellers of liquidity also had the same trade on. Since most of these positions require buying and selling large quantities of bonds on a leveraged basis (using repo/reverse trades or forward settles) to magnify the returns from the relatively small liquidity premium, the investors were heavily exposed to shocks to the financing mechanism, all at the same time.

In a more recent study on the liquidation of Amaranth Advisors, in retrospect it was easy to see that small fluctuations could wipe out a substantial portion of investors' capital.[1] In what was then the worst loss experienced by a hedge fund over a relatively short period of time, Amaranth Advisors, a self-described multistrategy hedge fund, lost 65 percent of its $9.2 billion assets in approximately one week's time. In the paper "EDHEC Comments on the Amaranth Case: Early Lessons from the Debacle," Hilary Till, research associate with the EDHEC Risk and Asset Management Research Centre and principal of Premia Capital Management, LLC, examined the losses experienced by Amaranth investors together with the associated lessons.

Ms. Till's research identified a natural gas spread strategy employed by Amaranth and designed to benefit under a variety of different scenarios. While, according to Ms. Till, the strategy appeared to be economically defensible, the scale of the position relative to the underlying capital of the fund was not. Specifically, using returns-based style analysis, she concluded that it was likely that the fund suffered from a nine-standard-deviation event, leading to the widely publicized losses. Key conclusions from Ms. Till's research included but were not limited to the following:

- Holding-level transparency was not required to identify the underlying risk of the fund. However, if holding-level transparency was available, the size of the Amaranth positions in natural gas as a percentage of the open interest in the market would have revealed associated illiquidity risk.
- Traditional risk metrics based on historical data likely underestimated the risk given the degree of leverage and associated financing and liquidity risk. However, scenario analysis might have detected the underlying magnitude of the natural gas spread–related risk positions.

Financial engineering tools have made it possible for an investor who knows little or nothing about the fundamentals of a market to put on massively levered positions in the market in search for pricing anomalies. The paradigm of alpha-beta separation that is so in vogue today promises to optimize risk-adjusted return by separating the asset allocation decision (beta) from the active management decision (potential alpha) in one fell swoop. However, this all comes with leverage, and investors need to understand that with every extra unit of return comes possibly higher expected loss.

Different managers may also obtain different haircuts as a way of creating insurance for the leverage provider. The haircut is the difference between the par amount of the borrowing and the amount that can be put at risk, and is a way of effectively creating a risky funding rate. Haircuts can and do change with market shocks. The presence of an implicit contract between the investor, alpha strategy and derivatives-based beta exposure providers, and the counterparty also creates risk. The question of who is providing the leverage and who assumes the ultimate risk from deleveraging can impact the long-term viability of a portable alpha program.

The dependence on the ability to obtain leverage may also show up in other ways. For stock index replication, market distortions can create situations where rolling the equity index futures from the near-expiry contract to the next-to-expire contract (moving from the June to September contract as the June contract's expiration date approaches, as an example) becomes uneconomical. Similarly, to replicate commodity exposure many market participants use total return swaps (TRSs), but the swap providers replicate the returns using commodity futures. Depending on their ability to roll efficiently, the cost of the implicit leverage provided by the swaps can be exposed to market dynamics. The inherent complexity of modeling and replicating fixed-income securities with embedded optionality shows up nowhere more profoundly than in fixed-income index replication. Despite numerous attempts, there are few replication vehicles that use derivatives for replication of market indexes such as the LBAG (Lehman Brothers Aggregate) at reasonable prices.[2]

LIQUIDITY AND CORRELATION

As investor risk aversion changes with the changing state of the economy, the risk premium in certain asset classes changes with it. In periods of high risk aversion, there is a general preference for liquidity. If the haircuts or margin requirements change substantially, leverage can force liquidation of illiquid securities, creating substantial negative return shocks. Unfortunately, liquidity is a very hard risk factor to measure, and many alpha strategy providers assume that their portfolios can be marked to market as if they were liquid packages under all scenarios.

The variation in the economy not only creates different expected returns due to time varying risk premiums, it also creates changing opportunity sets.

It is no surprise that in the most recent five years, many asset classes are showing an almost perfect degree of co-movement. As the market has been pumped with liquidity, risk premiums in all asset classes have fallen. A movement in one asset class is rapidly transmitted through to global equity, commodity, currency, and fixed-income markets. The investment and related alpha opportunity sets compress, all else being equal, and the diversification from the breadth of many different types of risk factor exposures becomes a mirage.

In terms of the classic approach to active investment propounded by Grinold and Kahn, the reason for alpha-beta separation is to access a much broader opportunity set of alpha strategy providers with the skill, breadth, and ability to translate investment ideas into successful investment strategies. One of the risks to the portable alpha program thus arises from the risks to the skills, breadth, and ability to translate ideas into successful investment strategies. Periods of high liquidity can effectively create higher risks from low breadth, higher leverage used to harvest the lower marginal returns from skill, and fierce competition for the same positions. Thus, periods of high liquidity create the dangerous environment for a subsequent fat-tail scenario. If this is true, assuming that the future will repeat the past, using probability distributions conditioned on the past is likely to lull one into false comfort.

Alas, statistical risk measurement tools, even many sophisticated asset allocation tools, assume that risk can be adequately measured by variance (whose square root is volatility), and assume away the risks that may face a portable alpha program in periods of crisis. It is absolutely crucial, as discussed later in this chapter, to stress-test the parameters and the assumptions of the model in situations that have not been observed in the past.

Consider the hypothetical example of a portable alpha strategy that consists of stock market beta via stock futures, and a hedge fund alpha strategy. Assume further that the correlation between the stock market and the hedge fund position is zero for small, local movements of the stock market, but high for extreme sell-offs in the market. Clearly such a strategy would not provide an attractive return profile relative to a traditional stock index investment in all scenarios. In scenarios of severe sell-offs, investors would be exposed to margin calls on the index futures while the alpha engine is falling in value. If such a situation were to happen, the futures would get liquidated at the same time that the value of the collateral (alpha strategy portfolio) was falling. In short, leverage combined with tail risk would lead to a position to exit at exactly the point where it should otherwise be scaling up its risks.

One may wonder if this is an artificial example. To the contrary, the portfolio described here accurately reflects the profile of an alpha source that sells puts on the S&P 500, and a beta source that replicates the market via stock futures. A careful investor would be much better off combining the same source of beta with an alpha provider who promises a lower alpha but ensures that the strategies will remain uncorrelated with the beta even when there is an extreme move.

For a large class of alpha strategy providers, selling liquidity means receiving compensation for selling crisis insurance. While crises are by definition rare, when they do happen, their severity is very large. By looking at short periods of history, or assuming the popular normal distribution for returns, there is simply no chance of discovering the large expected loss hidden in many of these strategies. Using these idealized assumptions, one is lulled into thinking that there is risk-free money to be made, and this naturally leads to leveraging up of free-money trades. It is also a fact that the differential availability of leverage to different market participants makes it possible for the market equilibrium to shift, and for more risky assets to be held by all investors, leveraged and unleveraged.

Harry Markowitz, one of the original founders of modern portfolio theory, recently explored in a simple yet elegant paper how the capital asset pricing model (CAPM) crumbles in the real world (Markowitz, 2005).[3] A striking consequence of this paper, which he does not mention but which is relevant for investors today, is that the increasing availability of leverage for some investors may actually drive all risky security prices higher, even those not held by leveraged investors, potentially leading to a market far from equilibrium and with an ultimately destabilizing outcome.

To recap Markowitz's new conclusions briefly: If you leave out the ability to leverage as an assumption, or limit borrowing, two consequences ensue:

1. The market portfolio is no longer the mean-variance efficient portfolio.
2. The returns of securities are no longer proportional to their beta with the market portfolio.

Markowitz's analysis is strikingly simple. Assume that there are three investable securities. For simplicity, the securities are taken to be uncorrelated and their expected returns, standard deviations, and Sharpe ratios are given in Table 9.1 (we assume risk-free rates are zero).

Figure 9.1 (taken from his paper) illustrates the difference in portfolio allocation between two investors, one who can use leverage (i.e., does not have the constraint that all weights be positive) versus another investor who cannot use leverage.

TABLE 9.1 Expected Return, Standard Deviation, and Sharpe Ratio for Three
Investable Securities

Security	Expected Return	Standard Deviation	Sharpe Ratio
1	0.15	0.18	0.83
2	0.10	0.12	0.83
3	0.20	0.30	0.66

Source: PIMCO; hypothetical example for illustrative purposes only.

The horizontal axis is the allocation to asset 1 and the vertical axis is
the allocation to asset 2. The allocation to the third asset is determined by
the budget constraint

$$X_1 + X_2 + X_3 = 1$$

where X_1, X_2, and X_3 are the fractions in the three assets. For an unleveraged
investor, the point (1,0) denotes full allocation to asset 1 only; point (0,1)
full allocation to asset 2 only; and point (0,0) full allocation to asset 3 only.

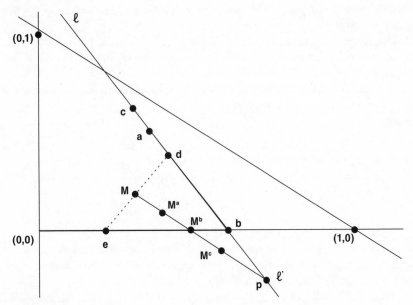

FIGURE 9.1 Market Portfolios with and without Nonnegativity Contraints
Copyright © 2005 CFA Institute. Reproduced and republished from *Financial
Analysts Journal* with permission from CFA Institute.

The following four consequences ensue (and the qualitative results do not change if investors have only the ability to lever limited amounts):

1. Point c is the minimum variance (risk) portfolio and is unique. Being on c pre-determines the portfolio return (12.4 percent, obtained by plugging in the weights 0.28, 0.62, and 0.10). To increase return, one has to take more risk. The optimal portfolio with more return (and risk) lies along the line *l'* moving down toward point b.

2. As return needs increase, a leveraged investor can move down beyond point b (say to point p), but an unleveraged investor has no choice but to move along from point b to point e. The unleveraged investor cannot go any further than point (0,0), at which his return is maximized. If an unlevered investor tries to compete with a levered investor for returns, he can only access higher-yielding, risky securities. As a consequence, the presence of leverage for some investors drives down the risk-premium for *all* securities, including the riskiest securities with worse risk/reward profiles.

3. The market portfolio is obtained by taking the wealth-weighted average of the portfolio allocation of various investors. If everyone remains on the line *l'*, then the market portfolio also lies along *l'*. The market portfolio is efficient (i.e., it has the least risk for the desired return). However, if some unlevered investors lie along the line connecting (0,0) and (1,0), and some investors lie along *l'* between points c and b, then the market portfolio is at M, which is not mean-variance optimal. Further, assuming the sharks (using a term coined by Stephen Ross and applicable in the current context to those who can leverage) are based at point p, the overall market portfolio in the presence of all three types of investors (unleveraged lying on mean-variance frontier, leveraged lying on mean-variance frontier, and unleveraged off the mean-variance frontier) is somewhere like the point M_a, M_b, or M_c. This portfolio is off line *l'*, so it is clearly not optimal for the sharks.

4. Security returns: Markowitz shows in his paper that the returns of securities are no longer proportional to their betas relative to the portfolio M, since M is not the mean-variance efficient market portfolio. Rather, returns are now proportional to the levered optimal portfolio P.

THE CONSEQUENCES OF LEVERAGE

We can now take the Markowitz paradigm one step beyond to explore the dynamic impact of leveraging on the market portfolio, pricing of risk, and security prices. As more and more investors are able to leverage, they buy securities that can be leveraged and move further out and down the ll' line. This puts pressure on investors who cannot lever, and they move further out to the left on the (0,0), (1,0) line, until they are all the way at (0,0) (i.e., they hold only the riskiest asset). Clearly, easy Fed policy of years past and the implicit put provided by a faith in the government, along with affordability products that have enhanced Main Street to access this leverage, have created a perfect environment in which leveraging was easy. We want to ask: What are the consequences?

First, unleveraged investors are forced to hold the riskiest security 3, which has the highest return but also the lowest Sharpe ratio. The market portfolio of the unleveraged investor lies along the line connecting d and e, which in the limit lies right on top of the point (0,0). In this limit, there is zero net demand for both security 2 and security 3, which are ex ante more attractive on a risk/reward basis. The market is distorted in that high Sharpe ratio securities are not held at all by unleveraged investors. Note that the point labeled M_c cannot be in equilibrium because there is net negative demand for security 2. The consequence is that the demand for the riskiest security drives up their prices, and drives down the price of the securities with better risk/reward profiles.

Second, unleveraged investors eventually begin to realize that leverage constraints are forcing them to hold the wrong securities, so they begin to relax their leverage constraints either explicitly or implicitly (e.g., with packaged solutions that allow leverage to be had via a structured note). They would like to do what the leveraged investors do, but the only ways to do this are to (1) sell off the large unleveraged holdings of risky securities and exchange them for a more optimal, leveraged mix; or (2) wait until the leveraged investors reduce their leverage and come back inside the triangle. Of course, if they choose the second path, they run the risk of holding an underperforming portfolio that is suboptimal. To avoid this, they might throw in the towel, sell the risky securities, and start to use leverage.

At this point, the leveraged investors and the unleveraged investors are all completely committed to holding market-optimal but highly levered portfolios. However, the very definition of risk using variance entails unhedged, embedded vulnerability to fat-tail shocks, such as a crisis of confidence or liquidity/financing potholes. If unrealized fat-tail events occur, the weaker hands, or those with implicit leverage, will reduce their leverage first and rapidly move the holdings back into the triangle toward point c. Market equilibrium returns with a vengeance and, depending on the overall magnitude of shorts in security 2, may set the stage for the next set of security price distortions.

One way of dealing prospectively with the threat of fat-tail events in the presence of leverage is to build in a return penalty, ex ante, as the leveraging dial of the investor's optimal allocation is dialed up. Another approach is not to chase the mean-variance optimal portfolio but to set hard limits on the maximum amount of leverage allowed at security level. A final approach is to purchase options, either explicit or implicit, as embedded in security prices. In selecting between these choices an investor has to carefully analyze the trade-offs between the prospective loss of returns from not being fully invested in risky securities, versus the immediate cost of purchasing options. Once in a while, an investor with patience is given the opportunity to get paid to purchase insurance *and* invest cash in prospectively higher returning securities with lower risk.

As we have seen from Markowitz's new analysis, the selective ability to leverage can create significant market distortions, and astute investors are well served by positioning themselves for the inevitable state when the unraveling of these distortions bites back those who have not paid attention to the underlying structures that have enabled them to arise in the first place. To understand these risks requires having a stress-testing framework that can not only subject portfolios to past stress events but also enable travels through imaginary market stresses that are possible though improbable.

STRESS TESTING: MEASURING RISK IN PORTABLE ALPHA

What are the ways we can measure the risks of a portable alpha program? In our view, simply depending on past return history to forecast the future return volatility is fraught with danger. There is notable research to support the idea that statistical tools for risk measurement are inadequate for measurement of idiosyncratic and other types of risk. There is also the challenge of risk modeling, even if holdings level transparency is available for a given alpha strategy. For example, while most hedge funds are reluctant to provide holdings-level data, the use of this data would be severely limited without good models to process the data. So good data and good models that are suitable to the portfolio's investment objectives need to be simultaneously obtained.

Second, one should be very careful not to aggregate prematurely. Any aggregation model such as value at risk (VaR) assumes that the underlying risks can be combined using particular assumptions for how the risks move together, and this aggregation results in a net loss of information. While not the last word, a careful, well-thought-out stress-testing methodology is perhaps one of the more robust ways to measure portfolio risk and adequately control the negative impact of leverage in periods of stress. We discuss stress testing as a risk-management tool in some detail here. When stress testing is used as a risk-management tool, it is crucial that both the alpha strategy and the market beta components are subjected to the same set of complete and consistent shocks, using the same set of building blocks described shortly. It is also important that they are subjected together, as the investor's capital is exposed to the combination of risk factors that is inherent in each of the two components—even if they are managed separately.

Portfolio risk measurement begins with the identification of a set of fundamental market variables that drive the prices of the securities that constitute the portfolio. The values taken by fundamental market variables are determined by demand and supply, perceptions of security-specific return and risk, liquidity, and the overall level of risk aversion of investors. Stress testing is the measurement of the sensitivity of an aggregate portfolio to certain predefined scenarios of the market variables—this should include both the alpha strategy and the derivatives-based market exposure (beta) components. Separating and performing the stress testing separately will completely miss the correlation or interaction effects between the holdings in the two components. Reasonable shock magnitudes and the probability of occurrence can be determined either by doing a distributional analysis of past history of the market factors, or by overlaying the forecast of economic conditions to forecast factor realizations. End users of the scenario analysis determine whether the factor shocks should be defined by reference to orthogonal (uncorrelated) factors or with respect to correlated factors. End users are also usually responsible for estimating the relative likelihood of different stress events happening—that is, for the estimation or forecast of the risk factor distribution—since stress tests intrinsically carry no probability information.

In principle, knowledge of all the moments of the full distribution of factors, including the factor covariances, is required to determine the total risk of the portfolio, either with correlated factors that are intuitive to the end user, or orthogonal factors that are usually nonintuitive but economical. In practice, however, the risk of sufficiently diversified portfolios can be replicated by just retaining the leading moments of the full portfolio distribution. However, it is important to go beyond mean-variance analysis. Finally, the time horizon relevant to the stress test has to be identified.

To ensure that the chosen stress shock algorithm is dynamic and leads to real-time risk management, the first step is to identify the variables that are the drivers of security prices. For instance, the level of all rates along the yield curve determines the price of a Treasury bond. One can choose these market rates to be par yields, spot yields, or forward yields of the Treasury curve, or, if one chooses, a different rate benchmark can be used. Increasingly, the LIBOR swap curve is being used as the benchmark. This is not a fundamental change in the paradigm, but simply a change of measurement reference. If one uses the swap curve as the benchmark, then the risk of the Treasury bond needs to be measured with reference to two variables: the swap yield curve, and the swap spread between the Treasury curve and the swap curve at each forward point. Choosing a good benchmark simply makes interpretation of the output of the stress-testing system more useful and efficient.

As the portfolio becomes more complex—holding, for instance, corporate bonds, mortgage-backed securities, inflation-linked bonds, tax-exempt bonds, and equity-linked structures—the market variable set has to be appropriately generalized to include credit spreads, implied volatility, prepayments, implied inflation rates, equity prices and implied volatility, and so forth. For equity variables, we can use any one of the broad market indexes, such as the S&P 500, the Russell 2000, and so forth, as well as the volatility benchmarks such as the VIX. This, along with investment-grade, high-yield, and emerging-market spreads, can also be used for stress testing credit components. For commodities, we can either use easily available total return swap indexes (GSCI, AIG) or independent commodity futures contracts. Finally, for currencies, we can use the spot and forward currency rates, as well as their implied volatilities. We emphasize the use of not only the underlying markets but also the implied volatility measures because so much of the alpha generation in the hedge fund community recently is a result of embedded sales of options.

Representative traded securities can be selected whose linear combinations give measurements of each of these factor exposures. In short, this is nothing but the extension of the classic option pricing approach of creating a dynamic portfolio of idealized systematic risks that can be replicated by holding positions in a certain complete set of benchmark securities to keep a hypothetical portfolio locally hedged. This point is absolutely key to any stress-testing analysis: Unless all possible dominant stress factors are included in the risk management, and representative securities that are carriers of those factors are found, the approach will not capture portfolio risk.

To translate market variables to risk factors, a model is required. The model can be very simple or very complex, and the degree of complexity really depends on the needs of the end user. For instance, for a Treasury bond, the sensitivity of the price of the bond to parallel shifts in the yield can be computed in closed form by a formula for duration, or duration plus convexity. By contrast, the sensitivity of the bond can also be computed to all orders by simply shifting the underlying yield curve in parallel by a predetermined amount. The impact of actual shifts of the yield curve depends on how the dynamic evolution of the yield curve itself is specified and calibrated. There are again numerous choices for yield curve construction—one can use a simple single-factor model calibrated to points on the yield curve, or more complex multifactor models that are calibrated to the benchmark yield curve, volatilities, and correlations of instruments, and allow for more sophisticated yield curve dynamics.

There are two key points to remember in choosing a model. First, if there are not enough securities with liquid traded prices, then a complex model can fail in the calibration step, and it can actually be worse as a tool than a simple approximation. Second, going to a complex model drastically increases the number of computations that need to be done, and is really only justified if the portfolio consists of complex securities with embedded options that cannot be priced using simple approximations. So, whereas the stress testing of a portfolio heavy in mortgage-backed securities will benefit from a complex model for yield curves, prepayments, and volatilities, a portfolio that consists simply of noncallable Treasury bonds will not benefit appreciably.

Once models for each class of securities are available, to obtain the stress risk, we simply move the underlying factors in a self-consistent (arbitrage-free) way, read the change in prices, and compute the risk-factor exposures. For a complex fixed-income portfolio, the risk factors that span the portfolio might consist of impact due to level shifts (in many different countries if the portfolio holds global bonds), curve steepening or flattening shocks, shocks to spreads via changes of option-adjusted spreads, and so forth. At any given point in time, the risk manager will look at this veritable zoo of factor exposures and decide which ones are of concern and which ones are not, given his belief in the possible impact of market movements. Then the partial sensitivity of the portfolio to a given factor shock is simply the product of the factor shock and the expected magnitude of the factor shock. Nonlinear variables can be used as right-hand variables by using representative option positions that replicate the various strategies.

Two different portfolios, or for that matter any number of investors, may be ranked for their skill by first benchmarking them to the same index, and then by limiting them in terms of the maximum relative exposures they can take for each systematic factor shock. Given a set of such portfolios, the residual dispersion in performance is by definition due to nonsystematic factor exposures. The immediate question then is, how does one do scenario analysis for nonsystematic, or security-specific, risk?

For example, in the world of fixed-income arbitrage, a common trade is to short the on-the-run bond (the most current issue) and buy the off-the-run bond (an older issue). The difference in yields between the two issues is commonly thought to be a free gain, and most stress-testing systems will capture no risk due to the spread trade (especially if the two bonds are close in maturity and coupon). But this ignores possibly one of the biggest systematic risks of all—that of liquidity risk.

The reason behind the spread between the on-the-run and off-the-run bonds is due to the differential performance of the two securities in periods of crisis. In a very real sense, during periods of crisis, holders of the new issue find it easier to raise cash against the security as collateral in the repo market. In periods of crisis the value of the liquidity premium can get to be enormous, such as in 1998 when the market saw almost a 15-standard-deviation event! This example points to two principles. First, the underlying distributions of security pairs may frequently be non-Gaussian (i.e., not normally distributed) and the apparent normal behavior is due to the fact that the liquidity risk factor is being ignored due to its rare large impact. Second, and more important, it points to the completeness problem in its naked glory—in other words, if any factor is ignored, the risk system can be fooled to think that there is no risk when there is actually an enormous amount of risk (especially when the assumption of no risk leads to leveraging the opportunity).

It is also good to remember, as described in the Chapter 5 appendix, that what seems to be a nonsystematic or security-specific factor will in time get arbitraged away and will become a systematic risk factor that needs to be stress-shocked. So alpha and beta portfolios constantly morph into each other, and—for this and the many other reasons highlighted previously—it is much more important to focus on the underlying risk factors and allowable risk factor ranges in order to measure the risk associated with a portable alpha investment. Capital losses that result from leveraged risk factor exposure are still capital losses even if the beta is dynamic as opposed to systematic.

How does one measure the liquidity risk factor, and how does one shock the liquidity risk factor? Clearly, one cannot just use the history of the bond versus old bond spread to measure the distribution of the liquidity factor, since it is very fat-tailed, and there might not be enough data for calibration. However, the lack of probability information does not mean that one cannot shock the liquidity risk factor to measure its impact on the portfolio. A simple approach is to assume that as liquidity gets spotty, the cost of funding rises by a large amount—for example, the repo-reverse differential blows out—and measure the impact of this assumption on the portfolio. Another, more sophisticated approach is to think of liquidity shock as equivalent to taking correlations to extreme values. Explicit models for such regime-switching behavior may also be built.

The magnitude of each factor shock has to serve three important purposes. First, the shock magnitude has to be large enough to capture a large portion of the factor risk. For example, a one-basis-point shock will not really serve the scenario analysis well for mortgage-backed securities since it does not capture much of the negative convexity, especially when the embedded optionality is more complex. The shock magnitude has to be chosen larger. Second, the shock magnitude has to be realistic in the context of historical and anticipated future outcomes. For instance, shocking interest rates by 500 basis points would certainly capture the negative convexity of a mortgage security, but would probably be useless as a tool to illuminate risk management on a daily basis, and thus useless for risk taking as well. Arbitrage bounds on possible outcomes correspond to the final and most important constraint on stress testing. In many realistic cases it may simply be mathematically inconsistent to simultaneously shock a number of correlated risk factors by independent large amounts. There are numerous practitioners who advertise stress shocks across various correlated factors that are large and are designed to make investors psychologically comfortable, but unfortunately many of those stress shocks cannot simultaneously occur.

To take an extreme example, assume that there are two independent stress shocks of the currently low-yielding Japanese yield curve; the first one is a parallel shift up or down by 50 basis points, and the second one is a steepening or flattening of 50 basis points. Now, given the low yields in Japan as of this writing, you cannot reasonably have a 50-basis-point steepening and a 50-basis-point downward parallel shock simultaneously since that would drive some yields below zero. However, you can have a shock of the level upward of 50 basis points with a 50-basis-point flattening. The point is that the correlation matrix of stress shocks is highly constrained, and it is simply not possible to imagine any and all scenario shocks as equally likely. There are systematic ways to take correlations to their extreme values in the context of portfolio risk models.

HISTORY AND TIME HORIZONS

Of course, the analysis can also be turned on its head. Given a portfolio with factor exposures and a covariance matrix of the factors (and higher moments if a tail analysis is of interest), one can solve for the combination of factor shocks that would lead to maximal loss, or to a given threshold loss.

If one were to use historical periods to estimate the shock magnitudes and shock correlations or particular crisis days, one is assured that there would be no mathematical inconsistencies. However, history-based stress testing assumes that the future will repeat particular days or combination of days from the past. Obviously, this rarely holds true in real markets. Every crisis is different in its microscopic details. Future probabilities, especially in stressed situations, are not similar to past probabilities. Stress tests are tools to gauge potential vulnerability to exceptional but plausible events. The risk manager who is really interested in assuring portfolio safety for the future instead of the past needs to forecast what elements of the portfolio stand to negatively impact the portfolio, and stress-test them simultaneously and consistently. This is necessarily subjective, but very flexible, because the risk manager has the ability to visualize outcomes that have never been realized and create them consistently. Weighing the likely outcomes higher than the unlikely ones, the risk manager then has the ability to apply the relevant controls to the portfolio according to the risks that make sense.

Details of this approach are presented in Bhansali and Wise (2001). First, the risk manager identifies which factor exposures have the most loading—in other words, which factors can impact the portfolio the most both independently and in conjunction. Then the risk manager chooses magnitudes for the factor shocks and the level of correlation between the factor shocks—that is, how likely is it that the shocks happen simultaneously. Of course, changing the correlations for some factor shocks cannot be done by freely changing many other factor correlations at the same time (otherwise the correlation matrix can become mathematically inconsistent). But since the risk manager usually has different degrees of confidence in certain correlation forecasts, the approach gives the risk manager the ability to weigh how the correlation matrix adjusts itself to be mathematically consistent, while at the same time creating a shocked environment that is complete.

The choice of stress-test time horizon also becomes very important for portfolios that run a mismatch between assets and liabilities. For leveraged portfolios, the impact of stress tests has special relevance for the time interval for which securities are lent out or borrowed, not only because an adverse market movement can result in margin calls and forced liquidation, but also because defaults of counterparties can lead to significant loss of mark to market. Most stress-test algorithms assume that the scenarios are realized over an instantaneous period. While this is simple to implement, it has the significant shortcoming that for portfolios that derive significant income from options or carry trades, the overall risk of the portfolio is overstated. In principle, we find that it is better to shock the arbitrage-free market realization for a forward horizon date, where the horizon date is chosen to be the average time to which the portfolio is expected to perform. This approach has an added benefit—it provides a way of performing the cost/benefit analysis for holding a long-term position against the risks that this entails.

CONCLUSION

When looking at the risks of a portable alpha program, it is important to recognize that there is no one unique measure that will capture all the nuances. Multiple risk tools, scenario analysis supplemented with reasonable amount of aggregation, measurement of nonlinear effects, emphasis on understanding the tails of the return distribution and what causes these tails, and just plain commonsense notions such as matching risk with investment horizon and liquidity needs are key components in a well-managed portable alpha program.

CHAPTER 10

Liability-Driven Investing

Jim Moore

The past few years have witnessed the beginnings of a rethinking of asset allocation for pension plans in the United States and Europe. For much of the past half century, assets were invested with a decided tilt towards equities. The rationale behind this focuses on the equity risk premium—over the long run, equity holders are compensated for bearing higher risk. As pension plans invest for the long run and are perpetual entities, they can weather market storms and lower cash funding costs by holding these higher return assets.

The combination of the so-called perfect storm of a simultaneous drop in equity markets and decrease in interest rates seen in 2000–2002 raised questions about the sustainability of the traditional investment model. The traditional model ignored what was happening on the liability side of a benefit fund's balance sheet and consequently the total risk to the plan's funded status. If equities went up, that was good—but did they go up enough? If they fell, that was bad—but how bad? If we could wait long enough all should work out in the wash, but concomitant with market turbulence are bankruptcies, and as plan sponsors are the ultimate backstop to pension liabilities, not all plans can wait out a market downturn.

The term *liability-driven investment* (LDI) arose on the investment landscape shortly after this period and began gaining prominence and attention as LDI surfaced more and more on conference programs and it became a three-letter acronym that was hard to avoid. One London-based colleague recently asked the question, "What is the greatest number: a) the number of portable alpha conferences, b) the number of LDI conferences, or c) the number of pigeons in Trafalgar Square?"

A more appropriate question has been asked by a number of clients: "What is LDI?" Before we answer this, let's take a moment to set our course through the rest of the chapter. We begin by asking the aforementioned question and examining the natural follow-on, "Why now?" The "now" question is the result of a confluence of recent capital market history and institutional catalysts on the regulatory and accounting front. We spend a few pages discussing how changes to the measurement mechanisms drive a more focused attention to different measures of volatility and their management. In order to appropriately deal with this volatility, the first step is to understand the nature of the liabilities themselves, which we cover over the following few pages.

Once we have set the landscape and objective, we can then delve into some detail of liability-driven investing and its connection to portable alpha. We explore three different phases of a shift in asset allocation, the latter two having direct relevance to portable alpha. In addition, the last phase utilizes a broader array of investment classes, namely alternatives and hedge funds, combined with portable alpha approaches. We then consider a case study of a plan sponsor exploring a Phase III approach and examine the implications of changes in leverage or funded ratio. We conclude by looking to a future beyond LDI—one that includes other factors beyond the liabilities that are being hedged, which recognizes that the pension plan is part and parcel of a sponsor's financial structure and that there are meaningful things worth considering on that front. But before we get there, let us begin by returning to our first question.

WHAT IS LDI?

At its core, liability-driven investment is simply putting the liabilities into the picture when making investment decisions. From a modeling perspective, this amounts to looking at the plan, recognizing that the liabilities are fundamentally a short position in the portfolio. While traditional asset allocation decisions focus on the trade-offs between the returns on assets and their *absolute* volatilities, relying on correlations to affect the weights to minimize volatility for a given expected return, in the LDI framework the focus is on surplus volatilities or tracking errors of assets *relative to liabilities*. For example, while the historic annualized volatility of the S&P 500 equity index is roughly 16 percent, relative to a typical defined benefit liability it is closer to 19 percent. This is a function of (1) the volatility of the liabilities, which would typically be 9 to 11 percent per year, and (2) the relatively low correlation of equities with liabilities.[1]

In most cases, for traditional defined-benefit liabilities, the largest single liability-related risk factor that is underrepresented in assets is interest rate sensitivity. Even core bond portfolios reflecting an aggregate market index, while highly correlated with liabilities and sharing the same principal risk factor, will be more volatile when viewed versus liabilities than on a stand-alone basis.

Figures 10.1a and 10.1b illustrate the different risk characteristics when viewing a range of asset allocations in a traditional asset-only space or in asset-liability space. Figure 10.1a traces the familiar arc of an efficient frontier in mean–standard deviation (volatility) space. The extreme lower left end on the frontier represents an all intermediate- or short-term bond portfolio—lowest risk and lowest expected return—while the upper right-most point is the highest expected return and highest risk asset class. This can be typically thought of as private equity or emerging market equities, but the pattern is the same regardless of the asset class, provided there is one in the set of investable assets that has higher expected returns and volatilities than the others. Moving along the frontier is simply a matter of finding the

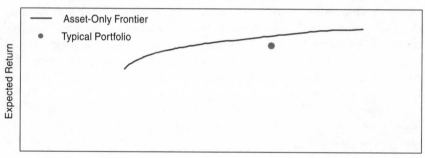

FIGURE 10.1A Optimization in Asset-Only Space

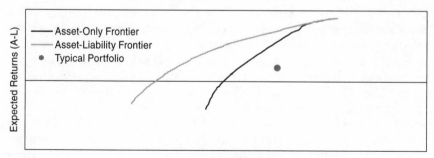

FIGURE 10.1B Optimization in Asset-Liability Space
Source: PIMCO.

mix of asset weights that maximizes the expected return for a given level of risk and then iteratively changing the desired risk level and reassessing portfolio weights.

The degree of curvature of the frontier reflects the correlation or, more precisely, the lack thereof in the returns of the chosen assets. If all assets were perfectly correlated, the frontier would be a straight line with a slope represented by the difference between the maximum and minimum returns divided by the difference between the maximum and minimum volatilities. To the degree that there are assets with lower correlations, there are efficiency gains from diversification and the frontier bows upward and to the left. A typical pension plan allocation is shown for comparison. For most plans this would be inside a frontier, but not too far from the frontier representing sponsor-specific limitations in investment policies or constraints on various asset classes.

Figure 10.1b revisits asset allocation by inserting some liabilities as a short position in the optimization exercise. Economically we can think of the liabilities as *borrowing* from plan participants (or policyholders).[2] Because these liabilities have their own risk characteristics, when viewed in this risk space, the previously determined efficient frontier is no longer optimal. A second frontier is shown that uses the same underlying asset classes but where portfolio weights are optimized allowing for the short position in liabilities. Here the minimum risk portfolio is not the one that has the lowest absolute volatility, but the asset that *looks most like the liabilities.* It is the one that covaries as closely as possible; one with a high correlation and similar volatility to liabilities.

For a typical U.S. defined-benefit pension plan, this asset class is long nominal bonds. If there is an explicit inflation component in the liabilities, such as in the United Kingdom, this could be long inflation-linked bonds. The highest-risk portfolio is generally the same as in the asset-only optimization except in the rare case where this high-risk asset class provides some meaningful correlation and hedging benefit. Tracing the arc of the frontier in this space is just a little more complex intuitively as there is an added element in the process. For a given level of risk—here, tracking error to liabilities—each move trades off diversification among the assets for the hedging benefit relative to liabilities. Some numerical illustrations later in the chapter will hopefully make this clearer. Note our typical plan allocation is much farther from the asset-liability efficient frontier than it is from the asset-only frontier. This illustrates the lack of focus on managing relative risk seen historically in U.S. and British pension funds. The typical U.S. pension plan has an asset portfolio with an annualized volatility of 9.5 to 11.0 percent, but an annualized tracking error to liabilities that exceeds this by 2 to 4 percent.

It is one thing to look at this in the context of a forward-looking theoretical model, but how have typical asset allocations done in practice? Has the higher risk paid off? Figure 10.2 illustrates the annual performance of the Ryan Labs Liability Index, a proxy for a typical defined-benefit plan's liabilities, versus a representative mix of stocks and bonds for a U.S. defined-benefit pension plan over the past 22 years.[3] In half the years the liabilities increased more than the assets did. The average return for the asset mix over the period was 11.3 percent per year, a number that most plan sponsors would have been very happy with. However, this failed to keep up with liability growth, which averaged 12.2 percent per year over the period.

The real issue isn't the difference in average return. It is probably surprising to most readers to see that the liabilities actually grew faster than the assets. If the difference in returns were a relatively constant and meager 90 basis points per year, that could be taken care of through modest and predictable annual contributions to the plan. The real issue is the volatility of the difference in growth rates. While the standard deviation of asset returns is a comfortable 10.9 percent, the standard deviation of the net returns, asset growth minus liability growth, is a much higher 15.7 percent. There is also an asymmetry in the benefit and pain associated with outperformance and underperformance. Once you are in a funding surplus and no longer making plan contributions, more surplus has limited current fiscal impact on the sponsor. As you fall into deficit and then further and further into deficit, requiring higher and higher contributions, the current pain increases. So the joy of a 26 percent net outperformance of assets over liabilities in 1999 is

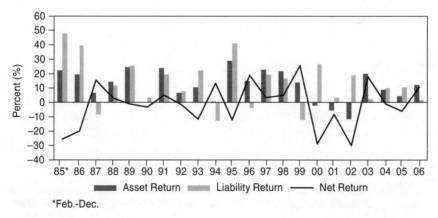

FIGURE 10.2 Assets and Liabilities: Ryan Labs' Historical Returns from 1985
Source: Ryan Labs.

less than the pain associated with return deficiencies of 29 percent and 30 percent in 2000 and 2002.

Another thing to note is that the runs of consecutive good or bad periods have a compounding effect, which can cause funded status to turn rather quickly. Figure 10.3 shows the aggregate funded status for those companies in the S&P 500 with defined-benefit pension plans from 1993 through 2006. The aggregate funding ratio built up slowly in the early 1990s, going from 98 percent in 1993 to 111 percent in 1998 before jumping to 128 percent in 1999. This reversed quickly once the peak of the funding roller coaster crested. In three short years, the funding aggregate dropped 5 percent, then 22 percent, and finally another 19 percent in 2002 to bottom at 82 percent in 2002. The climb back to full funding was aided by more cooperative markets as 2003 brought some welcome relief with strong asset returns, but also fresh contributions from sponsors—in some cases, substantial contributions.

It is also important to recognize that the aggregate position of the S&P 500—the sum of assets divided by the sum of liabilities—masks substantial variation among individual plan funded status. Bear in mind that in reality the excess assets of the plan that is 130 percent funded do not help the sponsor (or the plan participants) of the plan that is 80 percent funded. Arguably, there has not been a time in recent memory where there was a wider spread about the average funded status. Large plans rebounded to a greater degree and were more prevalent among those with surpluses. This is largely due to their larger asset exposure to international and emerging market debt and equity, which outperformed domestic markets as well as private equity and hedge fund holdings which have performed well in the 2003–2006 period. While the aggregate funding ratio was just under 100

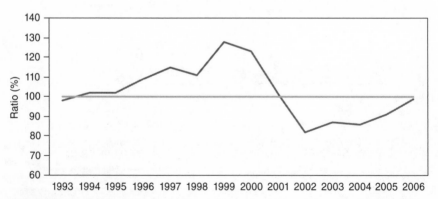

FIGURE 10.3 Aggregate Funding Ratio of S&P 500
Source: Credit Suisse.

TABLE 10.1   Funded Status of PBGC ($billions)

	2000	2001	2002	2003	2004	2005	2006
Surplus/(deficit)	9.7	7.7	(3.6)	(11.2)	(23.3)	(23.1)	(18.9)
Claims exposure	4	10	35	82	96	108	73

Source: PBGC annual reports (www.pbgc.gov).

percent at the end of 2006, and quite likely above it as of this writing, the majority of pension plans are still in deficit.

The extent of this *left tail* of exposed pensions is probably best seen by looking at the funded status of the Pension Benefit Guaranty Corporation (PBGC), the federal corporation established by ERISA[4] to ensure plan participant retirement benefits. Table 10.1 shows the PBGC's funded status and its estimate of its "reasonably possible" claims exposure as disclosed in its annual reports for the years 2000–2006.

Again, note how quickly the funded status deteriorates, dropping from an excess of assets over benefit liabilities of $9.7 billion, a surplus built up slowly over years, to a $23.3 billion deficit in four short years. Note also that the bottom in 2004 lags the bottom in S&P aggregate funded status by two years. As the PBGC inherits the plans of bankrupt companies, this process takes time and reflects the companies that did not have the wherewithal to hold out until a market turn. These plans are almost invariably more poorly funded than the average corporate defined-benefit plan. Also worth noting is the PBGC's estimate of claims exposure. This grew by more than a factor of 25 and has only recently bottomed. Although it improved measurably in 2006, it is clear that the U.S. defined-pension system is not out of the woods yet, and is still quite susceptible to a market downturn and also to falling interest rates.

LESS ROOM FOR COMPLACENCY

The rapid fall in funded status of ongoing corporations and the dire circumstances of the PBGC were noticed by commentators and regulators. Consensus mounted that the existing accounting and funding rules that allowed for smoothing of asset and liability gains and losses in order to make cash flows more predictable and avoid "noise" to income and the balance sheet needed to be revisited. The existing funding rules allowed smoothing of asset gains and losses of up to five years with additional smoothing of liabilities through interest rates averaging or corridors to determine materiality.

While this was a conservative measure in good times, it allowed plans to get materially worse in multiyear downdrafts.

This also coincided with the fall of Enron and Worldcom, and other financial improprieties, setting a mood for decreased acceptance of less than squeaky-clean presentation of financial status, and a heightened call for transparency and accurate mark-to-market bookkeeping. In 2005 the Bush administration and Congress began tackling a major rewrite of funding law, and the Securities and Exchange Commission (SEC) made a recommendation to the Financial Accounting Standards Board (FASB) that FAS 87, the accounting rule for pensions, was also due for overhaul.

No voice gets FASB's attention like that of the SEC. As one of its final obligations under Sarbanes-Oxley, the SEC conducted a detailed forensic audit of the 100 largest U.S. public companies and a random sample of 100 smaller ones. The SEC released its findings in June 2005 in a report entitled "Report and Recommendations Pursuant to Section 401c of the Sarbanes-Oxley Act of 2002 on Arrangements with Off-Balance Sheet Implications, Special Purpose Entities, and Transparency of Filings by Issuers."[5] The report escaped the notice of those looking for summer beach reading and most of the financial press, but its findings were not lost on those making accounting policy. The staff found that if pensions and other post-retirement benefits (health care) are combined, "approximately $535 billion in retirement obligations are not recognized on issuer balance sheets" (p.4). In the recommendations section, the report was fairly damning of the existing accounting standard:

> [F]irst, the accounting for defined-benefit pension plans deviates from the accounting required for other business and compensation arrangements, even when the economics are similar. While issues such as how to most appropriately measure the pension obligation and report pension items in the income statement should be considered, the Staff believes that work on accounting for defined-benefit plans should also focus on those areas that are inconsistent with the accounting for similar items in other areas, including:
>
> Consolidation... there is not an obvious reason why the plan should not be consolidated....
>
> Deferral of Actuarial Gains and Losses—It is not clear why changes in estimates related to retirement obligations should not be treated in the balance sheet the same way as changes in estimates related to other obligations....
>
> Valuation of Asset.... As the sponsor of a defined-benefit plan is affected by the gains and losses on pension plan assets in almost the

same way as it is affected by gains and losses on other investments, this distinction appears questionable.

[W]hile the disclosures are quite detailed, the Staff notes that it has long been accepted that "good disclosure doesn't cure bad accounting" (SEC report, pp. 107–108).

The end result of the Congressional and accounting focus was a tightening of pension regulations and disclosure with the added benefit of more consistency across the two oversight mechanisms. These changes came to pass in late 2006. On the funding side, asset smoothing was reduced from five years down to two, and the averaging of discount rates for liability valuation was similarly reduced from a four-year period to two years. Valuation rates were moved from a long Treasury or long corporate rate to a modified yield curve approach. In addition, amortization of unfunded liabilities was set at seven years to speed funding of unfunded benefit obligations. While this was not as dramatic a move to a full mark-to-market framework as some had hoped, it was a move in that direction and makes the volatility associated with asset-liability mismatches more apparent.

FASB's contemporaneous changes to the financial disclosure rules acquiesced to the SEC's request for change. Sponsors of defined-benefit pension plans now are required to reflect the mark-to-market funding status of pension plans on their balance sheets rather than providing the details in a footnote and smoothing the impact to the balance sheet over a number of years. Each year the changes in the mark-to-market value of the assets and liabilities are reflected in accumulated other comprehensive income and contribute volatility to shareholders' equity.

While this does not have the same visibility and impact as running these gains and losses through the income statement, it has meaningful consequences for a number of plan sponsors. Those sponsors who have large pension plans, either on an absolute basis or relative to their shareholders' equity, can see substantial volatility if plan assets and liabilities are not more closely aligned. This may be a concern for those focused on a particular credit rating or in an industry where the analyst community and investors pay attention to the balance sheet as well as the income statement. For industries like banking, where shareholders' equity is an element of regulatory capital, it can have material importance. For companies that have loan covenants tied to leverage ratios, this can be a material concern as well. The change makes the pension plan a more visible part of corporate capital structure. Essentially, the plan liabilities are borrowings from employees and former employees and are the liabilities of the plan sponsor. The assets, while dedicated to funding current and future benefit payments, are assets of the sponsoring firm.

These changes resemble what had already been done in accounting for pensions in the United Kingdom's revision to their pension accounting standard. Earlier in the decade, the British adopted FRS 17, which also brought mark-to-market gains and losses in funded status onto the balance sheet.

A more dramatic approach to deal with asset-liability volatility was taken in the Netherlands with the adoption of their FTK regulations that treated pension liabilities and funded status with the same framework that is used for life insurance regulation. The funded status of the plan is looked at prospectively as well as contemporaneously. There are risk charges associated with various risk factors—asset-liability duration mismatches, equity volatility, other asset class volatilities, and so forth. Depending on the amount of risk taken, a surplus over full funding is required. Plan sponsors must show solvency one year hence with a 95 percent certainty. Similar stress-test forward-looking funding standards are in place in some Scandinavian countries.

For many plan sponsors the increased visibility and more direct feed through to shareholders' equity are calls to do something now. Knowing exactly what that entails starts with taking a closer look at the liabilities.

EXAMINING THE LIABILITIES

Figure 10.4 gives a picture of the future cash flows for a representative pension plan. The mix of participants is relatively balanced between current employees and retirees. Benefit payments peak in 15 to 20 years as more of the covered boomer generation retires, but cash flows go on for another 60-plus years as younger plan participants have many years before retirement and then will live still more years as retirees.

A breakdown of the liability cash flows into the first 10 years, the next 20 years, and those beyond 30 years shows a disconnect between the contribution to the present value and the duration contributions of the segments. The first 10 years of benefit payments are responsible for 44 percent of the present value of liabilities, but only about one-sixth of the sensitivity to changes in interest rates. The benefit payments in years 10 through 30 contribute roughly half the value of the liabilities and three-fifths the duration contribution. Those payments more than 30 years out are less than one-tenth of the value of the liabilities, but represent nearly a quarter of the sensitivity to changes in discount rates.

The total duration of the liabilities at 14.0 years is approximately three times that of the U.S. market aggregate. Therefore to hedge these liabilities using the most typical bond allocation, the sponsor would need to buy three times as much in bonds as it has assets—a far cry from the typical 30 percent

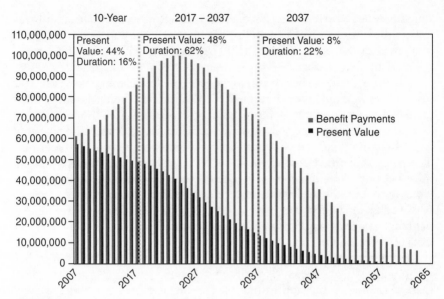

FIGURE 10.4 Defined-Benefit Liabilities
Source: PIMCO.

invested in bonds! This plan sponsor would also be poorly mismatched to exposure from anything other than a parallel move in the yield curve, as the bulk of market aggregate exposure is inside of 10 years. While exposure inside of 10 years comprises only 16 percent of the liability rate exposure, it is roughly 75 percent of the market aggregates.

A good example of the possible impact of this can be seen in 2005, when the U.S. yield curve flattened materially. The Lehman Aggregate Index returned 2.4 percent for the year while the U.S. Treasuries longer than 20 years in maturity returned 8.6 percent. If a Lehman Aggregate portfolio was levered to match the duration, the return would have been a scant 1.1 percent due to a rising cost of leverage over the period as the Fed raised rates.

The very long series of liability cash flows also makes pension liabilities quite convex. As interest rates rise, their duration shrinks, or as rates fall their duration extends, to a much greater degree than a market bond allocation. As the majority of the investment-grade bonds in the U.S. market aggregate index are mortgages or credit, a meaningful fraction of which are callable bonds, this contributes even more to the convexity mismatch.

This also raises the interesting question of what is the appropriate discount rate to use to value the liabilities. As these cash flows may have very long times to maturity, small changes in discount rates can have great bearing on the current value of liabilities. Table 10.2 shows the discount rate and present value of a single $100,000 liability cash flow due in 20 years for a variety of credit ratings.

Obviously, the higher the discount rate, the lower the present value of the obligation. Some would argue that the liabilities should be discounted at the sponsor's weighted-average cost of capital (WACC), which would include some equity expected return to be incorporated as well and probably look something like the discount rate for non-investment-grade securities. This ignores the fact that the holders of these liabilities almost certainly have a senior claim in bankruptcy to equity holders. Most plan participants would also probably feel a little uncomfortable if the security of their benefit had default likelihood consistent with junk bonds. If pension and benefit liabilities are pari passu to senior unsecured debtholders, the sponsor's cost of debt is a good first step.

Given the public policy issues associated with pensions and the fact that in a number of countries such as the United States and the United Kingdom there is mandated pension insurance, pension liabilities are generally discounted at a higher quality rate. In the past this was usually a government rate or some small multiple of the government rate (e.g., 105 percent of government bond yields). More recently accounting standards have converged around so-called high-quality obligations, generally taken to be on the order of a AA/Aa rating or a swap rate.

There may be other risks worth considering on the liability side in addition to the interest rate sensitivity and credit risk. In the United Kingdom, for example, some liabilities are defined in real terms as opposed to nominal terms. In cases where there is an explicit cost of living adjustment (COLA) for retiree benefits, this may also be an important factor to pin down and manage on the liability side. Mortality risk is drawing growing attention.

TABLE 10.2 A 20-Year Discount Horizon

Credit Quality	Discount Rate	PV of $100	Insufficiency Probability
U.S. Government	4.74%	$39.6	—
AA/Aa	5.58%	33.7	5.3%
BBB/Baa	6.04%	30.9	13.4%
BB/Ba	7.30%	24.4	30.8%
B	7.99%	21.5	46.1%

Source: Discount rates are from Bloomberg Fair Market Credit Indexes as of February 28, 2007. Insufficiency probabilities are Moody's default rates over 20 years for bonds with those initial ratings.

Currently, it is difficult to quantify precisely and more difficult to explicitly hedge (other than overfunding a plan). Also mortality adjustments progress slowly over time and it is hard to imagine sudden dramatic changes in life expectancy. As such, this is one factor that is probably best noted and monitored over time with continued adjustments to the liabilities, but is of lower importance in hedging than the other mentioned risk factors.

LIABILITY-DRIVEN INVESTING

The most basic liability-driven investment would be a portfolio that immunizes liabilities to the greatest degree possible. A high-quality bond portfolio that exactly matches liability cash flows may be a nice idealized construct, but it is seldom practical. First, given the nature of the actuarial process, there is an amount of measurement error necessitating adjustments on a periodic basis. Second, the long tails of the liability stream make it difficult to find bonds that can truly match liabilities. A factor-based approach that matches principal risk factors—duration, convexity, curve sensitivity—is a more practical approach and can generally match liabilities to acceptable tolerances at lower transaction and implementation costs. However, this too needs to be revisited periodically to adjust for slippages between the portfolio and the liabilities.

The general objection to immunization approaches is that they are *too costly*. Conceptually, any investment strategy that involves managing against some defined liability can be thought of as a trade-off between hedging and seeking excess return. Immunization strategies are all hedging with no excess-return seeking.

Traditionally, the bulk of excess-return seeking has come from investments in equities. Given the typical allocation weights in equities and the degree of mismatch that equities bring, it would seem that the majority of the focus has been on excess-return seeking or *reducing costs*. As expected returns run through the income statement, there is also a likely element of return seeking to boost earnings per share (EPS) in some quarters.

Figure 10.5a shows the yield on the Moody's long-term AA corporate index, a proxy for liability discount rates, 10-year Treasury yields, and the average spread between discount rates and the expected return on assets for S&P 500 companies with defined benefit-pension plans. Note that the spread between assumed returns on assets rises while the bond yields fall. Assuming a simple split of 65 percent equities and 35 percent fixed income, Figure 10.5b shows the implied equity risk premium (ERP). While the first year of the sample appears conservative with an ERP of 2.4 percent, recent implied ERPs may appear high considering current high levels of liquidity

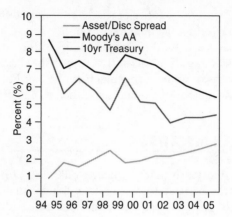

FIGURE 10.5A Expected Return versus Discount Rate

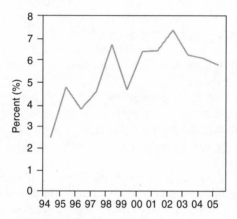

FIGURE 10.5B Implied Equity Risk Premium
Source: PIMCO, UBS, Bloomberg.

from global sources of capital and consultant and Wall Street estimates for the ERP clustering in the 3 to 4 percent range.

In retrospect this has proved costly. Risk is a cost! The mismatch between assets and liabilities can force a need for contributions when equity asset market performance is weakest. For cyclical companies this can be at especially inopportune times as they tend to be shortest of cash at exactly the same time that equity markets reach their nadir.

Figures 10.6a and 10.6b revisit the surplus efficient frontiers we saw in Figure 10.1, adding portfolios with the same ex-ante expected returns but ones that are efficient in asset-only space (A) and asset-liability space (B). Moving to the left is essentially a task in rebalancing a portfolio to achieve less risk in the two measures while holding the expected return steady. Moving to A usually involves moves out of equities into more exotic assets ranging from high-yield to emerging markets to commodities to hedge funds and private equities. An optimizer chooses the exotic asset classes for a combination of more potent returns and diversification properties. Going into a liability-relative space then re-norms the risk measure and trades off the new risk versus those return or diversification benefits.

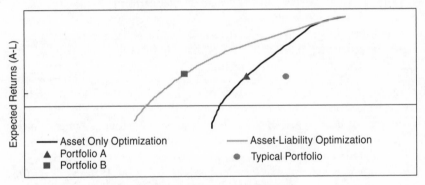

FIGURE 10.6A   Excess Returns versus Surplus Risk

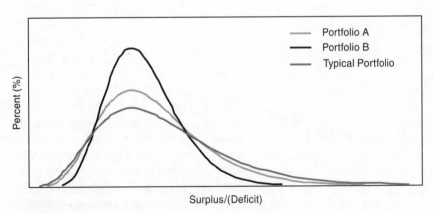

FIGURE 10.6B   Surplus Distribution in Five Years
Source: PIMCO.

The impact to the sponsor can be seen more clearly in Figure 10.6b. If we assume that the plan is currently just fully funded, the mode or peak of the future funding distribution would reflect a slight overfunding as the expected excess return is positive. Regions to the left would represent underfunding and those to the right would correspond to overfunding. Portfolio A gives slightly more certainty in the funded status five years hence than our typical portfolio, and portfolio B gives considerably more stability. Of course our starting portfolio provides the highest possible funding possibility, but it is also the one that presents the greatest downside risk as well. Given the asymmetry of pleasure and pain in funded status (and the spillover implications for the sponsor's balance sheet), many sponsors would likely give up some of the upside for the greater certainty.

The question arises as to the manner of portfolio change and degree of expected return give-up. From what we have seen of sponsor change in portfolio design, the move to LDI can generally be categorized into three phases. Two of these involve elements that are broadly consistent with the portable alpha strategies and philosophies seen elsewhere in this book.

Phase I: Starting from a 70/30 portfolio where the 30 percent bond allocation is as a market aggregate portfolio, simply change the bond benchmark to a long bond index or customized portfolio that more closely resembles liabilities (e.g., duration matched). This is the first step in the move and to some is tantamount to a baby step, but it is generally a move in the right direction. If the typical 70/30 allocation covers 10 to 15 percent of the interest rate exposure of the liabilities, and that with a mismatch in yield curve exposure, moving the bond allocation out the curve to more closely match duration raises the cover to 30 to 35 percent. An improvement, but still a (sizable) bet on the direction of future interest rates. To date, we would estimate that roughly 70 to 75 percent of the clients we have seen move in the United States are still in this first stage.

Phase IIa: Realizing that they are still running meaningful dollar duration gaps between assets and liabilities, these plans will use a derivatives overlay (interest rate swaps or bond futures) to effectively extend the duration of their assets to more closely match that of their liabilities. This approach falls into the broad category of a portable alpha-based strategy in the sense that these plans are obtaining their desired market risk factor exposure—in this case, long-duration interest rate exposure—using derivatives. The collateral for the derivatives market exposure is the existing plan assets. Those that are derivatives-averse can effect much of the same impact by running STRIPS-based portfolios, albeit with some loss of flexibility. Typically a plan will try to cover 60 to 80 percent of its interest rate exposure, making some allowance for the inherent uncertainty of equity moves with interest rates or to express some degree of an interest rate view. This is analogous to viewing the liabilities as a beta and implementing a portable alpha approach where the existing asset portfolio is seeking alpha, or excess performance, and the duration overlay is used to obtain the liability-hedging beta.

Phase IIb: These sponsors come to the realization that even if they used derivatives overlays to completely eliminate the interest rate mismatch, tracking error of assets to liabilities is still much higher than they would like. However, they are still highly conscious of expected return assumptions (EROA). In addition to extending duration through derivatives overlays, they move more money into cash fixed income—or example, moving to a 50/50 allocation with a much more complex fixed-income portfolio. To mitigate some of the drop in expected return, they increase the degree of risk in the elements of the fixed-income portfolio. For example, the average credit quality may be reduced from an AA average to something with an A/BBB average quality. The portfolio may take on decided elements of high yield, emerging markets, or leveraged loans to effect the increased spread. To compensate, the higher-quality bonds tend to be even longer and derivatives use is prominent to effect the desired aggregate.

In the United States, perhaps 15 to 20 percent of those who have moved down the LDI path are in Phase II with the majority pursuing Phase IIa rather than IIb. Those pursuing Phase IIb tend to be in stronger funding circumstances where the pension earnings are less material, but balance sheet volatility is a more pressing concern. Phases I and II are gradualist approaches, while Phase III generally is a more fundamental shift in philosophy.

Phase III: Redesign pension asset allocation as a complete clean sheet. While Phases I and II can be thought of as incremental changes, movers in this phase are going back to the drawing board to start anew. While the previous two phases are incremental approaches that keep a firm eye on the EROA and keeps it as a primary yardstick, the view in Phase III usually involves setting a risk budget and keeping it as a driving principle. Return is optimized subject to the risk budget, but the risk budget, expressed either in tracking error or more commonly in terms of value at risk (VaR), is usually the dominant decision variable. Some use of the leverage afforded by the portable alpha investment application, either to effect part of the interest rate cover or to give exposure to multiple risk factors, is a common element to achieving sponsor objectives.

Figure 10.7 gives a visual example of some of the trade-offs seen in the approaches in tracking error and absolute asset volatility in a simple two asset class (equities and bonds) context. Starting with a 70/30 allocation, moving to a long bond portfolio reduces tracking error to liabilities by a percent or so. Absolute asset volatility is virtually unchanged as the additional bond volatility has low correlation to the equity volatility, which dominates aggregate asset volatility.

Moving to a sizable duration completion overlay reduces tracking error another couple of percent, but increases asset-only volatility meaningfully. Some are surprised by the changes seen in the two bars. First, they expect the reduction in tracking error to be more meaningful. Recall, however, that if you completely eliminate the risks in the liabilities, you are left with the risk (absolute volatility) in the assets. If we assume that equities have an annual volatility of approximately 16 percent, and the 30 percent in bonds plus overlay completely matches the risks embedded in liabilities, we are left with the risk associated with the 70 percent equity allocation or 11 percent volatility (0.7×16 percent $= 11.2$ percent). As Figure 10.8 illustrates, there is only so much reduction in tracking error that can be accomplished by hedging the rate exposure in the liabilities. To really reduce tracking error, at some point the fundamental overall asset allocation needs to be addressed.

The second surprise is the increase in absolute asset volatility associated with putting on a duration overlay. The easiest way to conceptualize this is to view it in the form of levering the portfolio. Using a duration overlay

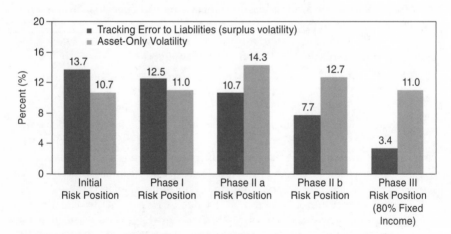

FIGURE 10.7 Risk of Different Investment Strategies
Source: PIMCO.

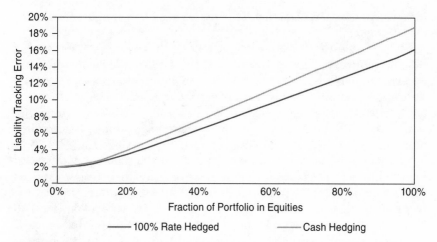

FIGURE 10.8 Portfolio Composition and Liability Tracking Error
Source: PIMCO.

is economically borrowing at floating rates to synthetically invest in a long swap bonds. On the asset-only side, the portfolio is economically 170 percent invested—100 percent in long bonds with a volatility of 9 to 12 percent in addition to the 70 percent investment in equities.

While this does reduce volatility relative to liabilities, the asset-only volatility does merit some concern. Suppose interest rates back up 100 basis points. Economically, the assets decrease in tandem with the liabilities so there is a better match—the loss on the asset side is balanced by the gain on the liability side. However, the gain on the liabilities cannot be effectively monetized, and there is a financial obligation to either the swap counterparty or the futures exchange. If the derivatives counterparty is calling for cash collateral, this cash must come from somewhere. This can take the form of liquidating other securities in the portfolio or tying up existing cash.

Asset-only volatility remains important as a proxy statistic indicating the potential liquidity risk in the asset portfolio, similar to portable alpha strategies more broadly. For moderate overlays this is quite manageable, but becomes a more pressing concern when overlays are quite large and/or the cash investments in the portfolio are rather illiquid. This is exactly the same issue that is faced when managing other derivatives-based market exposures, like equities, where the liquidity of the collateral is changed. The only thing that differs is the nature of the market move that causes potential event risk. If duration overlays are being run in tandem with multiple other derivatives-based market exposure positions and the underlying collateral is of an illiquid nature, it becomes quite important for the plan management to have contingency plans for liquidity management as tail risks can be magnified greatly.

Lastly in Figure 10.7 we see the two Phase III strategies. This simplified example illustrates that here is where we see meaningful reductions in tracking error to liabilities. These two asset examples lose some of the richness we will delve into shortly as much of the focus in these cases is usually on fundamentally rethinking the core risk assets and selecting them for inclusion in the portfolio because of their roles as hedging tools, concentrated return generators, stable return generators, or risk diversifiers.

As more and more investors reach beyond the standard equity/bond opportunity set, the choice is from which asset class they remove assets to put them into hedge fund strategies. Figure 10.9 illustrates the risk dimension of the choice in asset-liability space for a pension plan with an initial 60/40 portfolio where the bonds are invested in a long-duration portfolio. Before the investment change, the tracking error of the assets to the liabilities is approximately 12.5 percent. Equity volatility and the duration mismatch are the dominant sources of volatility, with trace amounts coming from credit risk, convexity mismatch, actuarial uncertainty, and other factors. The path to the upper right illustrates moving 10 percent of the portfolio

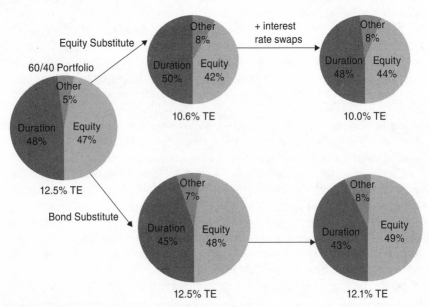

FIGURE 10.9 Moving 10 percent to Hedge Funds
Source: PIMCO.

from equities into diversified hedge fund exposure, and the lower path shows the effects of taking the allocation from bonds.

Taking the allocation from equities yields meaningful reduction in tracking error, reducing it from 12.5 percent down to 10.6 percent. The net effect is to diversify the risk assets and take advantage of the relatively low (assumed) correlation between the equity and the hedge fund return source. The contribution of equity to tracking error is reduced meaningfully and there is greater diversification in the sources of tracking error to liabilities. Overlaying the 10 percent hedge fund investment with interest rate swaps of like duration to the liabilities further reduces tracking error. The implication on expected returns is a function of the difference between the assumed equity risk premium and the estimated alpha in the hedge fund return source with the change being 10 percent of the difference.

In the case where the hedge fund allocation replaces a bond allocation, tracking error is initially virtually unchanged. The additional diversification of the risk sources is offset by the increase in mismatch between assets and liabilities. If the swap is used in addition to the asset move—a portable alpha implementation—the initial degree of duration mismatch is returned and there is a small overall reduction in tracking error associated with the modest diversification of risk factors. Here the switch is much more about attempts to deliver higher expected returns than about balancing risk sources and tracking error to liabilities.

CASE STUDY: INTO PHASE III

To illustrate some of the trade-offs and sensitivities associated with a wholesale change in strategy, let us examine a case of a plan looking to achieve a constant 4 percent annual tracking error to liabilities. The plan is relatively mature with approximately two-thirds of the liabilities associated with benefits in payment to retirees and future pensions associated with individuals who have left the company and are no longer accruing benefits. Service cost, the cost of providing additional benefits to active plan participants as they accrue additional service for benefit determination, is running at approximately 1.5 percent of liabilities per annum. The plan is $1 billion in size and is fully funded. The sponsor would like to ensure enough cash on hand or bonds maturing to ensure liquidity for benefit payments in the first three years of the portfolio.

The first step is to examine the liability cash flow stream provided by the plan's actuary to determine duration, convexity, and yield curve shape sensitivities and to construct the best hedging portfolio. The liabilities have duration of 11.5 years and convexity of 2.1 years. Because the duration of the liabilities is relatively close to that of the Lehman Long Government/Credit (LLGC) index (11.5 versus 10.8 years) and they are of similar AA credit quality, this will anchor the benchmark for the liability-hedging portfolio, representing 81 percent of the portfolio benchmark. The rest of the benchmark trades off the desire to match the duration, come close on convexity, and cover the cash flow requirements of the first three years' benefit payments. The additional duration is achieved using 20- and 30-year zero-coupon swaps (13 percent), which also extends the convexity of the portfolio to more closely match the liabilities. The balance of the portfolio is invested in shorter instruments to cover benefit payments not covered by the yield of the LLGC core portfolio and to hold cash to provide collateral to support the long zero-coupon swaps.

If the portfolio were fully invested in the hedging portfolio, there would not be enough excess return to cover the service cost, despite an assumed 75 basis points per annum after-fee excess return from active management around the benchmark. The tracking error to the liabilities is estimated at 1.8 percent, coming from active management of the fixed-income hedging portfolio and actuarial uncertainty, so there is some room to take on additional risk assets to cover the service cost.

For the purposes of this example, three additional assets are used to generate excess return. The first is a hedge fund strategy expected to generate 400 basis points per annum over LIBOR with 6 percent annual volatility. This strategy is coupled with a 10-year swap overlay that gives it approximately eight years of incremental duration. In addition, equity with an assumed 300 basis point equity risk premium and commodities with an assumed 200 basis point risk premium are included. Given the higher expected excess return and lower tracking error to liabilities than either equity or commodities, an optimizer would naturally load up on the hedge fund strategy with overlay. Given the sponsor's lack of familiarity with hedge funds, and to limit concentration exposure to gaining expected excess return from an unfamiliar source, exposure is capped at 10 percent. Cash is also allowed as an investment choice or when leverage is used, as a short position to represent the cost associated with beta overlays.

The initial optimization of the asset classes versus the liabilities with the tracking error constraints, without allowing leverage, gives the result with the 4 percent tracking error budget (see Table 10.3).

Note that the investment constraint on the hedge fund strategy with swaps binds. Without the constraint, the optimizer would put nearly 50 percent of the assets into the strategy, which would effectively create two problems. First, it would require all the excess return in the strategy to come from the wide range of highly variable risk factors that may comprise the opportunity set of a typical hedge fund or group of funds. Compared to more

TABLE 10.3 Optimal Portfolio Weights, 4 Percent Tracking Error Budget

Excess Return Expected		Portfolio Weights					Estimated Asset Volatility	
(%)	($M)	Custom Hedging Portfolio	Hedge Fund plus Swaps	Equity	Commodities	Cash	(%)	($M)
1.64	16.4	66%	10%	19%	5%	0%	8.31	83.1

Source: PIMCO.

easily quantifiable market return sources, this creates a greater reliance on manager risk factor and security selection skill as the sole source of excess return generation. Second, relying to such a degree on a relatively illiquid investment would necessitate reconfiguration of the primary custom hedging portfolio, requiring it to hold more cash for benefit payments and very long securities to obtain duration and convexity. This would reduce opportunities for spread in the portfolio and constrain active management opportunities.

The optimizer next moves to equities, as the assumed return is higher and they display marginally lower tracking error to liabilities. As the allocation to excess return assets increases, commodities enter the picture to diversify the equity exposure, with roughly one dollar in commodities to every four in equities. Note that with a 4 percent tracking error to liabilities, the absolute asset volatility of the strategy is 8.3 percent, which is 1.3 percent less than the volatility of the liabilities. The inclusion of other assets beyond the hedging portfolio reduces total asset volatility as the lack of correlations to equities and commodities provides asset diversification.

The 1.64 percent expected excess return covers the service cost, but just barely. The sponsor is more than comfortable with the asset volatility levels and wishes to see if using a modest amount of leverage can improve the expected return cover while still maintaining the 4 percent tracking error budget. The excess return from equities and commodities, as well as elements of the hedging strategy can be achieved synthetically. This provides some flexibility in portfolio design.

This strategy is illustrated in Table 10.4; 10 and 20 percent leverage strategies are examined.

The use of leverage has the intended effect—increasing expected returns. The trade-off is some additional volatility on the asset volatility, as there is an increased allocation to risk assets. It is interesting to note that of the additional 10 percent effectively invested, 6 percent goes to the liability hedging portfolio while 2 percent each goes into equities and commodities.

TABLE 10.4 Optimal Portfolio Weights, 4 Percent Tracking Error Budget, Allowing Leverage

Leverage	Excess Return Expected		Portfolio Weights					Estimated Asset Volatility	
	(%)	($M)	Custom Hedging Portfolio	Hedge Fund plus Swaps	Equity	Commodities	Cash	(%)	($M)
10%	1.78	17.8	72%	10%	21%	7%	−10%	8.96	89.6
20%	1.89	18.9	79%	10%	22%	9%	−20%	9.65	96.5

Source: PIMCO.

This can be thought of as a tug-of-war between the hedging portfolio and the risk assets over the 4 percent tracking error budget. Each dollar added to the hedging portfolio will reduce the tracking error, bringing it inside of the risk budget. Each dollar invested in the risk assets will move the tracking error outside of the risk budget, with a combination of equities and commodities doing less damage than either would do on its own. In this case, the ratio of three dollars to hedging for every two to risk assets holds the precarious balance.

The application of the leverage would most likely take place using swaps or futures. For a nontaxable investor such as a pension plan, outright issuance of debt would create tax and accounting concerns. There is some fungibility as to which exposure beyond the 100 percent level is taken through derivatives. It can be additional bond exposure (principally duration and curve positioning), equities, or commodities, or some combination of all three. The plan sponsor just needs to be cognizant of managing the risks of the overlays in such a way as to ensure sufficient liquidity and flexibility with the cash collateral as it is being asked to perform multiple tasks.

The asset allocations thus determined are not necessarily of the "set it and forget it" variety. Over time, performance of the assets and liabilities will lead to some drift away from full funding. If it is desirable to hold fast to the tracking error budget, the weights need to be reexamined periodically and rebalanced. Table 10.5 shows how the weights change if the funded ratio increases or decreases by 10 percent due to changes in the asset level in the case where the sponsor is implementing a strategy with 10 percent leverage.

Note that as the asset level rises relative to liabilities, more assets move into risk assets. In dollar terms, the hedging portfolio actually increases

TABLE 10.5 Optimal Portfolio Weights, 4 Percent Tracking Error Budget, Varying Funded Ratio

Funded Ratio	Excess Return Expected		Portfolio Weights					Estimated Asset Volatility	
	(%)	($M)	Custom Hedging Portfolio	Absolute Return plus Swaps	Equity	Commodities	Cash	(%)	($M)
110%	2.28	25.2	69%	10%	22%	9%	−10%	8.80	96.8
100%	1.78	17.8	72%	10%	21%	7%	−10%	8.96	89.6
90%	1.23	11.1	77%	10%	18%	5%	−10%	9.23	82.6

Source: PIMCO.

modestly, but not as much as the investment in risk assets. The reciprocal of the funding ratio (1/FR) enters as a scaling multiple on the trade-off between hedge fund diversification and hedging. *The higher the funded ratio, the lower the fraction of assets that is needed to hedge the liabilities.* As the funded ratio falls, a greater portion of the asset allocation is moved into hedging. Those familiar with constant proportionate portfolio insurance (CPPI) strategies or other dynamic optionlike structures will recognize this behavior. This is essentially what the constant expected tracking error strategy is—a version of a CPPI strategy where the control variable isn't an absolute level, but the funded ratio of the pension plan. Note that if the funded ratio falls to 90 percent, the expected excess return is below the service cost of the plan, and either cash contributions should be made to bring the funding back into balance or the anticipated trajectory of funding changes from positive to negative as active participants accrue additional benefits.

BEYOND LDI: INCORPORATING FACTORS OUTSIDE THE PENSION PLAN

It is important to note that for many if not most of the participants, the pension plan does not exist in a vacuum. For active employees the pension plan is part of an ongoing employment arrangement. For the sponsor, it represents future known and contingent liabilities. If the plan becomes too much of a burden, it may be frozen with future accruals curtailed. It may also be a strategic asset for attraction and retention of loyal employees with long time horizons. For the sponsor, the plan may be a very important part of its capital structure.

Ultimate payment of benefits does not always come from asset growth, but also comes from employer contributions. If the assets do not perform, the sponsor is obligated to make good on its promises and top up funding. If the sponsor has potential business situations under which additional contributions would create hardship, it may be prudent for the asset allocation in the plan to hedge these states of the world. The most obvious of these would be corporate bankruptcy.

While it would probably draw criticism or worse for the plan to short sponsor equity or buy credit default protection on the sponsor, some element of proxy hedging may make sense. This could take the form of basket hedges of sponsor industry stocks or credit exposure, or at the very least underweights relative to market aggregate index levels. Highly procyclical companies may want to think about reducing their aggregate beta exposures in asset portfolios to reduce co-cyclicality of earnings and plan funded status. Firms with margins susceptible to increases in input factor prices may wish to tilt asset allocations in the plan to hedge a need for contributions at the time margins reduce net income.

Other factors worth considering in the pension plan are the interaction with corporate capital structure and tax incentives. As pointed out decades ago by Fischer Black and Irwin Tepper,[6] holding equities in the pension plan is an inefficient use of the tax-preferred nature of the plan and the deductibility of corporate interest payments. Reducing leverage in the pension plan by selling equities, and introducing it on the sponsor balance sheet by issuing debt to buy back the company's shares, is value-enhancing to shareholders while leaving aggregate leverage unchanged. While this strategy has seen little adoption, it has some appeal if the sponsor and plan are looked at in aggregate.

If we revisit the preceding case study, suppose that the strategy of a 4 percent risk budget is adopted with the 10 percent leverage. Offsetting the roughly $400 million move from the prevailing 70/30 portfolio to a portfolio with 72 percent hedging bonds, the company outside the plan issues $400 million of debt at 8 percent to buy back $400 million of its own shares, which are paying a 2 percent dividend yield. Assuming a corporate tax rate of 35 percent, the interest cost effectively borne by the government amounts to $10.6 million ($400 million × 8 percent × 35 percent). Add to that $8 million of dividends not paid. If the sum is attributed to the pension plan, the effective return on assets is enhanced by 1.86 percent, which more than makes up for the drop in expected return on assets from reducing equity exposure. Value is increased for the pension participants as their benefits are more secure. Value is created for shareholders as more efficient use is made of the tax code.

CONCLUSION

The move to liability-driven investments is the conflation of a number of factors: aging demographics and maturing pension plans, accounting and regulatory changes, the increasing comfort with leverage as a portfolio management strategy, and the increased availability and liquidity of derivative instruments providing an ever-broadening set of tools to customize and increase the efficiency of strategies generally through the use of an LDI-driven portable alpha application. Much of the theory and tools touched upon in this chapter have been with us for decades, yet it is only now that we are seeing large-scale adoption of newer strategies. This highlights the importance of the accounting and regulatory landscape—if we mismeasure the risk it will be mismanaged, if it is managed at all.

The catalysts of regulatory and accounting change will probably lead to more innovations in pension fund management in the next 5 years than we have seen in the prior 30. Hopefully some of these innovations will also recast light on the benefits that defined-benefit pension plans offer as parts of capital structure and compensation schemes that provide enduring value to the organizations that sponsor them. If we focus too much on the problems and risks associated with these institutions and what they mean for plan sponsors, we may be blinded to the fact that the problems associated with the alternatives may be far, far worse.

Hopefully, thoughtful and measured combination of the lessons learned since 2000 and more of a mark-to-market view of the liabilities with the increased flexibility of capital markets instruments will lead to better portfolio management solutions. Ideally this combination will lead to more consistency of returns and tighter tracking between assets and liabilities. In turn, this should lead to better security for plan participants, and plans that are better able to weather future market storms.

APPENDIX 10.1 BUILDING BETTER BETAS THROUGH FINANCIAL ENGINEERING

A Further Extension of the Portable Alpha Concept to LDI

As discussed in the previous chapter, in the circumstance where an investor is short a liability with materially different risk characteristics than a given asset, the net volatility position is greater than the stand-alone asset. Take for example, U.S. equities and a typical pension liability with duration of 14 years. Assume the volatility of the equities is 16 percent, consistent with historic experience for U.S. equities; the volatility of liabilities is 80 basis points per year of duration, or 11.2 percent; and the correlation between the annual returns of stocks and long bonds is 10 percent. The net volatility of a long position in equities and a short position in the liabilities is 18.6 percent.[7]

One approach to rectify this problem for the investor who fervently believes in the equity risk premium as a way to outrun his pension liabilities is to create equities with more duration. Essentially, get two betas in one asset. This can be achieved in two ways. Put some duration in your equities, or put some equity in your long bond portfolio. From a theoretical perspective, this is largely a matter of semantics or preference. It is simply a matter of deciding which beta the investor wants to achieve in cash markets and which he wants to get through derivatives. However, from a practical implementation perspective, there are some important differences.

The first strategy, adding duration to equities, is simply a matter of attaching an interest rate swap or Treasury futures to the equity investment. Figure 10.10 illustrates the nature of the transaction. The investor puts $100 into a cash equity investment and then either receives a fixed rate on a long maturity (e.g., 30-year) interest rate swap and pays the floating rate (LIBOR) or goes long the desired number of long futures contracts. In this case, the exposure is

$$\text{Equities} + (\text{Long Bonds} - \text{Financing Cost})$$

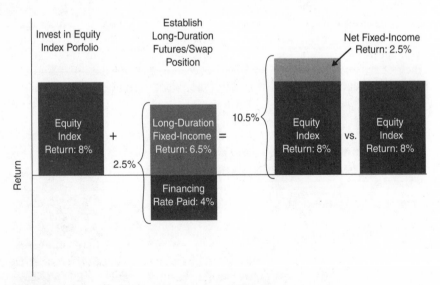

FIGURE 10.10 Strategy 1: Adding Duration to Equities
Source: PIMCO; hypothetical example for illustrative purposes only.

The second approach, adding equity exposure to a long bond portfolio, is a matter of entering into a total return swap in which the investor receives the return on a chosen equity index and pays a financing rate (LIBOR). Alternatively, the investor can use S&P 500 futures or some other futures market to gain the equity exposure. This parallel case is shown in Figure 10.11. Here the exposure is

$$\text{Long Bonds} + (\text{Equities} - \text{Financing Cost})$$

It is essentially the same thing, only what is inside and outside the brackets has changed.

However, as the saying goes, the devil is in the details. Bonds have superiority as collateral for financing. They are less volatile. In the case of Treasuries, they are almost certainly more liquid than equities. This has benefits when markets move and variation margin calls are required to hold overlay positions. This is especially true in times of financial turmoil. In addition, yields on bonds are higher than dividend yields on stocks. As the embedded financing costs (short rates) are closer to bond yields than dividend yields, this implies lower need to liquidate collateral to hold positions. This increases the stability of the strategy if it is to be implemented for an extended period and reduces transaction costs.

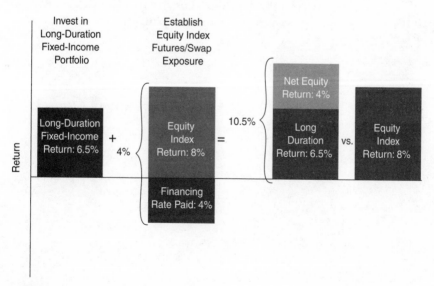

FIGURE 10.11 Strategy 2: Adding Equity Exposure to Long Duration Bond Portfolio
Source: PIMCO; hypothetical example for illustrative purposes only.

What would this long-duration equity look like? From a return perspective, it would generate the returns on the chosen equity index plus that of the long bond portfolio less financing costs. The return spread between long bonds and financing costs varies over time as the yield curve moves, but is generally positive and has averaged 3.4 percent over the 20-year period ended December 2006. Of course the absolute volatility is higher than a cash equity investment, at 2.8 percent over and above the S&P 500 index over the same period.

Though more volatile on a stand-alone basis, the strategy is less volatile when compared to a traditional equity strategy. Using the same assumptions from our earlier example and assuming that our collateral is invested in a bond portfolio similar to the Lehman Long Government Credit Index with a duration of 11 years, the net volatility is 15.9 percent,[8] which is not only decidedly lower than the 18.6 percent seen for the straight equity investment, but a tiny bit lower than the stand-alone volatility of the equities. How can this be? It results from the low correlation between the long bond returns and the equities. Here the duration mismatch is small and acts as a slight risk diversifier as opposed to when it is large and amplifies risk.

The same approach can be used to create better betas for pension plans in other asset classes for which there are liquid derivatives markets by combining these betas with long bond collateral portfolios. Commodities are an obvious extension of this reasoning. Long-short equity style or sector strategies are another. As the menu of options grows, so, too, will the array of better betas.

CHAPTER 11

Portable Alpha Theory and Practice: Wrapping It Up

Sabrina Callin

Investing has always been about the fundamental relationship between risk and return. While this has not changed, investors today are more open than ever to different sources of risk in addition to new investment tools and strategies, including portable alpha. The impetus for the broad-based shift appears to have been the 2000–2002 equity market sell-off combined with the associated decline in bond yields. Many not only experienced a material decline in their investment capital base, but at the same time were faced with lower prospective investment returns from traditional asset classes and strategies. As a result, change was not as much a choice as a requirement and the need to explore different approaches to investing become readily apparent.

The ensuing focus on both alpha and diversification was coupled with a great deal of excitement in the investment management community over the portable alpha investment application and related concepts like alpha-beta separation. Regardless of the impetus, it is true that portable alpha investment applications offer investors the potential to increase the return on capital from an investment allocation to a given asset class or sector while maintaining a similar level of risk. In some cases, portable alpha investment strategies can even provide an increase in expected return with a decrease in risk. Powerful concepts indeed!

All of the interest in portable alpha comes at a time when investors are recognizing that they may not be able to rely on the equity markets as the primary source of investment portfolio risk and expected return, at least for the foreseeable future. Dividends are very low by historical standards and relative to bond yields. In order for stocks to even provide a 1 percent return premium relative to bonds, per share earnings growth would have to be 4.5 percent (relative to earnings growth of just over 4 percent in the twentieth century). Getting to a risk premium that is closer to 3 to 5 percent may be a lot to ask! Therefore, with return targets of 8 percent-plus looming, many investors are actively taking steps to increase returns from other sources of risk, and ideally risks that offer attractive diversification to equity market risk.

ABILITY TO BORROW THROUGH THE DERIVATIVES MARKET SETS THE STAGE FOR PORTABLE ALPHA

At first blush, the potential investment benefits of portable alpha strategies may sound too good to be true. However, the ability to borrow through the derivatives markets to obtain desirable market exposure allows investors to incorporate a degree of diversification in (1) risk factor exposure and (2) investment manager skill that is not possible in a traditional asset management framework. This is not to say that portable alpha strategies universally offer an improved risk/return profile relative to traditional investment strategies. In many cases the increased expected return is accompanied by a similar or even greater increase in risk. The portable alpha investment application also does not make sense for all asset classes or investment categories for a number of reasons. However, the concepts behind portable alpha undeniably expand the universe of investment opportunities, making return profiles achievable that may not have previously been available to investors. Of course, it is still up to investors and their advisers to carefully consider the risk, return, costs, liquidity, and other relevant characteristics of any given investment strategy—including portable alpha strategies—on a stand-alone basis and also as a constituent part of the broader investment portfolio.

The term *portable alpha* is most commonly used to describe an investment approach that collateralizes derivatives-based market exposure, often referred to as *beta*, with an unrelated investment in a strategy designed to generate alpha (*alpha strategy*). The ability to employ a portable alpha approach is dependent first and foremost on the availability of a liquid, cost-efficient derivatives market for the desired beta exposure. Derivatives provide investors with the ability to finance beta exposure, generally at a money market rate–based cost, which frees up all or the majority of an investor's initial capital to be invested elsewhere. If the capital retained is invested such that the total return on capital is equal to the money market rate–based financing cost, then the return on the portable alpha strategy should be approximately equal to the beta market return. Of course, the goal of most portable alpha investment strategies is to generate attractive alpha—or risk-adjusted excess return—in addition to the beta market return. As such, most alpha strategies seek to outperform the money market rate–based cost of the beta derivatives exposure.

Portable alpha strategies that back S&P 500 futures with a high-quality enhanced cash portfolio date back to at least 1986 with the launch of PIMCO's StocksPLUS approach. Some investors have also used the same underlying concepts to obtain attractive alpha by investing in a traditional actively managed strategy, hedging the benchmark exposure and then obtaining a different market index exposure by holding long futures or swap positions. In these cases, the alpha strategy is the combination of the investment with the active manager plus the hedge to remove undesirable market exposure. More recently, however, investors have been combining an increasingly wide variety of beta derivatives and alpha strategies within a portable alpha context. Today the alpha strategies vary from the relatively low-risk enhanced cash alpha engines all the way to the higher-risk hedge fund alpha engines—and everything in between. Of course, as is true of investing more broadly, there is no such thing as a free lunch. The portable alpha strategies that claim to provide significant expected incremental return over stocks and bonds may involve a material increase in risk as well.

CENTRAL UNDERPINNINGS TO MODERN PORTFOLIO THEORY ARE HIGHLY RELEVANT

Investing, in the most basic sense, starts with the decision to forego consumption today with the goal of achieving a positive return on capital such that the future value of the capital is greater than the current value. With the exception of an investment in instruments like certain money market securities that effectively bear no risk of capital loss, most investments involve risk. As a technical matter, even a money market fund involves an uncertain return, money market instruments are generally thought of as the most liquid, lowest-risk investments available in the increasingly broad universe of choices. Perhaps the most important consideration is the potential that an investment will yield a negative return or capital loss over an investor's time horizon. This is what prevents investors from simply investing all of their investment capital with the goal of maximizing return without any thought to the downside risk.

An investor's risk tolerance is one of the most important guideposts when it comes to constructing an investment portfolio. While the true so-called risk-free investment may vary from investor to investor, the fundamental principles underlying most of modern portfolio theory focus on the still entirely relevant trade-off between expected return and risk—and also the benefits of diversification. The optimal risky investment portfolio is one that benefits to the maximum degree from diversification, thereby providing the greatest expected return at a given level of risk. The risk level of a given investment portfolio can be adjusted by holding varying combinations of the risk-free investment and the optimal risky portfolio such that investors with higher risk tolerances will hold more of the optimal risky portfolio than investors with lower risk tolerances. In addition, investors with a risk tolerance that exceeds the level of risk in the optimal risky portfolio can borrow and invest the proceeds in the optimal risky portfolio.

In the real world, the optimal portfolio is not readily identifiable as an investment option. As a result, borrowing can be employed not just to increase the risk and expected return profile of an investment portfolio but also as a means to accomplish greater diversification, a more efficient risk/return trade-off and potentially even a reduction in risk. *This is the basic premise behind the portable alpha investment application.*

Another interesting theoretical concept that is tangentially relevant in a portable alpha context is the idea of market efficiency. In theory, if the markets are perfectly efficient, then the price of a given investment should simply be a function of the associated nondiversifiable risk (the market risk). Beta was originally used in an investment context to quantify market risk in the capital asset pricing model (CAPM), a single-factor regression analysis that relates the return on a security over the risk-free rate to its sensitivity to the market portfolio or, equivocally, its market risk. Of course, in reality there is not one market portfolio, just as there is not one optimal risky portfolio—at least not one that we can identify and measure. Furthermore, skilled active management can result in additional return beyond the return that is expected as a function of the underlying risk. Therefore, the concept can and has been extended to allow investors to measure the sensitivity of investment returns to a variety of different market risk factors and also to measure any additional risk-adjusted returns or alpha derived from active management.

The bottom line is that the central underpinnings of modern portfolio theory are as relevant today as ever, and particularly so in a portable alpha context. It is generally necessary to take some type of risk in order to achieve an expected return premium over the risk-free rate. The key to optimal investing is to identify, measure, and diversify the risk.

ALPHA AND BETA—IT'S THE COMBINATION THAT MATTERS

It is hard to argue with the merit behind the decomposition of investment returns into alpha and beta. Doing so helps investors distinguish between the return earned as a direct consequence of the risk assumed and the returns that are not explained by the risk and therefore must be due to manager skill—or at least luck. This knowledge provides investors with not only a better ability to compare different managers and strategies, but also insight on the underlying risks factors. However, the terms *alpha* and *beta* are used today in an increasingly broad and often theoretically incorrect context. Unfortunately, this somewhat common use or misuse of the alpha and beta terms can be particularly problematic in a portable alpha and alpha-beta separation framework.

Beta is a sensitivity measure while alpha explains the return that is not accounted for by the beta relative to one or more market indexes or factors. Therefore, alpha cannot exist without beta, and both are wholly dependent on the factors (typically one or more market indexes) used in the associated regression equation. The same holds true for ex-post alpha where investment returns are compared against an appropriate market benchmark. For incremental return to truly be alpha, the market benchmark or risk factors used to calculate the alpha should be representative of the characteristics and most specifically the risk of the associated investment strategy. While an investor can select strategies that exhibit highly variable beta (sensitivity) to an increasingly wide variety of different risk factors, there is no such thing as stand-alone alpha. Even the alpha of a low-risk, actively managed, enhanced cash strategy that produces cashlike risk with incremental excess return is still a relative term, where the beta and alpha are measured relative to a cash benchmark as a close proxy for the risk of the actively managed enhanced cash strategy.

Investors can invest in an actively managed strategy and then hedge the benchmark exposure or undesirable risk factor exposure, but even then the investor will not necessarily receive the same alpha result when the original alpha is coupled with a different beta. This is due in part to variations in cost and bid-ask spread considerations associated with different derivatives contracts plus any associated implementation, liquidity, and operational costs. More fundamentally, it is due to the fact that the market indexes or risk factors used to calculate the betas are not the same.

Why is the more casual use of the terms *alpha* and *beta* potentially problematic in a portable alpha context? Ultimately, an investor has chosen to borrow with the goal of achieving higher returns. As a result, the investment capital is exposed to both the alpha strategy and the derivatives-based beta market. While true alpha does represent the residual return not accounted for by one or more relevant risk factors or benchmarks, much of what is marketed as alpha is not risk-adjusted return. Rather, it is just return over the risk-free rate—even though the risk inherent in the investment strategy is often materially greater than the risk inherent in a Treasury bill or money market investment. Therefore, investors cannot simply combine an alpha strategy with any given beta and assume that there will not be a material increase in risk.

All of this does not mean that the concept of portable alpha or alpha-beta separation is without merit. It simply means that, while an alpha source can be obtained entirely independently from the desired beta market exposure, it is still necessary to consider the two together. This is true for purposes of calculating the expected return, beta, and alpha of the portable alpha strategy and, more important, it is true for calculating the resulting investment risk. Regardless of the technicalities of the alpha and beta statistics, the end result from combining any number of different investment strategies and market risk factors may be an improvement in risk/return relative to either of the stand-alone components due to the power of diversification.

A WIDE VARIETY OF ALPHA SOURCES ARE AVAILABLE

Although the decisions are fundamentally related, one of the key elements of value inherent in the portable alpha concept relates to the ability to select an alpha source that is independent from the desired market (beta) exposure. The broader opportunity set carries with it the potential for higher return and powerful diversification benefits—although the decision process is more complex.

As a starting point, the alpha strategy decision fundamentally relates to how much and what type of risk an investor is willing to assume relative to a risk-free investment, not unlike the most basic of investment decisions. However, with portable alpha approaches, investors are also obtaining exposure to a second set of market risk factors via the beta derivatives exposure. In addition to evaluating a given alpha source on a stand-alone basis, it is important to evaluate the value of the alpha source in combination with the derivatives-based beta market exposure. Therefore, correlation and similar measures are very relevant.

Globally, there is an increasingly broad set of opportunities to add value relative to a risk-free rate through a combination of market risk factors and active management. Risk factor exposures and associated alpha opportunities encompass both traditional and alternative asset classes and include but are not limited to factors such as stock market risk, vega/volatility risk, interest rate risk, liquidity risk, currency risk, credit risk, commodity risk, financing risk, and even accounting, regulatory, and tax treatment risk. Of course, any given risk factor may be expressed through one or a variety of different asset types, instruments, or combinations of instruments, and any given asset or strategy may have exposure to multiple risk factors. The value of active management is manifest in selecting (market timing) and determining the optimal way to express risk factors (security selection) that will deliver an attractive risk/return profile.

All investment strategies that are expected to outperform the risk-free rate (or money market rates as a proxy) should theoretically result in an increase in expected return relative to the beta market exposure when combined with the associated derivatives contracts in a portable alpha context (at least this is true before fees and costs!). The key from an investor's standpoint is to select an alpha strategy (or strategies) that will produce the optimal result (maximum return at an acceptable level of risk) when combined with the desired beta market exposure(s) after fees and costs, on average over the investor's time horizon. Unfortunately, this is much easier said than done. Of course, the same is true of investing in a traditional context for the simple reason that ex-ante expectations do not always match ex-post results. Good investment decisions can yield bad results—and vice versa. Portable alpha and alpha-beta separation can be even that much more potentially complicated, however, due primarily to the derivatives and associated leverage components.

THE KEY IS IDENTIFICATION, MEASUREMENT, AND DIVERSIFICATION OF RISK FACTORS

Thanks to financial innovation, the universe of available risk factor exposures continues to expand, along with the array of different instruments, vehicles, and associated investment strategies, increasing the potential value that can be derived from intelligent investing and diversification. Fortunately, even in this increasingly complex investment arena, most investment portfolios and strategies can be decomposed into a set of primary risk factors.

With equity-based strategies, the common risk factor referenced is equity market risk (the original beta!). However, many actively managed equity strategies may assume additional risk in an effort to capture market risk premium. Common strategies along this vein include long small cap and short large cap stock positions and also long emerging market and short developed market positions. These risk factor exposures are associated with both traditional active equity strategies and also long-short equity hedge fund strategies, although the exposure to equity market risk in the latter case is likely to be much more variable over time. The primary risk factors evidenced in actively managed fixed-income strategies and fixed-income hedge fund strategies are typically interest rate risk, credit risk, volatility/vega risk, and liquidity risk—although, again, the exposure and magnitude can vary substantially over time. Globally diversified portfolios, which have been shown to offer improved investment results, also may incorporate currency risk.

In cases where a good investment benchmark has been identified that is reflective of an investment strategy's primary characteristics and, most important, the investment risk, the identification and measurement of the primary risk factor exposures may be relatively straightforward. In other cases, most typically with strategies that afford managers a large degree of freedom to vary the risk factor exposures over time, the risk factor exposures may require more effort to identify and monitor.

Extensions of the CAPM and related factor models can be helpful when it comes to identifying the market risk factors and residual alpha associated with a given approach or strategy that is expected to outperform the risk-free rate. Ultimately, though, it is important that investors obtain a reasonable level of transparency specific to the underlying risk factor exposures.

IT'S IMPORTANT NOT TO LOSE SIGHT OF THE POLICY PORTFOLIO

Studies show that asset allocation decisions have historically accounted for the majority of the return and related risk profile of an investment portfolio. To the extent that the asset allocation process incorporates an especially thoughtful strategic and tactical decision-making process and a broad opportunity set, the potential value-added on a risk-adjusted basis from asset allocation is even greater. This is not to say that the potential for alpha from a given strategy or manager is not important—true alpha is always valuable. However, given the importance of asset allocation decisions, any potentially material impact of the strategies designed to generate the alpha on the overall asset allocation risk/return profile should be carefully evaluated on an ongoing basis as part of the asset allocation and associated risk budgeting decision-making process.

Portable alpha avails investors of additional value-added opportunities that can be incorporated into the asset allocation decision-making process due to the ability to efficiently gain certain asset class and/or risk factor exposures by borrowing via the derivatives markets, thereby retaining capital to allocate elsewhere. However, portable alpha also creates the possibility for unanticipated and material alterations to a given asset allocation if the asset allocation only considers the risk factors associated with the beta components and not the risk factors of the alpha strategy or strategies. For example, the substitution of a bond swap plus alpha engine for a traditional investment in bonds within a given asset allocation may produce disastrous results in a period of equity market stress if the alpha engine collateralizing the bond exposure exhibits a meaningfully positive correlation with equities. The value-added potential of the portable alpha investment application is great—but there are important complexities and related considerations that must be carefully evaluated by investors.

PRUDENT DERIVATIVES-BASED BETA MANAGEMENT IS NOT FREE

Careful consideration by investors should not be limited solely to the alpha strategy and the combination of the investment risk factors in the alpha strategy and the derivatives-based beta market exposure. Available, liquid, low-cost derivatives serve as the fundamental building block for portable alpha implementation. Unfortunately, however, this piece of the equation is often oversimplified when it comes to the true costs, risks, and skills necessary to optimally manage the derivatives positions. One misperception is the idea that beta should be free. The notion that investors can obtain exposure to a wide variety of different market exposures for the same price (free!) is not at all reasonable—nor is free anywhere close to the right price for maintaining derivatives-based beta exposure.

As previously discussed, the borrowing cost component of derivatives-based beta exposure is typically tied to a money market interest rate. Using LIBOR as a base rate and looking at the spread relative to LIBOR associated with obtaining derivatives-based beta exposure, there is a fair degree of variation of costs even in the futures markets. Swaps, OTC-traded instruments that are negotiated directly with a counterparty and may involve complex legal agreements, typically trade at a premium to futures. This is due to the fact that the swap counterparties usually hedge their exposure using futures and they do not provide swaps for free. For indexes without liquid futures contracts, the swap cost may be closely related to dealer balance sheet cost, although the costs can vary substantially depending on market dynamics, liquidity, and other factors. Special swap terms that require the dealer to take additional risk or otherwise incur additional costs will likely be priced at higher levels.

Derivatives-based beta cost also varies by market participant. Unlike exchange-traded funds (ETFs) or mutual funds, the cost of obtaining beta exposure through the derivatives markets is not the same for everyone. Skill is relevant not only in terms of obtaining beta derivatives exposure at the lowest possible cost, but also for maintaining an appropriate amount of derivatives exposure, the associated cash flow management, and the investment and operational risk management processes and procedures. And, as is often the case, you get what you pay for.

PORTABLE ALPHA IMPLEMENTATION CAN BE COMPLEX AND COSTLY

A growing number of portable alpha implementation options are available to investors that may prove helpful in terms of addressing the complexities associated with the alpha strategy (and even the alpha strategy selection), the risk measurement process (including, in some cases, risk factor selection and hedging), and also the operational aspects, specifically with the derivatives and also more broadly with the portable alpha program.

Although the details vary from provider to provider and also from investor to investor, there appear to be three basic approaches to portable alpha strategy implementation: a fully integrated approach, a completely segregated approach, and something in between that we call *semibundled* for purposes of our analysis. The key components of each can be further broken down into four primary elements as a means to understanding the different approaches: (1) the alpha strategy (the strategy that houses the majority of the cash allocated to the portfolio alpha investment); (2) the beta derivatives exposure, sometimes referred to as an overlay; (3) liquidity to meet margin or collateral calls associated with the beta derivatives exposure; and (4) consolidated risk management, risk monitoring, and reporting.

In a truly integrated strategy, one manager manages all four elements in, as the name implies, an integrated fashion. In the segregated approach, all four elements are typically segregated and the end investor generally plays a key role in terms of the ongoing implementation and risk management. The third category, the semibundled approach, offers investors the ability to work with one central provider who in turn oversees and/or manages the four elements. The elements are still segregated as a technical matter, although they appear bundled from the investor's standpoint.

Each approach has distinct advantages and disadvantages and it is very important for investors to understand the complexities, costs, risks, and risk controls associated with a given approach before investing. The cost component may be particularly relevant when investors consider the trade-off between investment risk—which is necessarily tied to gross-of-fee return—and expected after-fee return.

RISK MANAGEMENT IS A CRITICAL COMPONENT OF SUCCESS

While investors have become much more open to new ideas and strategies, at the same time there seems to have been a marked increase in risk appetite. Importantly, while higher risk should theoretically lead to higher returns over the long term, there is no guarantee that this will occur. In fact, the more compressed that risk premiums become, by definition the return from taking risk decreases—but it does not follow that actual risk decreases if the sole reason for the compression in risk premiums is demand for risky assets.

Portable alpha strategies necessarily involve at least one form of leverage and the use of derivatives and may also include illiquid alpha engines with additional layers of leverage, nonnormal return distributions, and a high degree of optionality. As such, the investment risk associated with a given portable alpha strategy may not be as straightforward as is the case with traditional stock and bond portfolio investments. Nonetheless, because the capital allocated to a portable alpha strategy typically has 100 percent exposure to both the beta derivatives and the alpha engine component, it is important to have a clear understanding of the risk factors inherent in each component, the likely correlation between the two under various market scenarios, and, on an ongoing basis, any associated assets or liabilities. The last point is relevant for purposes of calculating the net asset value of a portable alpha strategy as of a given point in time, which is necessary as a first step to measuring risk factor exposure (percent allocations, etc.). To the extent that the risk factors within either component are likely to vary appreciably over time, the ongoing monitoring and measurement process is of particular importance, as is a reasonable level of transparency with respect to the risk factor exposures.

One relevant measure for purposes of understanding the aggregate risk profile of a given portable alpha strategy may be the historical and/or expected volatility of returns (taking into account both the beta and the alpha strategy components). However, volatility is generally not a good stand-alone measure of investment risk, especially for strategies that are relatively illiquid, have significant underlying optionality, or embed material rare event risk.

To have a more complete understanding of the risk and magnitude of potential losses, other risk measures are important as well, in particular stress testing. The related derivatives and leverage components are also worthy of special consideration. Not only may some types of leverage result in magnified losses, but liquidity requirements associated with the derivatives-based beta exposure and/or derivatives positions within the alpha engine may result in forced liquidations of strategies at disadvantageous times.

One of the most noteworthy challenges associated with portable alpha strategy selection, which is also a challenge to successful asset allocation more broadly, is that volatilities and correlations are notoriously unstable. This fact, when coupled with the reality that market shocks seem to happen much more frequently than statistics predict they should, makes it more difficult to ensure that the risk of a particular investment exposure is acceptable to the end investor.

All of that said, portable alpha strategies can reap powerful risk-reducing diversification benefits—it is just critically important for investors to consider not only the extra return potential but also any associated incremental risk.

PORTABLE ALPHA IS ALSO VALUABLE FOR INVESTORS FOCUSED ON LDI

Interestingly enough, given all of the focus in our industry on portable alpha, the portable alpha concept may be particularly relevant and beneficial in another area that has received a great deal of focus in recent years, liability-driven investing (LDI). Many pension plan sponsors face two major, yet seemingly irreconcilable, concerns: return targets that appear high relative to prospective asset class returns *and* a need to reduce the volatility of their asset portfolios relative to their liabilities. The former challenge might invoke increased investment allocations to risky assets in an effort to achieve higher returns, while the latter challenge may call for increased investment allocations to high-quality fixed-income securities with a similar duration to the duration of plan liabilities. The irreconcilable difference relates to the fact that high-quality, longer-duration fixed-income securities do not typically carry a high enough risk/return premium to help meet the former objective at the same time as the latter. Investors have responded with a variety of strategies to help reconcile this difference—or at least to navigate the associated issues.

Portable alpha applications are one area that is receiving an increasing amount of attention from investors who are focused on liability-driven investing. The LDI-related portable alpha applications generally allow investors to obtain/retain exposure to a risky asset class or investment strategy and therefore (on an expected basis) capture the associated risk premium and, at the same time, obtain/retain exposure to an investment that is highly correlated with plan liabilities. The key to this solution, as is the case with all portable alpha strategies, is derivatives. Investors can add interest rate exposure to a given portfolio or investment via the derivatives markets without deploying any or a material amount of cash. Alternatively, an investor can invest in an appropriate long-duration bond portfolio (effectively the risk-free asset from the standpoint of a pension plan sponsor) and then assume additional risk—in exchange for additional expected return—by obtaining desirable risk factor exposure via the derivatives markets. The optimal choice for a given investor will be contingent on a number of factors. Ultimately, though, in addition to balance sheet volatility and actuarial return target considerations, the answer to the following question is very important: Will the assets cover the liabilities?

PORTABLE ALPHA PROVIDES TOOLS FOR BETTER INVESTMENT RESULTS

This liability question is not limited to just pension plans or other investors with explicit long-dated liabilities. The endgame of investing for most is ultimately about covering future liabilities or, if not technically liabilities, implicit obligations or return targets designed to sustain spending targets. Even with individual investors, the reason for investing may not be so much about additional consumption as it may be about necessary retirement savings, college educations, planned charitable donations, and the like. At the same time, most investors do not have limitless capital to invest, and capital losses can be particularly painful as losses necessarily reduce the base on which investment returns can be earned. It takes a 25 percent return to bring an investment portfolio up to its starting value following a 20 percent loss for this reason [$100 − ($100 × 20 percent) = $80; $80 × 1.25 percent = $100].

As such, most investors do not simply invest in such a way that they believe will achieve the highest return. Rather, careful consideration is (or should be) given to the downside risk as well. Risk is a two-way street, and higher risk may lead to higher expected return—but it also comes hand in hand with the greater possibility of capital losses. This can be problematic in an environment where prospective investment returns are lower, yet future obligations and associated return targets are unchanged. This is where portable alpha and associated concepts may be particularly helpful.

There are two key ways for investors to increase their return without increasing their risk—or, alternatively, to decrease their risk without decreasing their return. One is improved diversification and the other is increased alpha. While not a simple investment application by any means, portable alpha allows investors to capitalize on both, often to a significant degree. For this reason, we believe it is well worth the time, energy, and effort that investors may need to devote in order to benefit from this powerful investment application.

Portable Alpha—The Final Chapter

Schemes, Dreams, and Financial Imbalances: "There Must Be More Money"

Chris P. Dialynas

In the movie *The Rocking Horse Winner*, adapted from a D.H. Lawrence short story, a boy was haunted by a chant from his house, "There must be more money!" in reference to his mother's constant need for more money to make extravagant ends meet. The dedicated child, who adored his mother, responded to the chant by partnering with the gardener, who regularly bet on horses. The boy would rock on his rocking horse faster and faster until he determined the winning horse upon which he could place his bet and satisfy the needs of the house. In the end, the heavy demands of the house were so great and the difficulty of choosing the winner so onerous that the boy died after picking a big winner. The mother, ignorant of and unsupportive of the boy's activities, refused the big payoff, saying, "I'll have nothing to do with blood money." In the movie, the boy had to do more and more to keep up with the "wants" of the house. So, too, are the demands on absolute return managers, and the greater required energy is manifested in greater leverage. Ultimately, death of the strategies occurs for the house (the investor loses money) and the blood money is in the hands of the investment manager. In this final chapter we will learn how and why this is happening and why we believe it is a very relevant epilogue to *Portable Alpha Theory and Practice*.

The investment landscape is much different today than at any time in the past. Investor dreams of double-digit returns have provoked leveraged investment schemes—often-referred to as alpha engines—of dubious quality.

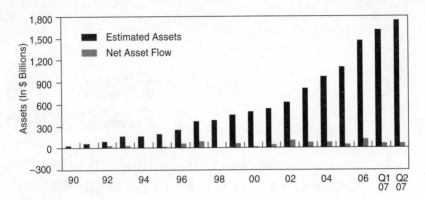

FIGURE E.1   Estimated Growth of Assets/Net Asset Flow for the Hedge Fund
Industry (1990–Q2 2007)
Source: Courtesy of Hedge Fund Research, Inc.

Structured products, hedge funds, private equity funds, and other so-called
absolute return investment strategies are all increasingly important market
participants. The capital deployed in these products by investors is enormous
and has been growing at a very fast rate. By way of example, the hedge fund
industry has grown from essentially nothing in 1990 to about $1.5 trillion
in 2006 and is rapidly approaching $2 trillion, as noted in Chapter 6 and
depicted in Figure E.1.

These investment strategies commonly employ derivatives and abun-
dant leverage to generate "excess" returns. In contrast, in my early days
at PIMCO in the 1980s, we utilized the inherent ready-made leverage
of financial futures and the to be announced (TBA) mortgage market in
an unleveraged manner to produce alpha. The concept was simple and
elegant—arbitrage the low implied cost of financing imbedded within the
futures contract and the higher prevailing high-quality market rates of interest for short-term bonds, a strategy we referred to as "BondsPLUS." At
that time, financial futures were the only derivatives available, and high-
quality, unleveraged investment standards were rigid. An additional landscape change is the growth of the cumulative U.S. current account deficit,
representative of investment funds in foreign investors' hands, from nothing
in 1984 to over $6 trillion today. The combination of leveraged invest-
ment schemes and foreign investors is a potentially lethal one. As a result,
the new leveraged financial market architecture and system have profound
implications for both investment strategies and public policy.

The rapid growth of the credit derivatives market to approximately $25
trillion as shown in Figure E.2 reflects the demand for ready-made LIBOR
financing and leverage.

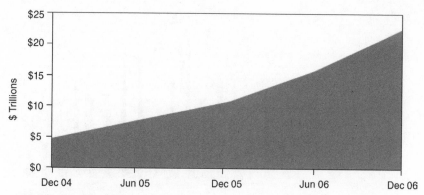

FIGURE E.2 Credit Default Swaps Market (Notional Amounts Outstanding from End-December 2004)
Source: Data from the Bank for International Settlements (www.bis.org).

The transformation of alpha engines from high-quality financing arbitrage to leveraged beta strategies, called alpha, stands in sharp contrast to the prevalent conservative attitude of the 1980s. The structured products market is a good example of statistical engineering, whereby leverage is used as a tool to create products with return promises too good to believe. Structured corporate bond products provide leveraged exposure to the corporate market and benefit from book value accounting. Structured product is engineered and dependent on statistical default and correlation data. The engineering of cash flows transforms well-diversified leveraged portfolios of corporate bonds, primarily BBB rated, into assets rated AAA, AA, and A. Growth in this market is shown in Figure E.3.

Unfortunately, few investors seem to understand that statistics are environment dependent. The structures resemble Pascal's wager in that if the statistics are unreliable, the value of the structured product can drop rapidly as the short convexity cliff is hit. The radically changed financial markets, influenced by increased globalization and characterized by high leverage in the United States, exchange rates pegged cheap to the U.S. dollar, and enormous technological advances, suggest that it is highly likely that the statistical conclusions are unreliable.

The investor in leveraged hedge fund or other absolute return strategies, the leveraged structured product investor, and the foreign investor all represent sources of demand that drove down risk premiums and market volatility in the period from 2003 to 2006. The lower risk premium and lower volatility premiums mean that an even greater amount of leverage is required to achieve a stipulated nominal return objective. The leveraged absolute return schemes are viable as long as funding is plentiful. However,

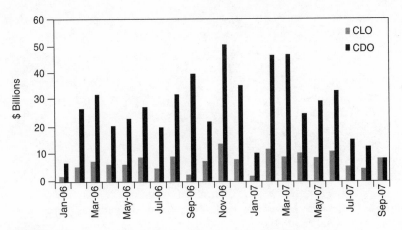

FIGURE E.3 Growth in Structured Product Markets (January 2006–September 2007)
Source: Data from Merrill Lynch.

if funding is withheld, the highly leveraged strategies can unwind quickly. This dynamic is akin to the portfolio insurance strategies of the mid-1980s. The increase in leverage bids up the value of assets, compressing risk spreads and simultaneously increasing the fundamental risks associated with those assets. It is incorrect to assume that compressed spreads and low volatility imply low risk. *Quite the contrary.*

RISK ASYMMETRIES: VOLATILITY, SPREAD, LEVERAGE

Another challenge relates to the compensation schemes afforded to hedge fund managers that may actually inhibit, rather than encourage, rational decision making that is in the best interest of the investor. The typical 20 percent participation in excess returns is a call option. Increasing the risk of the fund maximizes the call option's value. Consequently, the fund manager will rarely return assets to investors or hold the assets in cash when valuations are poor relative to risk. Negative carry trades require good timing or strong conviction. It is rare for a hedge fund manager to engage in such a trade, because the call option on fees is worthless if an event does not occur. If the hedge fund manager is engaged in a carry trade when the downside of the associated risk emerges (the bad event happens), the client loses a lot of money but the hedge fund manager merely loses business. Perhaps a clever hedge fund manager should divide his business into two portions, positive carry and negative carry, and thus always be assured of great fees. (See Chapter 3 for greater elaboration about manager fees and market asymmetries.)

We have already established the linkage between high leverage, low volatility, and low risk premiums. These dynamics invalidate traditional investment assumptions of normally distributed returns and create significant risk/reward asymmetries. Investors should disinvest or short leveraged asset markets offering little premium and minimum volatility. Leveraged carry strategies in these markets are extremely dangerous as they are ripe for a violent mispricing. Investors should sacrifice yield in these situations, because the maximum opportunity is the sum of the yield spread plus the product of the yield spread times the bond's duration, whereas the gain from a short position is potentially large because an increase in volatility and spread is positively correlated and negatively related to leverage. Perversely, a reduction in leverage in the macro system increases volatility and increases spreads.

The simplest example of a risk/return asymmetry is a corporate bond. An investment in a corporate bond provides investors with the product of the initial yield advantage times the term of the bond in the best case and possibly negative 100 percent in an extremely negative case. Minimal risk premiums imply minimal yield advantage. An example will illustrate the point. Assume an investor has a 1-year investment horizon and is considering an investment in a 10-year Baa corporate bond with a duration of 6.5 years and a yield that is 75 basis points greater than the yield on a 10-year Treasury note (i.e., a yield spread of 75 basis points). We can see the very poor risk/return profile in Table E.1. Because of the asymmetry shown in the table, Schumpeter

TABLE E.1   Corporate Bond Return under Different Yield Spread Change Scenarios

Spread Change	(75bp)*	0	50bp	100bp	Infinite*
Market Value Change	5.00	0	(3.25)	(6.5)	(100%)
Spread	.75	.75	.75	.75	0
Total Return	5.75	.75	(2.50)	(5.75)	(100%)

Returns are expressed in percentage terms.

*It is a highly improbable event that the yield spread would decline to zero, as this would mean that investors do not demand any compensation for the credit risk that they are assuming. Nonetheless, the price gain associated with the elimination of the yield spread plus the initial yield represents the maximum possible return to an investor who holds a long position in a corporate bond. Conversely, as noted earlier and shown in Table E.1, the downside to the same investor is theoretically infinite, as there is no limit to the possible increase in the yield spread.

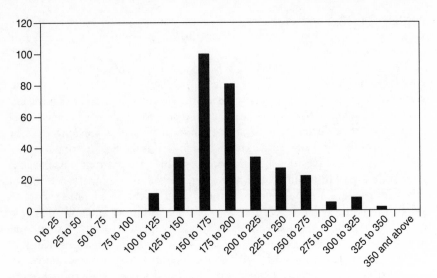

FIGURE E.4 Distribution of Spreads on Baa Corporate 10+-Year Index
(1980–2007)
Source: Data from Citigroup.

believed the bond investor was the hero of capitalism (the risk taker), not
the entrepreneur.

Figure E.4 depicts the distribution of spreads on 10-year Baa corporate
notes from 1980 to 2007. As shown in the chart, when spreads are already
at very low levels, the asymmetry between the reward of further yield spread
declines and the risk of (possibly material) increases in yield spreads is
strikingly apparent.

Of course, if leverage is involved, even a relatively modest change in
yield spreads can lead to devastating losses, as demonstrated in the following leveraged carry trade example. We now know the structured subprime
mortgage asset-backed market valuations in 2006 were exemplary of this
risk profile.

Leveraged Carry Trade Example

5-year bond, duration of 3.5 years   Higher-volatility yield spread = 1.50%
Current yield spread = .35%   Average yield spread = 1%
Leverage = 10×
Finance @ .10%

Leveraged Return in a Stable Market:

$10(.35 - .10) = 2.50\%$

Leveraged Return when spreads increase to 1.50% (50bps above average):

Higher-volatility market: $10[(.35 - .25) - 10(\text{Duration} \times \text{Yield Spread Change})]$

$$2.5\% - 10(3.5 \times 1.15)$$
$$2.5\% - 10(4.025)$$
$$2.5 - 40.25$$
$$= -37.75\%$$

ABSOLUTE RETURN DYNAMICS

Hedge fund returns tend toward subpar during periods of heightened market volatility. Higher volatility results in higher bid-ask spreads, more costly money (borrowing), and margin calls, leading to the unwinding of positions. Highly leveraged strategies geared to high absolute returns are strategies that can be characterized as the sale of options at the tail of the assumed distribution.

We can think of a dynamic game where there is only one participant. This participant can set the leverage such that the strike price of the option sale is where he pleases and receive a market volatility premium. Under normal conditions, the participant can fare well because the game is fair. A nominal return distribution approximates reality. However, the high leverage is incompatible with high volatility, particularly in a VAR framework. In fact, a review of historical data indicated that the performance of hedge funds examined deteriorated very rapidly during periods of heightened volatility once the strike price approached. This relationship is exhibited in Figure E.5 by the inverse correlation between hedge fund returns, on average and across most style categories, and the VIX as a proxy for market volatility. (The VIX is a volatility index created by the CBOE to measure equity market volatility.)

We found the same relationship when examining individual hedge fund strategies. In the case of the individual funds analyzed, they were hand selected by an institutional investor with the goal of diversifying risk across different managers and strategies, yet all exhibited a negative correlation with volatility. Therefore, on average, when volatility increased the performance for all of the funds declined. As a result, during periods characterized by sharp increases in volatility the investor may find the theoretical diversification benefits provided by the group of hedge fund strategies to be sorely disappointing.

This is consistent with the idea that performance is very negatively convex at the strike price, resembling a cliff, as illustrated in Figure E.6.

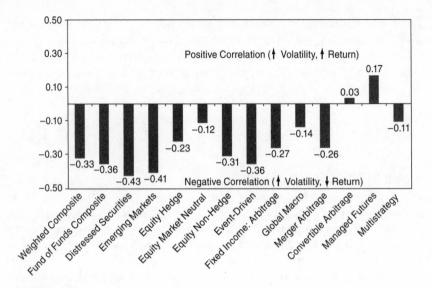

FIGURE E.5 Correlation of Hedge Fund Strategies with VIX (10 Years Ended September 2007)
Source: Data from FHRI and CS/Tremont.

The increased systemic leverage and foreign participation negate normally distributed return assumptions. The correct distribution is impossible to specify, and, if specified, the equation is very difficult, if not impossible, to solve.

The dynamics become more interesting when we introduce many more participants who hold similar investment objectives. The competitive desire

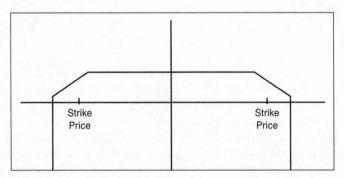

FIGURE E.6 Cliff Return Distribution (Leveraged Structured Products and Hedge Funds)
Source: Data from PIMCO, hypothetical example for illustrative purposes only.

for a given return objective leads to three possibilities: (1) more leverage, (2) a strike price closer to the spot price, or (3) a combination of (1) and (2). The greater leverage provides for more of a given spread, and striking the option closer to the money yields more premium. As more and more investors enter the game, each must get in front of the others to retain competitive status. Fund managers get in front by engaging in one of the three possibilities, which lead to similar increases in risk/reward and hold similar implications for public policy. Moreover, the compensation structure of the hedge fund industry provides incentives consistent with the postulated behavior, which is inconsistent with a rational investor's utility function.

The dynamics become even more interesting when we introduce large players who hold political objectives: foreign investors. A large foreign investor can influence yield premiums, particularly if the stock of assets held is large and the inflow also is large. This investor can induce volatility if he abruptly alters his investment strategy, impacting the pricing of risk in a material way. The range of corporate bond spreads shown in Figure E.4 highlights the potential for variation in Baa (investment grade) credit risk premiums as an example. The abrupt change in strategy results in increased volatility, which then causes the hedge fund investors to experience the downside of the negatively convex cliff illustrated in Figure E.6.

THE U.S. CURRENT ACCOUNT DEFICIT, WAR, AND HEDGE FUNDS: BRIEFLY

The U.S. war on terror began in 2001 and continues today. Countries at war prefer: (1) well-functioning capital markets, (2) open trade, (3) minimal market volatility, (4) low risk premiums, and (5) rising markets. These conditions lead to low financing costs and efficient production. Historically, market price deterioration results from losing a campaign or diminishing public support for the war initiative. It is at this point that government controls over trade and finance substitute, in the name of patriotism, for open trade and finance. Markets tend to perform very poorly when this occurs—assuming they remain open.

Leveraged strategies directed to higher-yielding assets reduce risk premiums and suppress volatility. An overvalued U.S. dollar and the consequent large current account deficit support dis-saving in the United States and provide funds to foreigners to reinvest in the U.S. markets, further suppressing risk spreads and volatility and raising U.S. asset prices. (The impact on dis-saving in recent years is clearly evidenced in Figure E.7.) A risk management approach to policy at the Federal Reserve further reinforces the market

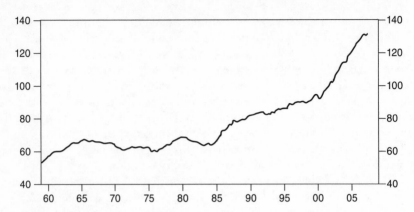

FIGURE E.7 U.S. Household Total Debt to Disposable Income Ratio Difference (Year to Year)
Source: Data from the Federal Reserve.

behavior. U.S. consumers and investors alike feel great because foreigners finance U.S. consumption, and asset appreciation creates wealth.

The war effort is advanced by an economy operating efficiently with low volatility/low risk premiums. The price appreciation of the U.S. housing market for 2002 through 2006 is a result of this policy attitude. Moreover, the U.S. government has an organized market surveillance committee to ensure market stability and, presumably, the consequent economic efficiency. Distortions in capital allocation that result are largely ignored. Unsurprisingly, hedge fund leveraged strategies, the large trade imbalance, and U.S. war efforts serve to reinforce each other. The importance of the accumulated misallocations of capital will be realized very dramatically when a meaningful change in the war campaign occurs. Investors are wise to avoid leveraged absolute return strategies when that day arrives.

PUBLIC POLICY IMPLICATIONS

The present financial schemes that incorporate highly leveraged strategies concurrent with a horribly imbalanced global economy are very binding on public policy. The greater and greater leverage and closer and closer cliff strike prices imply that the range of tolerable market movement and volatility increases is becoming a smaller and smaller segment. This suggests that policy makers must respond to market volatility more quickly, as depicted by the narrower public policy discretion interval in Figure E.8, or risk a major credit contraction as leveraged strategies delever and disintegrate.

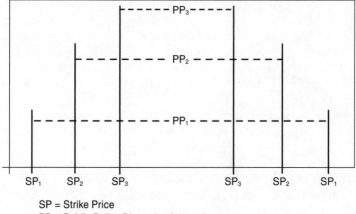

SP = Strike Price
PP = Public Policy Discretion Interval

FIGURE E.8 Public Policy Implications Chart
Source: Data from PIMCO, hypothetical example for illustrative purposes only.

Increases in leverage and credit are very beneficial to an economy until, as Schumpeter posited, credit contraction produces deflationary results, and, as Miller-Modigliani showed, the increases in leverage disproportionately increase bankruptcy risk. So, too, with the general economy.

CONCLUSION

Ironically, what began in the early 1980s as a simple finance arbitrage PIMCO portable alpha strategy has evolved in some cases to highly levered, unregulated portable alpha hedge fund strategies. Both are referred to as the alpha source in a portable alpha context, but they are vastly different in terms of the potential downside risk. Coincident with a globalized financial system completely out of balance wherein "Renegade Economics"* rules the public policy front, disintegration of many of these highly levered schemes is not the question. The questions are when and how bad. The leveraged schemes were created to fulfill investor dreams. The schemes perpetuated the increase in global liquidity, global imbalances, financial risk, and geopolitical risk. A sharp reversal in liquidity that could result from

---

*As described in "Renegade Economics: The Bretton Woods II Fiction" by Chris Dialynas and Marshall Auerback (September 2007, www. pimco.com).

a necessary risk reassessment may be difficult to contain. The reversal in liquidity will most likely derive from an abrupt foreign reallocation away from U.S. assets, as losses on prior investments of presumed high quality are realized, marking the secular peak in global trade. Moreover, the newly created so-called *sovereign wealth funds* will eventually be viewed as imperialistic vehicles further exacerbating global political tensions and will therefore increase market risk.

Financial engineers quantify the risk inherent in a strategy in very precise statistical and Greek terms. The credentials of the engineers and complexity of the models further authenticate the output. The application of math, physics, and statistics to financial assets has provided a security blanket to investors. The quants prove things. However, economics and investing have never been precise sciences. Highly leveraged investment schemes appear stable. No doubt there is a wide range of quality among the many absolute return schemes, as well as a wide range of hidden embedded risk. The embedded risk is hidden in the model derivation and the assumptions therein. Understanding the embedded risks, assumptions, and changing risk character of the various types of portable alpha strategies, as embedded options are attached and alpha morphs into beta, is the main point of this book. To truly accomplish this for portable alpha approaches and other investment schemes more broadly, politicians, policy makers, and investors alike must recognize that double-digit investment returns in a low single-digit interest rate world are inconsistent, likely of very high risk, unsustainable, destabilizing, and subject to severe loss potential.

Notes

Chapter 1   Overview of Book and Key Concepts

1. Jonathan Burton, "Alpha and Bets: Investment Consultant Peter Bernstein on Sharpening Your Portfolio's Edge," *MarketWatch,* April 30, 2007.

Chapter 2   Portable Alpha Definitions and Trends

1. William Sharpe, Gordon Alexander, and Jeffery Bailey, *Investments* (Prentice Hall, 1995), 759.
2. Exceptions include situations where an investor appropriately evaluates an investment but underestimates the true inherent risk due to fraudulent representations made by others.
3. William Gross, "Consistent Alpha Generation through Structure: Bold Thinking on Investment Management," *Financial Analysts Journal 60th Anniversary Anthology* (2005).
4. Peter Bernstein, *Capital Ideas Evolving* (John Wiley & Sons, 2007), 179.
5. This is not to say that there were not and are not skilled equity managers out there, but the equity market itself is volatile and returns might sometimes even be referred to as irrational (or even irrationally exuberant?), often rendering excellent company and industry level research somewhat meaningless.
6. Bernstein, 182–190.
7. Treasury bill data is first available starting from January 1978.
8. Amaranth Advisors LLC was a multistrategy hedge fund managing over $9 billion (U.S.) in assets. In September 2006, it lost well over half of its asset value in a single week due to losses on natural gas futures. The use of Amaranth as an alpha engine within a portable alpha program is of public record. See Chapter 9 for additional discussion regarding the risks that were taken by Amaranth.

Chapter 3   Back to the Basics

1. An interview with Bill Sharpe by Jonathan Burton, "Revisiting the Capital Asset Pricing Model," *Dow Jones Asset Manager,* May/June 1998, 20–28.
2. Edward Qian, "Risk Parity Portfolios: Efficient Portfolios through True Diversification," PanAgora Asset Management, September 2005.
3. Jonathan Burton, "Alpha and Bets: Investment Consultant Peter Bernstein on Sharpening Your Portfolio's Edge," *MarketWatch,* April 30, 2007.

Chapter 4   Asset Allocation and Portable Alpha

1. Ignoring potential incremental costs, liquidity requirements, and other details.
2. This was also the name of a well-received book on marketing by Rick Page (McGraw-Hill, 2001).
3. The fifth percentile is 1.6 standard deviations below the mean. The standard deviation of 15 percent times = 1.6 means that there is a 5 percent chance of stocks performing 24 percent below this 5 percent mean outperformance, for a shortfall of 19 percent relative to bonds.
4. Robert D. Arnott and Peter L. Bernstein, "What Risk Premium is 'Normal'?" *Financial Analysts Journal,* March/April, 2002.
5. STRIPS is an acronym for "separate trading of registered interest and principal of securities." Treasury STRIPS are fixed-income securities sold at a significant discount to face value and offer no interest payments because they mature at par ("Treasury STRIPS," *Investopedia*).
6. This is based on dividing the portfolio value by the cost of a 20-year inflation-indexed annuity priced based on the long TIPS yield. For the first seven months of the series before TIPS were available, we used the yield on long-term U.S. government bonds, less the three-year rate of inflation, as a proxy for real yields.

Chapter 5   Alpha, Beta, and Alpha-Beta Separation

1. Keith Ambachtsheer, "Alpha, Beta, Bafflegab: Investment Theory as Marketing Strategy," *The Ambachtsheer Letter—Research and Commentary on Pension Governance, Finance and Investments,* no. 243, April 2006.
2. William F. Sharpe, "Capital Asset Prices: A Theory of Market Equilibrium under Conditions of Risk," *Journal of Finance* vol. 19, no. 3:425–442.
3. Michael C. Jensen, "The Performance of Mutual Funds in the Period 1945–1964," *Journal of Finance,* May 1968.
4. Jonathan Burton, "Revisiting the Capital Asset Pricing Model," *Dow Jones Asset Manager,* May/June 1998:20–28.
5. The market model was developed in Bill Sharpe's doctoral dissertation paper, published in 1963, "A Simplified Model of Portfolio Analysis" and first mentioned in a footnote in Harry Markowitz, "Portfolio Selection: Efficient Diversification of Investments," published in 1959, as described in the 5th edition of *Investments,* by William F. Sharpe, Gordon J. Alexander, and Jeffery V. Bailey.
6. M. Barton Waring and Laurence B. Siegel, "The Myth of the Absolute-Return Investor," *Financial Analysts Journal,* vol. 62, no. 2, March/April 2006.
7. For example, we assume lognormal distributions for credit bond prices, even though a credit bond embeds a short put position on the assets of the firm. Because option returns are nonstationary, the lognormality assumption can be questionable, particularly for low bond ratings.
8. For example, if the true model is

$$R = \beta_1 f_1 + \beta_2 f_2 + noise$$

and we decide to regress R on f_1 only, then the upward bias on the f_1 coefficient will be

$$\beta_1 + \beta_2 \frac{Cov(f_1, f_2)}{Var(f_1)}$$

9. The puzzle can be solved in one of two ways: Either, as Barro argues, a world with rare disasters is compatible with a high premium because investors will require such a premium to compensate them for the inconvenience of these events; or, as has been explained by Jorion and Goetzmann, the measured world risk premium, when taking into account all past disasters in a large pool of countries as opposed to just the United States, turns out to be much lower than previously thought—in the order of 1 to 2 percent.
10. The probability of exactly k jumps happening over a period of time t is

$$\frac{(\lambda t)^k \exp(-\lambda t)}{k!}$$

Chapter 6 Global Sources of (Portable) Alpha, Associated Risks, and Active Management

1. Eugene F. Fama and Kenneth R. French, "The Cross-Section of Expected Stock Returns," *Journal of Finance* vol. 47, no. 2, June 1992.
2. H. Chen, G. Noronha, and V. Singal, "Index Changes and Losses to Index Fund Investors," *Financial Analysts Journal* vol. 62, no. 4, 2006:31–47.
3. Hedge Fund Research 2006 annual industry report.
4. Ibid.
5. National Association of College and University Business Officers. 2006 NACUBO Endowment Study Results (released January 22, 2007).
6. M. Hutchinson and L. Gallagher, "Convertible Bond Arbitrage," working paper, University College Cork and Dublin City University, 2004.
7. V. Agarwal, W. Fung, Y. Loon, and N. Naik, "Risks in Hedge Fund Strategies: Case of Convertible Arbitrage," working paper, Georgia State University and London Business School, 2004.
8. W. Fung and D. A. Hsieh, "The Risk in Hedge Fund Strategies: Theory and Evidence from Trend Followers," *Review of Financial Studies,* vol. 14, no. 2, 2001:313–341.
9. Hedge Fund Research 2006 annual industry report.
10. W. Fung and D. Hsieh, "Extracting Portable Alphas from Equity Long/Short Hedge Funds," *Journal of Investment Management* vol. 2, no. 4, 2004:1–19.
11. A. Patton, "Are 'Market Neutral' Hedge Funds Really Market Neutral?" London School of Economics, March 11, 2004.
12. Clifford Asness, Robert J. Krail, and John M. Liew, "Do Hedge Funds Hedge?" *Journal of Portfolio Management,* Fall 2001:6–19; and Clifford De Souza and Gokcan Suleymann, "Allocation Methodologies and Customizing Hedge Fund Muulti-Manager Multi-Strategy Products," *Journal of Alternative Investments,* Spring 2004:7–21.

13. Mark Mitchell and Todd Pulvino, "Characteristics of Risk and Return in Risk Arbitrage," *Journal of Finance,* October 2000.
14. J. Duarte, F. A. Longstaff, and F. Yu, "Risk and Return in Fixed Income Arbitrage: Nickels in Front of a Steamroller?" Anderson Graduate School of Management, University of California–Los Angeles, May 2005.

Chapter 9   The Real Holy Grail

1. As further described in study.
2. As of this writing, some providers provide total return swaps on fixed-income indexes, but since they are usually one-way, dealers are reluctant to do them in volume. Lehman Brothers, PIMCO, and some other market participants also provide derivative-based replication strategies. Finally, futures exchanges are ready to launch futures on the indexes, but their success remains to be seen.
3. Harry M. Markowitz, "Market Efficiency: A Theoretical Distinction and So What?" *Financial Analysts Journal,* vol. 61, no. 5, 2005:17–30. Also presented at the 25th anniversary of the Q-Group, Fall 2006, Santa Barbara, California.

Chapter 10   Liability-Driven Investing

1. Consistent with average liability durations of 11 to 14 years and 80 basis points annualized interest rate volatility.
2. In the pension context, this is consistent with the legal status of pension obligations in the United States. The liabilities are first secured by the assets in the pension trust and then are similar to senior unsecured debt obligations of the sponsor. Those familiar with the pronouncements of Warren Buffet of Berkshire Hathaway will recognize the concept of *float.* In the aggregate a book of insurance policies has some largely predictable payout pattern. As the policies are generally purchased up front, the insurer has the cash in hand to invest to meet a future liability payout patterns. The characteristics of the liabilities are a function of the factors dictating payout amounts, but also importantly, the time to claim.
3. The asset mix is 55 percent U.S. equities as represented by the S&P 500, 10 percent International Equities (MSCI EAFE), 30 percent U.S. bonds (Lehman Brothers Aggregate), and 5 percent cash.
4. ERISA is the Employee Retirement Income Security Act of 1974, the principal framework for laws governing qualified pension plans in the United States. In addition to establishing the PBGC, it also codified rules and regulations as to the funding standards for benefit plans, fiduciary liability of plan sponsors, tax status of pension plans, and rules and regulations for investing plan assets.
5. The report is available at http://www.sec.gov/news/studies/soxoffbalancerpt.pdf.
6. See Black's "The Tax Consequences of Long-Run Pension Policy," *Financial Analysts Journal,* July/August 1980; and Tepper's "Taxation and Corporate Pension Policy," *Journal of Finance,* March 1981.
7. The square root of $[0.16^2 + (14*0.008)2 - 2*0.10*0.16* (14*0.008)] = 0.186$.
8. The square root of $[0.16^2 + (3*0.008)2 - 2*0.10*0.16*(3*0.008)] = 0.159$.

Bibliography

Agarwal, V., Fung, W., Loon, Y., and Naik, N. "Risks in Hedge Fund Strategies: Case of Convertible Arbitrage." Working paper, Georgia State University and London Business School, 2004.

Ambachtsheer, Keith. "Alpha, Beta, Bafflegab: Investment Theory as a Marketing Strategy." *The Ambachtsheer Letter*, no. 243, April 2006.

Ambarish, R. and Seigel, L. "Time Is the Essence." *Risk*, vol. 9, no. 8, August 1996: 41–42.

Arnott, Robert. "Risk Budgeting and Portable Alpha." *Journal of Investing,* vol. 11, no. 2, Summer 2002: 15–22.

Asness, Clifford S., Krail, Robert J., and Liew, John M. "Do Hedge Funds Hedge?" *Journal of Portfolio Mangement,* Fall 2001: 6–19.

Barro, Robert. "Rare Events and the Equity Premium." Working Paper, Harvard University, July 4, 2005.

Bernstein, Peter. *Capital Ideas Evolving.* Hoboken, NJ: John Wiley & Sons, 2007.

Bhansali, Vineer, and Wise, Mark. "Forecasting Portfolio Risk in Normal and Stressed Markets." *Journal of Risk*, vol. 4, no. 1, Fall 2001: 91–106.

Bhansali, Vineer. "Markowitz Bites Back: The Failure of CAPM, Compression of Risky Asset Spreads and Paths Back to Normalcy." January 2007. Retrieved June 4, 2007, from, www.pimco.com/LeftNav/Viewpoints/2007/Bhansali-+Markowitz+Bites+Back-+01–2007.htm.

Brittain, B., Callin, S., and Moore, J. "Portable Alpha, Alpha/Beta Separation: Separating the Trends from the Noise." January 8, 2007.

Burton, Jonathan. "Alpha and Bets: Investment Consultant Peter Bernstein on Sharpening Your Portfolio's Edge." *MarketWatch*, April 30, 2007.

Burton, Jonathan. "Revisiting the Capital Asset Pricing Model." Reprinted with permission from *Dow Jones Asset Manager*, May/June 1998: 20–28.

Chan, N.T., Gretmansky, M, Haas, S.M., and Lo, A. "Systemic Risk and Hedge Funds." MIT Sloan Research Paper No. 4535-05, AFA 2006 Boston Meeting Paper.

De Souza, Clifford, and Gokcan Suleymann. "Allocation Methodologies and Customizing Hedge Fund Multi-Manager Multi-Strategy Products." *Journal of Alternative Investments,* Spring 2004: 7–21.

Dialynas, C., and Auerback, M.. "Renegade Economics: The Bretton Woods II Fiction." *PIMCO Viewpoints*, October 2007.

Duarte, J., Longstaff, F.A., and Yu, F. "Risk and Return in Fixed Income Arbitrage: Nickels in Front of a Steamroller?" Anderson Graduate School of Management, University of California–Los Angeles, May 2005.

EDHEC Business School. "Alternative Investments: EDHEC Comments on the Lessons to Be Drawn from the Amaranth Debacle." October 2, 2006. Retrieved June 4, 2007, from www.edhec-risk.com/about_us/Press%20Releases/RISKArticle1048860368688218576/attachments/Press%20release%20-%20EDHEC%20comments%20on%20Amaranth%20case.pdf

Fama, E., and French, K. "Common Risk Factors in the Returns on Stocks and Bonds." *Journal of Economics* vol. 33, 1993: 3–56.

Fung, W., and Hsieh, D. "Extracting Portable Alphas from Equity Long/Short Hedge Funds." *Journal of Investment Management* vol. 2, no. 4 (2004): 1–19.

Fung, W., and Hsieh, D. "The Risk in Hedge Fund Strategies: Theory and Evidence from Trend Followers." *Review of Financial Studies* 14, no. 2 (Summer 2001): 313–341.

Goetzmann, W. and Jorion, P. "A Century of Global Stock Markets." Working Paper, National Bureau of Economic Reasearch, Inc, 2007.

Greenwich Associates. "Market Dynamics." Bond Management. 2006.

Hedge Fund Research. "HFR Year-End 2006 Industry Report." Retrieved June 11, 2007, from http://www.hedgefundresearch.com.

Hutchinson, M., and Gallagher, L. "Convertible Bond Arbitrage." Working paper, University College Cork and Dublin City University, 2004.

Ibbotson Associates. *Stocks, Bonds, Bills, and Inflation: 2000 Yearbook*. Chicago: Ibbotson Associates, 2001.

Ilkiw, J. "Missing Persons Found: Jensen Coined Beta and Alpha but Tito Cashed Out." *Canadian Investment Review*, Winter 2006.

Investment Company Institute. "Worldwide Mutual Fund Assets and Flow Fourth Quarter 2006." Retrieved on June 12, 2007, from, http://www.ici.org/stats/mf/ww_12_06.html#TopOfPage.

Jahnke, W. "The Asset Allocation Hoax." *Journal of Financial Planning*, Article 4, February 1997.

Leibowitz, M., and Bova, A. "Gathering Implicit Alphas in a Beta World." *Journal of Portfolio Management*, Spring 2007: 10–21.

Malkiel, B. G. *A Random Walk Down Wall Street*. W.W. Norton & Company, Inc., 2003.

Malkiel, B. G. "Returns from Investing in Equity Mutual Funds, 1971 to 1991." *Journal of Finance*, vol. 50, 1995: 549–572.

Markowitz, Harry M. "Portfolio Selection." *Journal of Finance* vol. 7, no. 1, 1952: 77–91.

Markowitz, Harry M. "Market Efficiency: A Theoretical Distinction and So What?" *Financial Analysts Journal* vol. 61, no. 5, 2005: 17–30.

Mitchell, Mark, and Pulvino, Todd. "Characteristics of Risk and Return in Risk Arbitrage." *Journal of Finance*, October 2000.

Northern Trust. "Executive Summary Findings". *Wealth in America 2006*. Northern Trust: December, 2005.

O'Rielly, W., and Chandler, J. "Asset Allocation Revisited." *Journal of Financial Planning*, Article 13, January 2000.

Qian, E., PhD. "Risk Parity Portfolios: Efficient Portfolios through True Diversification." *Panagora*, September, 2005.

Patton. A. "Are 'Market Neutral' Hedge Funds Really Market Neutral?" EFA 2004 Maastricht Meetings Paper no. 2691, March 11, 2004.

Schwert, Q. "Indexes of United States Stock Prices from 1802 to 1987." *Journal of Business* vol. 63, no. 3, July 1990; 399–426.

Sharpe, William F. "Capital Asset Prices: A Theory of Market Equilibrium under Conditions of Risk." *Journal of Finance* vol. 19, no. 3, 1964: 425–442.

Sharpe, W. "Asset Allocation: Management Style and Performance Measurement." *Journal of Portfolio Management,* Winter 1992: 7–19.

Sharpe, W., Alexander, G., and Bailey, J. *Investments, Fifth Edition.* Englewood Cliffs, New Jersey: Prentice Hall Publishers, 1995.

Shiller, R. "Do Stock Prices Move Too Much to Be Justified by Subsequent Changes in Dividends?" *American Economics Review* vol. 73, no. 3, June 1981: 421–436.

Statman, M. "The 93.6% Question of Financial Advisors." *Journal of Investing,* Spring 2000.

Tobin, James. "Liquidity Preference as Behavior towards Risk." *Review of Economic Studies* vol. 25, 1958: 65–86.

Waring, M. Barton, and Siegel, Laurence B. "The Myth of the Absolute-Return Investor." *Financial Analysts Journal* vol. 62, no. 2, March/April 2006: 14–21

Wright, C. "Tail Tales: Is Your Risk Model Telling You the Whole Story?" *CFA Institute Magazine,* March/April 2007: 36–43.

About the Authors

CONTRIBUTORS FROM PIMCO

Jamil Baz, PhD

Mr. Baz is an executive vice president, portfolio manager, and a member of Pacific Investment Management Company's (PIMCO) global team. He has more than 18 years of work experience in the financial industry. Prior to joining PIMCO in 2007, Mr. Baz was a managing director in macro proprietary trading at Goldman Sachs in London. His prior experience includes positions with Deutsche Bank, where he was the global chief investment strategist; Lehman Brothers, where he co-ran European fixed-income research; and the World Bank, where he worked in derivatives and liability management. He graduated from the London School of Economics (MSc), Massachusetts Institute of Technology (SM), and Harvard University (PhD). He is also a lecturer at Oxford University, where he teaches mathematical finance. Mr. Baz is widely published in the fields of derivatives, fixed income, and exchange rates.

Vineer Bhansali, PhD

Dr. Bhansali is an executive vice president, portfolio manager, firmwide head of analytics for portfolio management, and a senior member of PIMCO's portfolio management group. Dr. Bhansali joined PIMCO in 2000, previously having been associated with Credit Suisse First Boston as a vice president in proprietary fixed-income trading. Prior to that, he was a proprietary trader for Salomon Brothers in New York and worked in the global derivatives group at Citibank. He is the author of numerous scientific and financial papers and of the book *Pricing and Managing Exotic and Hybrid Options* (McGraw Hill, 1998). He currently serves as an associate editor for the *International Journal of Theoretical and Applied Finance*. Dr. Bhansali has more than 17 years of investment experience and holds a bachelor's degree and a master's degree in physics from the California Institute of Technology, and a PhD in theoretical particle physics from Harvard University.

Bruce Brittain, PhD

Mr. Brittain is an executive vice president and product manager for PIMCO's Absolute Return Strategies (PARS). He joined PIMCO in 2002 from Lyster Watson & Company in New York, where he was responsible for the firm's hedge fund institutional advisory business. Mr. Brittain has had a professional investment career spanning economic research, foreign-exchange product management, fixed-income capital markets, and equity derivatives at Salomon Brothers, Swiss Bank Corporation, and Lehman Brothers. He has more than 26 years of investment experience, including 5 in the hedge fund industry, and holds a master's degree in economics from the London School of Economics and Political Science, and a PhD in economics from the University of Chicago.

Sabrina C. Callin, CFA, CPA

Ms. Callin is an executive vice president and the head of the StocksPLUS product management team responsible for PIMCO's global portable alpha-based equity business. Prior to joining PIMCO in 1998, she was a manager in the assurance and business advisory services group at KPMG Peat Marwick, LLP. She has more than 16 years of investment experience and holds two bachelor's degrees with majors in finance, accounting, and economics from Texas Christian University, and an MBA from the Stanford University Graduate School of Business.

Richard Clarida, PhD

Dr. Clarida joined PIMCO in 2006 as executive vice president and global strategic adviser. Before joining PIMCO, Dr. Clarida had extensive experience in Washington—as assistant treasury secretary, in academia—as chairman of the Department of Economics at Columbia University, and in financial markets—Credit Suisse, Grossman Asset Management, the Clinton Group. Dr. Clarida is based in PIMCO's New York office and continues to teach at Columbia University. He has a master's and PhD in economics from Harvard University and a bachelor's degree from the University of Illinois. He has more than six years of investment experience.

Chris P. Dialynas

Mr. Dialynas is a managing director, portfolio manager, and a senior member of PIMCO's investment strategy group. He joined PIMCO in 1980. Mr. Dialynas has written extensively and lectured on the topic of fixed-income investing. He served on the editorial board of the *Journal of Portfolio Management* and was a member of Fixed Income Curriculum Committee of the Association for Investment Management and Research. He has more than 29 years of investment experience, holds a bachelor's degree in economics from Pomona College, and holds an MBA in finance from the University of Chicago Graduate School of Business.

William H. Gross, CFA

Mr. Gross is a founder and managing director of PIMCO and has been associated with PIMCO for more than 38 years. As chief investment officer of PIMCO he oversees the management of over $600 billion of fixed-income securities. He is the author of numerous articles on the bond market and has frequently appeared in national publications and media. Morningstar named Mr. Gross, along with his investment team, Morningstar's Fixed Income Manager of the Year for 1998 and for 2000, based on its own research and in-depth evaluation by its senior editorial staff. Mr. Gross was the first person ever to receive this award more than once from Morningstar. When presenting the award to Mr. Gross, Morningstar stated that he earned the award by "demonstrating excellent investment skill, the courage to differ from consensus, and the commitment to shareholders necessary to deliver outstanding long-term performance." In 2000, Mr. Gross received the Bond Market Association's Distinguished Service Award. In 1997, Mr. Gross authored *Everything You've Heard About Investing is Wrong,* published by Times Books/Random House. In December 1996, he was the first portfolio manager inducted into the FIASI's Hall of Fame for his major contributions to the advancement of fixed-income analysis and portfolio management. In a survey conducted by *Pensions and Investments* magazine in its September 6, 1993, issue, Mr. Gross was recognized by his peers as the most influential authority on the bond market in the United States. He has more than 38 years of investment experience and holds a bachelor's degree from Duke University and an MBA from the UCLA Graduate School of Business.

Brent R. Harris, CFA

Mr. Harris is a managing director and a member of PIMCO's executive committee. He also serves as chairman and president of PIMCO Strategic Global Government Fund, Inc.; chairman of PIMCO Funds; and chairman of PIMCO Commercial Mortgage Securities Trust, Inc. Mr. Harris developed and oversees strategic market initiatives at the firm and directs portfolio management in this area. Mr. Harris joined PIMCO in 1985, having previously been associated with the Claremont Economics Institute. He has more than 24 years of investment experience and holds a bachelor's degree in economics from Claremont McKenna College and an MBA from the Harvard Business School.

Steven Jones, CFA

Mr. Jones is a vice president and a product manager focused on PIMCO's portable alpha–based equity strategies. Prior to assuming current responsibilities he was a member of PIMCO's short-term portfolio management team and also an associate with PIMCO's institutional account management group. Prior to joining PIMCO in 2000, he worked as a hedge fund performance analyst at Collins Associates, a fund-of-funds investment management firm. Mr. Jones has more than 9 years of investment experience and holds a bachelor's degree in business administration/finance from the University of California at Riverside and an MBA from the University of California at Irvine.

James M. Keller

Mr. Keller is a managing director and portfolio manager, responsible for PIMCO's government/derivatives desks, and specializes in long-duration fixed-income portfolios. Mr. Keller joined PIMCO in 1996, previously having been associated with Merrill Lynch, Inc., and has been a member of the Chicago Board of Trade and the Chicago Mercantile Exchange. Mr. Keller has more than 20 years of investment experience and holds a bachelor's degree from the University of Illinois and an MBA from the University of Chicago Graduate School of Business.

Lisa Kim

Ms. Kim is a lead product associate for PIMCO's derivatives-based index and enhanced cash products. Prior to joining PIMCO in 2003, she worked as a financial analyst at Stanford Management Company, the investment firm for Stanford University's endowment, in the fixed-income and cash management desk. Prior to Stanford, she worked as a financial analyst at CM Capital, a fund-of-funds and venture capital investment firm. Ms. Kim has nine years of investment experience and holds a bachelor degree in economics and business administration from the University of California–Berkeley.

James F. Moore, PhD

Dr. Moore is an executive vice president and product manager for long-duration and pension products. He joined PIMCO in 2003 from Morgan Stanley, where he was in the Corporate Derivative and Asset Liability Strategy groups. At Morgan Stanley Dr. Moore was responsible for asset-liability, strategic risk management, and capital structure advisory work for key clients in the Americas and Pacific Rim. Previously, he was associated with Enhance Reinsurance, the Wharton Financial Institutions Center, and William M. Mercer Co. While at Wharton, Dr. Moore taught courses in investments and employee benefit plan design and finance. He has more than 13 years of investment experience and holds bachelor's degrees in applied mathematics and economics from Brown University and a PhD from the Wharton School of the University of Pennsylvania with concentrations in finance, insurance, and risk management.

Alfred Murata, PhD

Mr. Murata is a senior vice president and a portfolio manager with PIMCO's MBS and ABS teams. Prior to joining PIMCO he researched and implemented exotic equity and interest rate derivatives at Nikko Financial Technologies. He has more than eight years of investment experience and holds a Ph.D. in engineering-economic systems and operations research from Stanford University, a JD from Stanford Law School, and is a member of the State Bar of California.

Don Suskind, CFA

Mr. Suskind is a vice president and a member of the StocksPLUS product management team responsible for PIMCO's equity business globally and across distribution channels. Prior to joining PIMCO in early 2004, he was associated with the Geneva Companies, a subsidiary of Citigroup, where he was a merger and acquisition adviser. Mr. Suskind has more than nine years of investment experience. He holds a bachelor's degree in economics from the University of Virginia and an MBA from the Wharton School of the University of Pennsylvania.

Mihir Worah, PhD

Mr. Worah is an executive vice president, portfolio manager, and member of the government and derivatives desk. He joined PIMCO in 2001 as a member of the analytics team and worked on term structure modeling and options pricing. Previously he was a postdoctoral research associate at the University of California–Berkeley and at the Stanford Linear Accelerator Center, where he built models to explain the difference between matter and antimatter. He has a PhD in theoretical physics from the University of Chicago and is the author of numerous scientific papers.

CONTRIBUTORS FROM RESEARCH AFFILIATES

Robert Arnott, Chairman

Mr. Arnott is the chairman of Research Affiliates, a research-intensive asset management firm, focused on building cutting-edge new products and bringing them to the marketplace through affiliations wherever possible. Several unconventional portfolio strategies now in wide application figure among Mr. Arnott's pioneering innovations: tactical asset allocation, global tactical asset allocation, tax-advantaged equity management, and fundamental indexation, among others. He has served as editor of the *Financial Analysts Journal* and has published more than one hundred articles in the *FAJ*, the *Journal of Portfolio Management,* the *Harvard Business Review,* and other respected journals. Mr. Arnott has served as a visiting professor of finance at UCLA, and has served on the product advisory board of three exchanges and the editorial board of several finance journals.

In recognition of his achievements as a writer, Mr. Arnott has received five Graham and Dodd Scrolls and Awards, awarded annually by the CFA Institute for best articles of the year, and declined a sixth award during his tenure as editor. He was recently given a lifetime achievement award by Foundation and Endowment Money Management. Mr. Arnott graduated summa cum laude from the University of California at Santa Barbara.

Index